Ethics and Finitude

Ethics and Finitude

Heideggerian Contributions to Moral Philosophy

Lawrence J. Hatab

ROWMAN & LITTLEFIELD PUBLISHERS, INC.
Lanham • Boulder • New York • Oxford

LC N 1013186

ROWMAN & LITTLEFIELD PUBLISHERS, INC.

Published in the United States of America
by Rowman & Littlefield Publishers, Inc.
4720 Boston Way, Lanham, Maryland 20706
http://www.rowmanlittlefield.com

12 Hid's Copse Road
Cumnor Hill, Oxford OX2 9JJ, England

Copyright © 2000 by Rowman & Littlefield Publishers, Inc.

British Library Cataloguing-in-Publication Information Available

Library of Congress Cataloging-in-Publication Data

Hatab, Lawrence J., 1946-
  Ethics and finitude : Heideggerian contributions to moral philosophy / Lawrence J. Hatab.
    p. cm.
  Includes bibliographical references and index.
  ISBN 0-8476-9682-0 (alk. paper)—ISBN 0-8476-9683-9 (pbk. : alk. paper)
    1. Heidegger, Martin, 1889–1976—Ethics. I. Title.

  B3279.H49 H285 2000
  171'2—dc21

                                                                        99-086407

Printed in the United States of America

∞™ The paper used in this publication meets the minimum requirements of American
National Standard for Information Sciences—Permanence of Paper for Printed Library
Materials, ANSI/NISO Z39.48–1992.

To my wife, Chelsy

To be answerable to the claim of
presencing is the greatest claim
of humanity; "ethics" is this claim.

Martin Heidegger,
Zollikoner Seminare

Contents

Preface

Martin Heidegger insisted that philosophy cannot be grounded in techniques of proof and argumentation because it begins with being seized by moods (like wonder) that prompt questioning in the first place and that continue to animate inquiry. Philosophical development, then, cannot ignore the disposition of mood in both the inception and reception of intellectual discourse. My own disposition toward ethics has changed. Early in my career I was not interested in ethics as a discipline. In fact I was somewhat antagonistic, owing to a Nietzsche-inspired suspicion of ethics as the rule of normalization that suppresses heroic creativity, individual eccentricity, and the openness of life. I also experienced a visceral discomfort with the cool, detached logical machinations of analytic moral philosophy, which in large measure was dominated by the theoretical pursuit of necessary principles that could ground ethical practice and that could survive the gauntlet of trial by standards of consistency, universality, and indefeasibility. Something was telling me that whatever importance ethics does have was here being transmuted into the logistics of *academic* practice.

My suspicion and discomfort were shared by a large part of my tribe in continental philosophy. There was a sense of bemused disdain for ethics in general terms as either a cultural leveling force or a philosophical surrender to theorization. I came to be suspicious of my suspicion, however. It was clear to me that colleagues in my tribe were all decent, well-socialized people, and witnessing my friends and relatives raising children made it obvious to me how important ethical norms are in human development, all the way down. I gradually became embarrassed at the rather cavalier disregard of ethics in my philosophical environment. I came to read two philosophical studies that opened up a different vantage point on ethics, particularly by way of Aristotle, and this nourished my new disposition.[1] I realized that ethics need not be reduced to normalization or theorization. At the same time I learned of the degree to which Heidegger, one of my philosophical heroes, was inspired by elements of Aristotle's ethics in his early philosophical work. I wondered to what extent I could coordinate my new inter-

xi

est in ethics with the thought of Heidegger. Thus began a project that brought forth the present work.[2]

I hope to persuade readers that Heidegger's manner of thinking is well suited to moral philosophy. There are several obstacles along the way, which will be addressed as we proceed. Two obstacles in particular can be noted here, one in analytic circles that dismisses or fails to recognize Heidegger's importance as a thinker; the other in continental circles that would take my venture into ethics as a corruption of Heidegger's thought. In both cases I have to defend a particular approach to the quotidian world. One mark of Heidegger's philosophical importance is his attention to everyday practices and environments, yet he was more interested in extraordinary dimensions of thought and experience covered up by everyday life. A predilection for the extraordinary has remained a driving force in continental philosophy. In turning to ethics I will be concentrating on many issues and problems that members of my tribe might consider pedestrian. Yet what has always struck me about Heidegger's thought is the enormous potential it has to illuminate and affect concrete modes of life. (If I were to define my philosophical orientation I would call myself something of an existential pragmatist.) At the same time, a Heideggerian perspective on the everyday world will differ markedly from how that world is usually construed in analytic philosophy. With Heidegger we take notice of the complex finitude of the lived world, in ways that analytic philosophy has either missed, underplayed, or consciously ignored.

Because of my hopes for a broad audience, I have tried hard to cultivate an accessible writing style, which is not easy when dealing with a thinker like Heidegger. When I write I picture the reader at my side, as a co-traveler, so I labor for clarity and communication. Analytic readers may still be mystified by my text, but I hope not. Continental readers may hunger for more imaginative vision or intellectual thrills, but I suppose I should confess to having become excited by more prosaic topics.

Finally, a disclaimer: Ethics is an ocean of issues. I could not hope to cover every relevant topic or to treat adequately all the topics that I do take up. Very little of what follows can pretend to be definitive or comprehensive. The main concern is to open up applications of Heidegger's way of thinking to basic questions in moral philosophy. Some topics, such as virtue, empathy, and selfhood, will be given extended discussion. A host of other topics will be introduced to attest to the potential scope of my approach, but these will be advanced more in the manner of sketches and suggestions for further reflection. I also will treat references to other relevant thinkers mostly in endnotes, so as not to clutter the main text with such discussions. I am certain that many readers will complain about thin treatments of important figures in various movements who could and should be brought to bear on my analysis. Doing justice in this regard, however, is simply not possible within the range of my purposes.

There are many people I want to thank for their comments, encouragements, and contributions in the course of my project: William Brenner, Curtis Brooks,

Douglas Chismar, David Crownfield, Michael Davie, Gabe Ingram, David M. Levin, Steve Litherland, Anne Parrella Neill, Tom Neill, Richard Polt, William Richardson, Frank Schalow, and Robert Scharff. Special thanks to Maureen MacGrogan of Rowman & Littlefield for her early faith in this project, and to the former secretary in the Philosophy Department at Old Dominion University, Mary Hall, whose command of the office made it possible for me to write this book while chairing the department. The same thanks goes to the current secretary, Emily Pickering.

NOTES

1. The works in question are Alasdair MacIntyre, *After Virtue* (South Bend, Ind.: University of Notre Dame Press, 1981), and Martha Nussbaum, *The Fragility of Goodness* (Cambridge: Cambridge University Press, 1986).
2. Prior to the publication of this book, an article of mine with the same title appeared in *International Philosophical Quarterly*, vol. 35, no. 4 (December 1995): 403–17.

Abbreviations

Except for *NE*, all of the following are works by Heidegger. On occasion I have slightly modified published translations.

AI   "Aristotle-Introduction" (1922), *Phenomenological Interpretations with Respect to Aristotle: Indication of the Hermeneutical Situation*, trans. Michael Baur, *Man and World* 25 (1992): 355–93.

AM   *Aristotle's Metaphysics 1–3: On the Essence and Actuality of Force* (*GA* 33), trans. Walter Brogan and Peter Warnek (Bloomington: Indiana University Press, 1995).

BP   *Basic Problems of Phenomenology* (*GA* 24), trans. Albert Hofstadter (Bloomington: Indiana University Press, 1982).

BT   *Being and Time*, trans. John Macquarrie and Edward Robinson (New York: Harper and Row, 1962).

BW   *Basic Writings*, 2nd edition, ed. David F. Krell (New York: Harper and Row, 1977).

CT   *The Concept of Time*, trans. William McNeill (Malden, Mass.: Blackwell, 1992).

DT   *Discourse on Thinking*, trans. Joan Stambaugh (New York: Harper and Row, 1966).

ECP   "On the Essence and Concept of *Phusis* in Aristotle's *Physics* B, 1," in *PM*, 183–230.

ET   "On the Essence of Truth," in *BW*, 115–38.

FCM   *The Fundamental Concepts of Metaphysics* (*GA* 29/30), trans. William McNeill and Nicholas Walker (Bloomington: Indiana University Press, 1995).

GA   *Gesamtausgabe* (Frankfurt am Main: Vittorio Klosterman, 1975ff).

HCT   *History of the Concept of Time: Prolegomena* (*GA* 20), trans. Theodore Kisiel (Bloomington: Indiana University Press, 1985).

IM   *An Introduction to Metaphysics*, trans. Ralph Manheim (New Haven, Conn.: Yale University Press, 1959).

LH   *Letter on Humanism*, in *BW*, 217–65.

MFL   *The Metaphysical Foundations of Logic* (*GA* 26), trans. Michael Heim (Bloomington: Indiana University Press, 1984).

NE   Aristotle, *Nicomachean Ethics*, trans. Terence Irwin (Indianapolis: Hackett, 1985).

OWL   *On the Way to Language*, trans. Peter D. Hertz and Joan Stambaugh (New York: Harper and Row, 1971).

P   *Parmenides* (*GA* 54), trans. André Schuwer and Richard Rojcewicz (Bloomington: Indiana University Press, 1992).

PLT   *Poetry, Language, Thought*, trans. Albert Hofstadter (New York: Harper and Row, 1971).

PM   *Pathmarks*, ed. William McNeill (Cambridge: Cambridge University Press, 1998).

PS   *Plato's Sophist* (*GA* 19), trans. Richard Rojcewicz and André Schuwer (Bloomington: Indiana University Press, 1997).

QCT   "The Question Concerning Technology," in *BW*, 311–41.

TB   *On Time and Being*, trans. Joan Stambaugh (New York: Harper and Row, 1972).

WCT   *What Is Called Thinking?* trans. J. Glenn Gray (New York: Harper and Row, 1968).

WM   "What Is Metaphysics?" in *BW*, 93–110.

WT   *What Is a Thing?* trans. W. B. Barton Jr. and Vera Deutsch (Washington, D.C.: Regnery, 1967).

Introduction

The aim of this investigation is an application of Heidegger's thought to the practical sphere of ethics. From early on in his thinking, Heidegger subordinated the question of ethics to the question of being. Ethics, like other disciplines, is concerned with a sphere of beings and not the being of beings. For Heidegger, ethics could not be addressed adequately until the ontological question of being as such was given priority (*BT*, 37; *MFL*, 157). Heidegger often indicated that this should not be taken to mean a dismissal of ethics. The problem was that ethics, again like other specific domains, has concealed in its manner of thinking the primal finitude of being, a finitude shown in elemental modes of being-in-the-world, of how human beings exist in the lived world. My take on this distinction between ethics and finite ontology is as follows: Ethics has been rich in its analysis of normative topics but poor in its attention to being-ethical-in-the-world, in the fullest Heideggerian sense of such a phrase, particularly in how ethical life exhibits a situated finitude. In other words, ethics has not only concealed the finitude of being, moral philosophy has concealed the finitude of ethics. The coordination of ethics and Heideggerian ontology suggests the possibility of taking up moral philosophy anew once the ontological structure of finite being-in-the-world has been articulated.

Although Heidegger often gave the impression of segregating ontology from practical disciplines such as ethics, I am convinced that this was only a preparatory division and not a substantive one (see *BT*, 332). Much in Heidegger's thought has seemed promising for an investigation of ethics.[1] There is a good deal of suspicion, however, about ethical possibilities in Heidegger. Given the Olympian distance of Heidegger's later thought—for instance, the claim that thinking has "no result" and "no effect" (*LH*, 259)—and given his affiliation with National Socialism, together with the deceit and galling silence of the postwar years, Heidegger's segregation of ethics from ontology can be interpreted as a more heinous division, namely that Heidegger's thought was or became indifferent to ethics, or worse, inseparable from something dark and barbaric.

1

I am not entirely swayed by this suspicion. I am among those who believe that one can distinguish Heidegger the man from his thought in certain ways. One can even distinguish Heidegger's thought in its actual manifestations from the potential for ethics contained therein (in all periods of his thinking, but especially in the early writings). Moreover, I think it is possible to show, in some measure, that Heidegger's political commitments were not consistent with basic elements of his thought and its ethical implications. This is not to deny that Heidegger himself affirmed an idealized version of National Socialism that followed his thought in significant ways; it is simply to say that his political vision (however construed) did not follow necessarily from his philosophy. In this investigation I will not engage the notorious Heidegger Affair in the main text. There is a wealth of material on this topic, and I will confront some basic issues in the matter of Heidegger's politics in the epilogue. My motive in this study is not to rehabilitate Heidegger or to speak *for* Heidegger in the question of ethics, but to speak *from* the atmosphere of Heidegger's thinking with the hope of making significant contributions to ethical thought. This is *my* project, then, and one that I will not shy away from calling moral philosophy. I aim to explore familiar ethical questions, concerns, and social applications, rather than simply some arcane circulation of Heideggerian terminology. And yet, most of my inspiration has come from Heidegger's existential phenomenology. But I stress that my work is a Heidegger*ian* endeavor, an experiment in applying Heidegger's way of thinking that is not confined to or bound by Heidegger's texts.

The basic structure of this investigation is a coordination between Heidegger's alternative to modern philosophy and a Heideggerian alternative to modern moral theories. Modern philosophy, beginning with René Descartes, is governed by the subject–object binary unfolding out of scientific reason, where the world is construed as a set of objective conditions divorced from human involvement and meaning, a divorce accomplished by the disengaged subjectivity of rational reflection. Disengaged abstraction permits a deliverance from the contingency, flux, and limits of lived experience, and thus prepares foundationalist guarantees secured from the instabilities of time, history, and cultural diversity. Heidegger works to unravel the subject–object binary by arguing for the priority of an engaged being-in-the-world that precedes abstract reflection, in the sense that the self is already shaped by contexts of meaning (historical tradition, practical involvement, everyday concerns, social relations, moods, and language uses) before the world is subjected to objectification. Philosophy has tended to miss this prereflective dimension precisely because it is less manageable and shows itself to be radically finite, which undermines foundationalist guarantees.

It is important to stress what Heidegger means by the finitude of being. Finitude does not refer simply to spatial, temporal, definitional, or cognitive limits; it includes an indigenous negativity in being, where an absence or otherness is always part of a thing's being, so that being cannot be associated with full or constant presence. For human beings, finitude includes a sense of absence in the midst of presence (for instance, the meaning of death), an awareness of the pervasive possibility of loss and privation, and a coping with the intrinsic incompleteness of the human condition. The finitude of being-in-the-world also refers to the limits of human selfhood caught up in the encumbrances and contingencies of life, which is counterposed to the intimations of sovereignty and mastery contained in the modern conception of a self-grounding, autonomous subject.

Modern moral philosophy, particularly in its Kantian and utilitarian manifestations, has mirrored in many respects the basic features of the modern subject–object binary and its foundationalist aspirations. My contention is that modern moral theories repeat the problematic disengagement from finite being-in-the-world critiqued by Heidegger, and that ethics can benefit from Heideggerian phenomenology and its divergence from the modern project. The finitude of human existence is not only an ontological matter; it is also located in moral life, in the ways in which we exist ethically. Ethical matters are responses to finite limit-conditions, and ethics itself is finite in its modes of disclosure, appropriation, and performance. Moreover, an engaged being-in-the-world can show the ethical sphere as neither an "objective" nor a "subjective" condition, but as a mode of *finite dwelling*. Here a balance can be struck between foundationalist approaches to ethics that stress objectivity and antifoundationalist approaches that take ethics to be an utterly open project of the subject.

What is the sphere of ethics at issue in this investigation? Ethics is an interest in, and interrogation of, matters of existential weal and woe in social life, how we deal with, respond to, and affect each other's betterment and suffering. Ethical matters include (1) welfare (human development and flourishing), (2) help and harm, (3) justice (fairness and reciprocity), (4) freedom, (5) responsibility, and (6) virtue (dispositions and capacities that shape a person's character, social bearing, and course of life). As a social enterprise, ethics has a dialogical character, as a process of engaging each other's interests, needs, prospects, and actions. As a normative enterprise, ethics involves preferences and estimations of better and worse ways of living, along with the shaping of an "ought" as a measure or guidance for such evaluations. As a practical enterprise, ethics pertains to actions and modes of living; and in the face of multiple estimations and the openness of future possibilities, ethics calls for deliberation and decision.[2]

In such a setting, ethical interrogation unfolds as (1) action-guiding (What should I do?), (2) action-judging (Did I act well?), (3) value-disclosing (What is good or worth desiring?), and (4) life-shaping (What kind of life should I/we lead?). In these matters, moral philosophy should not be bound by the modern fixation on "theory," on the project of rational justification and the privileging of abstract principles over concrete situations. Ethics should be understood as the contingent, heuristic, interactive engagement of basic practical questions: How should human beings live? How should we live together? How should we treat each other? What do we owe each other? What are better and worse ways of conducting our lives?

In contrast with the overly theoretical approach of modern moral philosophy—where the practical environment is governed by preconceived principles and philosophical validity is measured by the consistency, universality, impartiality, and indefeasibility of such principles—I take moral philosophy to be an *engaged, interpretive, contextual, addressive discourse for the sake of disclosing ethical bearings in life*. Let me briefly discuss the terms in this characterization, since they will resonate throughout the text to come.

Since we are already informed by tradition and upbringing with an inherited ethical outlook, philosophical reflection will begin as an *interpretive engagement* with how we already live, as opposed to seeing the ethical field as a clean canvas or by way of some "view from nowhere." Moral philosophy should also favor a *contextual* approach, in that ethical issues are better engaged in terms of their specific circumstances and specific parties, rather than through overly formal generalizations. In its performative character, moral philosophy should be a mode of *address*, that is to say, an offering and exchange between people in terms of their actual interests and prospects. Such an encounter is dialogical rather than monological, personal rather than impersonal, in that ethics is an experimental, shared, living task. Accordingly, ethics should build from actual questions, doubts, disagreements, responses, and negotiations, as opposed to overly abstract, hypothetical, or theoretical techniques of analysis. Finally, I very much favor the notion of *bearings*, since it combines multiple connotations that will figure in my analysis: It conveys a sense of one's existential posture, comportment, and attitude in life (a noble bearing); it speaks of significance and relevance (having a bearing on a problem); it suggests a creative bringing-forth of possibilities (bearing as giving birth); it connotes a sense of direction (getting one's bearings); and it tells of withstanding the difficulties of life (bearing a storm). All of these meanings emerge in the course of this investigation as ethical articulations of what Heidegger means in a larger sense by finite dwelling.

Chapter 1 provides a rather detailed overview of Heidegger's thought, primarily his early phenomenology and its divergence from modern philosophy. The subject–object binary will be countered by the unitary structure of a situated, meaning-laden being-in-the-world. Foundationalism will be countered by the radical finitude of being and the temporal–historical character of existence. Accordingly, human thought and experience will be construed as an *engaged openness* rather than a detached quest for foundations. I labored over how much preparatory material to provide before turning to the matter of ethics. I decided in favor of a rather lengthy orientation in Heidegger's thought for two reasons: Readers unfamiliar with Heidegger need a good deal of guidance in fathoming this difficult thinker; and even many of Heidegger's learned readers have missed, distorted, or misinterpreted important elements of his thinking that need to be addressed properly if they are to bear fruit in this investigation. So I think the extensive setup is warranted. Although it might seem distracting or frustrating to delay the discussion of ethics in this way, my hope is that the sustained background preparation will pay off for readers.

Chapter 2 completes the preparatory material by laying out the features of a pluralistic conception of truth that can underwrite a robust alternative to philosophical treatments that either overestimate or underestimate the prospects for truth in the field of ethics. With Heidegger it is possible to talk about a world-disclosive sense of truth that need not be restricted to scientific objectivity and that need not collapse into some kind of subjectivism.

Chapter 3 parallels chapter 1 by first sketching elements of modern moral philosophy, and then launching from each of the main features of Heidegger's thought some applications to the sphere of ethics. Of particular importance will be Heideggerian alternatives to the modern emphasis on autonomy, rationality, and individuality, as well as a deconstruction of familiar divisions between facts and values, cognition and emotion, theory and practice.[3]

Chapter 4 takes a historical turn by exploring the relationship between Heidegger and Aristotle, and the possibilities for ethics implicit in this relationship. Heidegger's early interest in Aristotle's ethics as an opening for his ontological investigations will serve to open up both the ethical potential in Heidegger's thought and the prospects for some postmodern modifications of Aristotle's premodern ethical outlook.

Chapter 5 continues the association with Aristotle by addressing the recent revival of virtue ethics as an alternative to modern moral theories. Heideggerian modifications of Aristotelian virtue will be illustrated in discussions of *phronēsis*, desire, and courage. This chapter also initiates a consideration of the role of moral principles in ethical life.

Chapter 6 ventures an analysis of empathy along Heideggerian lines. Empathy will be construed as a mode of human attunement disclosing the existential weal and woe of others, and as such it serves the basic function of opening up moral import, interest, and motivation. With Heidegger we can overcome interpretations of empathy as a strictly subjective phenomenon, and we can also make better sense out of important findings in developmental psychology that suggest a natural human predisposition for empathic concern. The limits of empathy and its relation to moral principles are also discussed.

Chapter 7 utilizes Heidegger's analysis of social life and authenticity to argue for an ambiguous blending of socialization and individuation in ethical existence, as contrasted with polar oppositions implicated in debates between liberalism and communitarianism. The finitude of being and the engaged openness of the human self will be employed to explore Heideggerian perspectives on freedom, respect, identity, and responsibility.

I hope to persuade the reader in the pages to come that bringing Heidegger into a discussion of ethics will make a genuine contribution to moral philosophy. In general terms (to be defended in more detail as we proceed), the distinctiveness

6 *Introduction*

of a Heideggerian perspective will turn on how it improves upon modern and postmodern approaches to ethics in the following ways. The advantage over modern and postconventional approaches will involve how finite being-in-the-world (1) opens a space for ethical meanings that had been lost in the wake of scientific objectivism, (2) improves upon reason-based models by bringing affects, dispositions, prereflective habits, and tradition into the picture, (3) gives social relations a primacy that accordingly need not be defended or constructed in the face of supposed gaps between isolated, autonomous individuals, and (4) accords well with the openness, contingency, uncertainty, and ambiguity of ethical practice.

The advantage over other developments in continental philosophy that have taken up ethics (and that have usually owed much of their pedigree to Heidegger's thought) is that finite being-in-the-world is a *situated openness*, and many trends in continental philosophy have either underplayed openness in favor of situatedness or underplayed situatedness in favor of openness. The latter effect is especially true of many so-called postmodern approaches to ethics, where much of the ethical sphere has been understood as a regime of normalization that suppresses difference, creativity, and cultural transgression.

In the face of these various approaches, my contention is that Heidegger's thought can help advance moral philosophy by articulating a number of correlations that together shape the contours and the tensions of an ethical world: correlations of finitude and meaning, situatedness and openness, encumbrance and freedom, prereflective understanding and formal reflection, affect and cognition, sociality and individuation, tradition and innovation. My general aim is to show how Heidegger's way of thinking is able to articulate both the claim and the finite complexity of ethical existence.

NOTES

1. Some works that have explored ethical ramifications of Heidegger's thinking include Charles E. Scott, *The* Question *of Ethics: Nietzsche, Foucault, Heidegger* (Bloomington: Indiana University Press, 1990); Reiner Schürmann, *Heidegger on Being and Acting: From Principles to Anarchy*, trans. Christine Marie Gros (Bloomington: Indiana University Press, 1987); Lawrence Vogel, *The Fragile "We": Ethical Implications of Heidegger's* Being and Time (Evanston, Ill.: Northwestern University Press, 1994); Joanna Hodge, *Heidegger and Ethics* (New York: Routledge, 1995); Frederick A. Olafson, *Heidegger and the Ground of Ethics: A Study of* Mitsein (Cambridge: Cambridge University Press, 1998); Nancy J. Holland, *The Madwoman's Reason: The Concept of the Appropriate in Ethical Thought* (University Park: Pennsylvania State University Press, 1998); Werner Marx, *Is There a Measure on Earth? Foundations for a Nonmetaphysical Ethics*, trans. Thomas J. Nenon and Reginald Lilly (Chicago: University of Chicago Press, 1987); and Werner Marx, *Towards a Phenomenological Ethics: Ethics and the Life-World*, trans. Stefaan Heyvaert (Albany: SUNY Press, 1992).

2. I should add that, unlike some scholars, I use the terms "ethical" and "moral" interchangeably. I will reserve the term "ethics," however, for the enterprise of moral philosophy.

3. In this chapter and throughout the book, the reader will recognize a mix of metaethical topics (questions concerning moral psychology, ethical development, truth in ethics, the nature and status of values, and so forth) and normative topics (considerations of better and worse ways of living and defenses of certain ethical positions).

Chapter One

An Overview of Heidegger's Thought

To understand Heidegger's treatment of the being-question, it is best to begin with his criticisms of the subject–object distinction originating in the thought of René Descartes.[1] The narrative elements in Descartes's *Meditations* help us get started. Descartes's motivation for his philosophical project stemmed from the clashes, confusions, and controversies generated by the New Science and its departures from traditional beliefs and common sense. His intentions were to (1) justify the new scientific orientation in the face of customary powers and habits of thought, and (2) secure this orientation with a methodological ideal of strict certainty. In order to accomplish these aims, Descartes took a retreat from home, education, community, custom, and practical affairs by traveling and engaging in solitary reflection. With his strict criterion of methodical skepticism, Descartes found every form of thought and experience doubtful except the absolute certainty of the doubting consciousness itself, the *cogito*. Consequently, he located certainty in the thinking subject and thus in the realm of abstract ideas divorced from material things and the confusing flux of sense experience.

For Heidegger, Descartes's posture and findings dramatize and embody the path of modern science in its mathematical essence, in which the truths about nature are discovered through mathematical constructs, laws of motion, and mechanical causal relations. Accordingly, things in the world are now conceived as simply units of matter in motion, quantifiable locations on a grid of space–time coordinates, a framework uniformly applicable to any and all kinds of entities. The world is thus stripped bare of particular and variable features, customary meanings and values, common-sense beliefs, practical relations, human involvement—all accomplished through the reflective distance and "inward" turn of abstraction from the immediacy of lived experience. This turn is shown in the primacy of method in modern science and philosophy, where the rational mind constructs *in advance* the criteria and rules for how entities will be properly understood. With modern standards of abstract principles, mathematization, uniformity, causal necessity, and predictability, the world is disclosed as a set of "objects" that are shaped by way of preconceived constructions of a disengaged, rational "subject."

A momentous ideal that emerges out of such an orientation is the *free rational individual*, which is central to so much of modern thought. Here we have a heroic narrative of the critical thinker liberated from dependency on tradition, community, custom, and superstition, arriving at rational methods and truths that are *self-grounding*—an epistemological echo of the old theological *causa sui*. But in view of the new model of scientific objectivity, the cost of these developments is, in Max Weber's famous phrase, the "disenchantment" of the world. The world is rendered simply as an aggregate of brute objects explainable by mechanical laws, abstract properties, and causal relations. Notions of existential significance—meanings, values, and purposes—are no longer intrinsic to reality (as was the case in ancient and medieval thought). The world itself is devoid of such significance. If these meanings are to have a location, they cannot be found in objects but rather in the human subject: either in the epistemologically deficient sense of being "mere" human or individual projections upon nature that have little intellectual status, or in an alternative foundational sense of being traceable to certain necessary faculties in the subject. In either case, existential significance is no longer a feature of the world, but simply a human, subjective matter. The world itself is stripped of existential significance in deference to modern science's objective methods and discoveries.

Concurrent with this stripping effect is the rise of instrumental reason, where the disengaged subject can picture the world as a fund of resources and raw materials that is manipulable and controllable on behalf of human needs and interests (witness the Industrial Revolution and the growth of capitalism in this era). As Descartes himself indicated, the central benefit of the new mechanical model of nature is the power of technological control it unleashes for those who come to understand the secrets of nature's workings; humans then can become "the masters and possessors of nature."[2]

In sum, the modern philosophical orientation answers the question of being (of what things "are") with a dyadic ontology of subject and object, with each sphere receiving its respective grounding in (1) rational principles, faculties, and methods, and (2) measurable properties, causal relations, verification procedures, and prediction/control efficacy.

HEIDEGGER'S STARTING POINT

Heidegger's philosophical approach unfolds as a critical interrogation of this modern ontology. Why should we settle for this conception of being that involves such a complex disengagement from more original modes of thinking and experience? Why accept the discrediting or devaluing of these more immediate milieus? Heidegger employs a phenomenological approach that seeks always to disclose phenomena in the way they appear, without preconceptions or assumptions that conceal, ignore, or explain away such modes of appearing. In this way room can be made for disclosures that precede or exceed modern conceptions of subject and object.

An important example of Heidegger's phenomenological approach is that the question of being itself announces that being-in-question is a phenomenon that first demands attention. As we will see later, being-in-question is indicative of the openness and finitude of being, and it also brings into view that being for whom the question matters, the questioner, namely human being. Heidegger's coinage for human being is *Dasein*, which is chosen in part to subvert and sidestep subject–object, human–world polarities. In turning phenomenological attention to Dasein, Heidegger insists that we must begin with the way Dasein first normally understands its world, in everyday life and practices. We must start with what is disclosed "proximally and for the most part" (*BT*, 37), with what is initially and usually closest to us and part of our lives before philosophical reflection.

Before the detached, reflective standpoint of Cartesian subjectivity and scientific objectivity, we are "always already" (*immer schon*) shaped by everyday concerns, practical involvements, moods and affects, inherited customs and traditions, social relations, and language uses. These spheres cannot be bracketed or displaced in any philosophical inquiry that aims for a comprehensive understanding of the meaning of being, unless we commit to some fanciful story about an original defect of ignorance and subsequent deliverance or correction—a notion which indeed has been alive in the Western tradition in different forms (for instance, the Christian doctrine of the fall and the Platonic myth of recollection).³

Dasein is being-in-the-world, which means it is never separable from world involvement, and it cannot be understood as a discrete subject on one side of a self-world relation. Da-sein is the "there" of being, the disclosive opening of and to being. Additionally, Heidegger alters the meaning of two classic philosophical terms by claiming that Dasein's "essence" is its "existence" (*BT*, 67). For Heidegger, essence is not to be understood as a foundational, fixed determination of "what" something is; rather, essence (*Wesen*, connected to the verb *sein*) is to be taken in a verbal sense (*ET*, 137), as a coming-to-be in the *way* something unfolds. And existence is not to be understood in terms of mere empirical presence, or even Jean-Paul Sartre's characterization of consciousness as opposed to things in the world. For Heidegger, existence is to be understood in terms of the Greek *ek-stasis*, as standing out; that is to say, not the "inside" of a discrete consciousness, not even an outside as the "other side" of consciousness, but a standing *in* the out, an immersion *in* the "there" of being that characterizes Dasein's prereflective involvement in the world.⁴

BEING AND BEINGS

Heidegger establishes a central distinction between ontical and ontological analyses. The ontical refers to particular beings in the ways that they show themselves. The ontological refers to the being of beings, or how beings are understood in a general sense. It is important to stress that beings manifest themselves in different ways (*BT*, 37), which call for a pluralistic sense of "regional ontologies," or specific ways in which beings are disclosed (in history, mathematics, natural science, literature, ethics, and so on). Heidegger also calls for a "fundamental ontology," which inquires into the meaning of being that underlies beings and all regional ontologies. In this regard, Heidegger insists on the "ontological difference," in the sense that being will be fundamentally different from positive descriptions of beings and regional ontologies. Being is associated with the existential *meaning* that animates Dasein's involvement in the world, and with a negativity that exceeds conditions of actual beings and that generates existential meaning. For Heidegger, being is not a being or a collection of beings or an abstraction drawn from characteristics of beings (for instance, matter). Being is associated with the process of disclosing the meaning of the world in its finitude. Accordingly, being is "essentially finite" (*WM*, 108). The finitude of being does not refer simply to spatial, temporal, definitional, or cognitive limits, but also to how an awareness of absence is intrinsic to the presence of things (*BP*, 311). This will become clearer later when I discuss the meaning of possibility, temporality, and death.

The ontological difference does not refer to different realms of reality. Being and beings are distinct but never separate from each other. Being is always the being *of* beings (*BT*, 29). Correspondingly, Dasein's existence is understood by way of two distinct modes of analysis, the existentiell and the existential (*BT*, 33): The existentiell refers to the ontic sphere of Dasein's concrete living situations and tasks; the existential refers to the general ontological structures exhibited in Dasein's existence. An existential analysis is a philosophical inquiry into fundamental concepts, rather than attention to regional ontologies or specific modes of life. *Being and Time* aims for an existential analysis, but Heidegger is quick to point out that such philosophical constructions are always grounded in, and point back to, existentiell conditions (*BT*, 34).

FORMAL INDICATION

Central to the above discussion is Heidegger's important notion of formal indication (*formale Anzeige*), which is prominent in early works and lecture courses surrounding *Being and Time*.[5] For Heidegger, philosophical concepts are not a priori structures or transcendental conditions in the Kantian sense of fixed categories that ground thinking, but rather formal indications: formal in terms of abstract, conceptual generality, and indications in the sense of "pointing to" (*anzeigen*) concrete existentiell conditions of life and action that cannot be fully captured in, or exhausted by, conceptual forms. Indeed these formal concepts can only be discovered by phenomenological attention to concrete life experiences. It is the reflective "idleness" of philosophy that tempts us to think that conceptual constructions are ascertainable entities in and of themselves, but this is a mistake (*FCM*, 292, 294). Heidegger clearly states that "formal characterization does not gives us the essence" (*FCM*, 293); it simply indicates the *task* of philosophical thinking that can only be exhibited and played out in life.

Formal indication points positively toward life possibilities, but *as* possibility it has a negative, limiting character in refusing to reduce philosophical concepts to any particular worldview (*GA* 61, 141). Formal indication also does not provide any foundational or metaphysical comfort that would supersede the flux of life, but only a rough sketch that prepares a leap into the irreducible movements of existence (*GA* 61, 34, 37). One could say that, for Heidegger, traditional philosophy has stressed its formal aspects while overlooking or concealing its indicative aspects; in other words, the tradition has confused the map with the journeyed terrain.

THE HERMENEUTIC CIRCLE

Contrary to the idea of knowledge as the discovery of freestanding facts or truths independent of human involvement—some uninterpreted "given" out of which inferences can proceed from unadulterated, stable foundations—Heidegger insists that all forms of thought are saturated with prior modes of understanding that Dasein brings to any inquiry. Consequently, philosophical thought must work on and with already operating forces and capacities, rather than see itself as the search for some purely objective ground. For Heidegger, interpretation goes all the way down. As opposed to the ideal of transparent, self-grounding subjectivity in modern thought, Dasein "always already" has a historical understanding of being before it is subjected to reflection and analysis. Hermeneutics discounts the possibility of a "view from nowhere." No inquiry begins from scratch; it is always shaped by prior modes of understanding or direction that usually go unnoticed *because* of their tacit character.

For Heidegger, the "already" element shows that interpretation is not a one-sided construction or invention of Dasein. Yet knowledge is always historically animated and prepared, so we cannot assume that inquiry can arrive at some pure, unmediated starting point. Dasein, then, must always move within a hermeneutic circle, which is "vicious" only in light of the traditional linear model of demonstrative reasoning from clear and distinct foundations. For Heidegger, the circle is a virtuous one that simply needs to be acknowledged, entered, and explored (*BT*, 194–95).

What is already given for Dasein is shown in the prereflective background mentioned earlier: practical involvements, affects, social relations, inherited traditions, language, and especially an *interest* in whatever inquiry is at hand. I would add something that I explore later in some detail, namely child rearing. Each mature Dasein brings to any endeavor the effects and influences (both tacit and overt) of its enculturation since the first moments of life.

In a general sense, the questioning character of Dasein organizes well the contours of the hermeneutic circle. Being-in-question is a primal phenomenon that exhibits a temporal and historical structure, the openness of which preempts all attempts to ground thought in achieved or prospective answers. Questioning is an *engaged openness*, a mingling of presence and absence, of having and not having, which both situates us and exceeds actuality. In philosophy we put in question something with which we are already familiar to some degree (What is the good life?). Our inheritances and past engagements are what prompt the interest in the inquiry and its vague intimations of familiarity. But *as* questioned, the phenomenon in question is exceeded, since there is something yet to be disclosed; so we are not locked into any extant actuality, but open to future possibilities. Being-in-question does not mean that no answers are to be found, but simply that searching and discovering are not a means toward fixed and closed results.

The "already" character of thought, for Heidegger, is different from Platonic recollected essences that precede and transcend concrete existence, from innate ideas (Descartes), and from abstract, theoretical a priori structures that provide necessary, ahistorical "transcendental" conditions for the possibility of experience (Immanuel Kant, Edmund Husserl). Rather, philosophy involves formal indication, ontological generalizations that aim to elucidate and modify vague, everyday, prereflective understanding, but that also must pass through, be informed by, and refer back to, concrete conditions of life.[6]

Philosophy as interpretation, then, is not demonstration or proof, but descriptive phenomenology, the attempt to gather in language (*logos*) an elucidation of the phenomenon in question *as* it appears in its unfolding and already-given character. Philosophy is a linguistic/conceptual attempt to be faithful to prereflective experience. As phenomenology, it is a letting what shows itself appear in the way that it shows itself (*BT*, 51ff). In the letting-appear construction, the "letting" indicates that the showing requires Dasein's engagement, while the "appear" indicates that the showing is something *to* which Dasein responds. Phenomenology is a *responsive engagement* with the world. The interpretive character of philosophy is indicated both in what Dasein brings to inquiry and in how Dasein gears and adjusts its inquiry to its environment. Such a reciprocal relation precludes any reduction of thought to a subject or an object.

In sum, philosophy, as temporal–historical interpretation, is not the discovery of freestanding facts, causes, or fixed conditions, but more a movement from implication to explication (*BT*, 188–89). As such, however, philosophy is not arbitrary; since Dasein is *in* the world already, philosophy cannot be a mere "construction" superimposed on some raw, amorphous receptacle. As interpretation, though, philosophy is tenuous, searching, even experimental (Heidegger always referred to his thought as *unterwegs*, "on the way"). Hermeneutic inquiry presupposes a reflexive awareness of the contingent, historical situatedness shaping the inquiry, and thus it is different from an insular confinement to a particular historical framework. Hermeneutics implies an openness to other possible modes of thought.

Phenomenological philosophy is addressive formal indication, it can only offer itself for readers to gauge its appropriateness to experience; reader response is always presupposed. At one point in *Being and Time*, Heidegger acknowledges the circularity of his own text as interpretation; it cannot engage in proof, but only an "allowing to come into words" of an understanding of being, from which one can discern for oneself whether its formal–indicative sketch is disclosive of modes of being (*BT*, 362–63).

DESTRUCTION OF TRADITION

Because the philosophical tradition, especially modern philosophy, has overlooked or concealed the existential elements described above, Heidegger engages in a "destruction" of the tradition (*BT*, 41ff). Such engagement is not a destroying, but a destructuring of the tradition to open up its hidden or tacit dimensions, its "positive possibilities" (*BT*, 44). It is quite important for my purposes to establish that Heidegger does not dismiss the philosophical tradition and what it has disclosed; he frequently notes that various philosophical (and scientific) orientations have properly disclosed elements of the world. Heidegger aims to address what has been concealed in such disclosure. In general, what has been concealed in "positive" disclosures is the radically finite and temporal character of being. For Heidegger, "being" is more a verb than a noun, more a temporal–historical unfolding than a foundational "constant presence." Heidegger thus aims to open, deepen, and enrich the tradition rather than replace it with something entirely different.

When Heidegger critiques notions such as subject and object, he is not denying the phenomena of "self" and "things" in the world; he is only challenging the distortions and omissions of philosophical *theories* that are not adequate to the phenomena. In fact, Heidegger even admits that traditional theoretical constructions are disclosive in a way and even harbor deeper implications consonant with his own ontological searchings (*BT*, 72ff). The problem is that these traditions have become so encrusted they block any movement, and so they must be challenged and supplemented. Such is the task of the innovative philosophical language of *Being and Time*.

BEING-IN-THE-WORLD

We have already established that "subject and object do not coincide with Dasein and world" (*BT*, 87). Reflective disengagement from everyday practices and involvement creates the space of a supposed "internal" consciousness counterposed to "external" things in the world. Such a division makes possible classic philosophical problems that have marked the modern period: radical skepticism about the existence of the external world or other minds; bifurcations of fact and value, the theoretical and the practical; and a host of philosophical problems generated by these bifurcations. Heidegger's conception of being-in-the-world precedes such divisional thinking, and it also exhibits elements of existential meaning and movement, which undermine abstract, fixed constructions that have amounted to a stabilization and reification of being.

The tradition has tended to turn Dasein into a "positive" content (*BT*, 72ff): rational animal, creature of God, biological organism, psychological faculties, material properties, soul, subject, consciousness, spirit, life. Heidegger's alternative phenomenological rendering of Dasein is being-in-the-world. Dasein is *in* the world, not in the sense of a merely objective, spatial, locational "in," but more in the sense of being involved or at home, an in-habitive sense captured in the word "dwelling" (*BT*, 80). Heidegger writes emphatically: "Dwelling is the essence of being-in-the-world" (*LH*, 260). Dasein's existence is initially an involved familiarity, as opposed to a disengaged reflection on an object simply present to the gaze of consciousness, a reflection that presupposes a division and exchange between discrete spheres inside and outside the mind. Being-in-the-world essentially exhibits modes of concern (*Besorgen*)

> having to do with something, producing something, attending to something and looking after it, making use of something, giving something up and letting it go, undertaking, accomplishing, evincing, interrogating, considering, discussing, determining. . . . (*BT,* 83)

> caring is the care of livelihood, of profession, of enjoyment, of being undisturbed, of not dying, of being familiar with, of knowing about, of making life secure in its final goals. (*AI,* 361–62)

This latter text also mentions something quite important for my purposes, namely the performative element of being-in-the-world prior to objectification. Dasein's modes of concern involve forms of *Vollzug*, which means performance, execution, and actualization (*AI*, 362). The text also provides a threefold organizational structure for analyzing the concept of world that I want to employ: the world understood as a self-world (*Selbstwelt*), an environing-world (*Umwelt*), and a with-world (*Mitwelt*).

THE SELF-WORLD

The term "world" in this construction is meant to show that selfhood, for Heidegger, is not a matter of sheer subjectivity in the modern sense, but it does express and allow for the particular perspectives of individual selves. Heidegger goes so far as to say that the being of Dasein is "in each case mine" (*BT*, 67). The central concept of "mineness" (*Jemeinigkeit*) has been the source of a good amount of confusion and misinterpretation. First of all, the inclusion of *je* in the concept is meant to indicate the plurality and particularity of occasions of concern, rather than some kind of universal constancy. Mineness is a contextual specificity of existential mattering that is not equivalent to an ego or egoism, or a metaphysical self, but simply those meanings indicated in first-person pronoun usages (*BT*, 68). The upshot of mineness is that being *matters* to each Dasein in its modes of existence. Consequently, "I am a scientist" or "I want to help you" would be expressive of mineness. Additionally, the primacy of mineness stands as a warning against third-person biases and predilections in philosophy (talk of entities, properties, and so on, that take the third-person grammatical form). Philosophical activity is addressive in expressing and referring to a first-person element that cannot be severed from intellectual work.

Mention should be made here of another important concept that is prominent in early lecture courses, *Jeweiligkeit* (see *HCT*, 152–54). *Jeweiligkeit* names a temporal contextuality referring to each specific "while" or occurrence. Together, *Jemeinigkeit* and *Jeweiligkeit* gather a sense of mattering, specificity, and temporality that announces Heidegger's alternative to the predominance of strict objectivity, homogeneity, and universality in traditional ontology, an issue that will become quite important in this study.

THE ENVIRONING-WORLD

For Heidegger, being is not an object and the world cannot be understood as simply a collection of objects. The being of the world is a context of meaning organized around the phenomenon of care (*Sorge*). The analysis begins with a consideration of practical dealings with things in terms of use and production (*BT*, 96), something opened up by the phenomenon of tool use—the *using* of a tool, not just thinking about use (*BT*, 98ff). Tool use is characterized as *zuhanden*, which means in use or available for use, as opposed to something *vorhanden*, or merely present before an attentive gaze. *Zuhandenheit* refers to practical familiarity, competence, and involvement, which is generally designated as circumspection (*Umsicht*). In using my pen, for example, I am not considering objective properties of the pen or standing back and reflecting on the pen or my purposes. I am simply engaged in a purposive practice and tacit competence animated by the web of concerns that figure in my writing. Such practice is illustrative of various forms of in-order-to that exhibit Dasein's "to be" character. These tacit, purposive practices cannot be captured in object–property language, or in accounts of an "exchange" between internal intentions and external execution (for instance, writing with a pen as conscious or unconscious inferences and applications of beliefs). In engaged, purposive familiarity there is simply an environmental, practical field.

As is typical of Heidegger's approach, the meaning of this field of circumspective concern is disclosed by way of a certain negation; that is, in a breakdown of the practice field occasioned by a disruption or malfunction. As Heidegger puts it, "everything positive becomes particularly clear when seen from the side of the privative" (*BP*, 309). If my pen runs out of ink or seems too heavy or too small for comfortable use, I become more explicitly aware of the purposive background in the light of obstacles. And my reaction to a breakdown (being startled, annoyed, and so forth) *shows* the tacitly purposeful character of the practice for Dasein, which would not be exhibited by, say, a robotic writing device. The breakdown also turns my attention to relevant properties of the tool (the point of the pen, the ink supply, the shape, weight, and so on) that in use are not in my attention, and also to explicit purposes (I cannot write until I get another pen).

In general terms, then, Dasein's everyday existence is originally an interrelated web of practices and competencies, an intersectional confluence of self and world that is not *experienced* as a subject–object transaction, as an internal cognitive grasp of external things. It is less a knowing-that and more a knowing-how and knowing-for, whose tacit meanings and features are made explicit in disruptions. Heidegger is not denying objective reality in the sense of things or properties independent of Dasein or of use. Nor is he denying subjective reality in the sense of thoughts, intentions, and beliefs. His claim is simply that subject–object ontologies are not adequate to express prereflective practice. Indeed, for Heidegger, the notions of beliefs and objective properties are *vorhanden* constructions that are phenomenologically derived from *zuhanden* conditions, since the former emerge out of the latter (*BT*, 121), by way of disruption and disengagement and by way of the purposive background that provides the *interest* in *vorhanden* properties. The general point is that before we reflect on ourselves or the world, we are immersed in concrete, indivisible practices of purposive concern.

It is important to note that, for Heidegger, both the *vorhanden* and the *zuhanden* are genuine modes of disclosure. So disengaged descriptions can truly reveal certain elements of the world. The problem is that modern philosophy has taken scientific objectivity, which is a highly sophisticated extension of the *vorhanden* perspective (*BT*, 412–13), as the primary and exclusive ontological measure. Heidegger simply wants to challenge this priority by beginning with the *zuhanden*.

Since this is a crucial element in Heidegger's argument that will bear on my discussion, I will dwell for a moment on the relation between the *zuhanden* and the *vorhanden*. Surely objective descriptions and talk of mental operations show something important, but attention to unreflective practices that do not articulate a transaction between beliefs and objects would force standard models of cognition to suggest something like unconscious inferences, a maneuver that at least is phenomenologically suspect. But what about learning new skills or confronting unfamiliar experiences? In cases of, say, learning a new language or how to play the piano, there seems to be a clear sense of reflective distance from practice and clear analytical divisions between mental beliefs and conditions in the world separate from beliefs: That word *Welt* is the German term for my word "world." That note on the page refers to this key that I must remember to hit with this finger, and so on. This is quite true, but it is not a substantive challenge to Heidegger's position. First of all, Heidegger does not deny or exclude distinct spacings of reflective distance from practice, which are essential for learning new practices. We should notice, however, that such learning milieus always bank on other background competencies and tacit familiarities that make the learning possible. For instance, I already understand what words and notation are, how to follow instructions, how to converse, how to use relevant devices such as books and pencils, and so on—a background that is not explicitly thematized in the learning environment. In addition, when the new skill has been mastered, the learned practice then becomes an unreflective, skillful, familiar competency; that is, it becomes the "second nature" of habit, where one can speak the new language or play the piano without reflective distance, polarized spacings, and analytical divisions.

One strength of Heidegger's position is its comprehensiveness. His phenomenological analysis can incorporate and account for objective modes of disclosure as a derivative, disengaged abstraction from prereflective practice. Subject–object ontologies have a difficult task in accounting for prereflective practice (if it is treated at all). As we have seen, in using a pen, objective properties and self-consciousness are recessed: I do not normally experience the activity as a mental formation of beliefs and intentions that are transferred to bodily maneuvers linked up with external conditions judged to fit my intentions—I simply pick up the pen and write. The comprehensiveness of Heidegger's account can also be seen in its capacity to articulate engaged elements in even highly reflective activities that usually go unnoticed. Even advanced models of scientific objectivity cannot be divorced from (1) the tacit competencies of scientific practice, from basic skills to utilization of laboratory devices (see *BT*, 409), and (2) the interest in, and meaningfulness of, the scientific enterprise itself.

In considering the environing-world, Heidegger's phenomenology opens up not only Dasein's practice field, but also the deeper background of *potentiality* (*BT*, 119). In its practices, Dasein exhibits continual modes of "in order to" and "for the sake of." Such potentiality cannot be adequately captured in representational categories of intentions and goals—which amount to *vorhanden* constructions that limit, polarize, and freeze the meaning and movements of potentiality into subjective origins and objective outcomes. Dasein as being-potential is a rich and complex web of meanings, circumstances, desires, tasks, burdens, limits, concerns, and performances—for instance, the full story of *being* a teacher, a parent, or a scientist.

The complex, fluid field of Dasein's being-in-the-world is an elusive but tangible existential environment. Dasein inhabits a meaningful world before it is subjected to reflection and abstract organization. In everyday experience we do not originally perceive our activities in terms of raw, neutral data (mere sense impressions of colors, shapes, movements, and so forth) subsequent to which "meaning" and "value" are "added on" by some kind of psychic transfer (*BT*, 132). Contrary to modern philosophy and science, where the natural world is taken to be value-free, or independent of human interests, Heidegger maintains that Dasein's original experience of the world is interest-laden. Accordingly, from a Heideggerian perspective, phenomena such as interests, uses, purposes, and values can be said to "be" in the world, and not simply in the subject, because subject–object dichotomies are derived from a more original confluence of environmental meanings.

THE WITH-WORLD

The modern conception of the self has tended to be individualistic. Its internalization of reflection divorces the self not only from its environment but also from other selves. The prevailing view has taken social relations as a second-order sphere compared to the original immediacy of self-consciousness. And epistemologically, the emphasis has been on monological reason, where knowledge is understood from the standpoint of the individual mind, its faculties, and rational procedures. Heidegger, however, follows Georg Hegel in arguing for a social self. Dasein is "essentially *Mitsein* (being-with)" (*BT*, 156). For Heidegger, sociality goes all the way down. For instance, the practices of the environing-world are primarily social practices, as a relatedness to others and their practices (my writing for readers with pen and paper made by others, and so on). Again I would add the importance of child-rearing and the essential dependence on others to be enculturated into a world of practices.

Social relations are not inside-out connections between mutually secluded selves. Others are part of the disclosive "there" of Dasein's being. Being-with is part of Dasein's being-in, part of Dasein's inhabitive dwelling (*BT*, 155). In everyday dealings, I do not "launch" myself into social relations from the standpoint of a discrete, interior consciousness. I *am* with others in innumerable co-concerns and social transactions that continually occupy my life. This is not to deny individuality, or distinctions between self and others, or the inwardness of self-conscious reflection, but only to assert an interactive social milieu that is more original than the individualized model of the conscious self.

To summarize the preceding conceptions of Dasein's world: In contrast to the modern division between subject and object, between an interior self and an external world, Heidegger argues for an original ekstatic structure of Dasein, where the standing-out is rhetorically counterposed to the supposed interiority of consciousness. The "out" is not even a movement from the inside of consciousness, but an ekstatic dwelling *in* the world, *there* in Dasein's environment, and *with* other Daseins. Accordingly, Dasein's existence exhibits an original, ekstatic in/there/with structure.

Notice how various problems associated with modern philosophy can be dissolved in view of this ekstatic structure. With self-conscious, reflective disengagement and its concomitant subject–object dichotomies, it might seem plausible to question the existence of the external world or other minds, or puzzle as to how ideas relate to things in the world, or how beliefs relate to practices, or how values relate to facts. But say I am working with someone who is showing me how to restore an old piece of furniture, guiding me along in the various skills and handling of materials that mark the practice. Heidegger's phenomenology is able to express how the meaning of the task and its environmental, behavioral, and linguistic transactions are completely intrinsic to the practice, so that the aforementioned theoretical questions and puzzles would never arise (indeed they would surely undermine the endeavor).

Next we consider how Dasein's ekstatic in/there/with structure is *disclosive* of the world and the meaning of being, how Da-sein, as the "there" of being, opens up the world. Such disclosiveness occurs through three fundamental concepts in Heidegger's analysis: affective attunement (*Befindlichkeit*), understanding (*Verstehen*), and language (*Rede*).

AFFECTIVE ATTUNEMENT

A fundamental mode of being-in-the-world that discloses the "there" is found in Heidegger's coinage of *Befindlichkeit* and its manifestations in mood (*Stimmung*).[7] Mood can be called an affective attunement (drawing on connotations of *stimmen*), a precognitive disclosure of various ways in which the world *matters* to Dasein (*BT*, 176) and interests Dasein.[8] Heidegger insists that moods should not be understood as subjective or inner states, which is why "feeling" and "affect" can be misleading (*BT*, 178).[9] A mood is not an interior condition, because it is ekstatic in disclosing how the world matters, a kind of "atmospheric" background that precedes and makes possible any particular endeavor's pursuits and findings (*FCM*, 68). A mood, then, is what I would call "ambient attunement." And it is important to note that, for Heidegger, mood can be collective and public, not simply an individual locus of experience (*BT*, 178). Indeed, mood is something that constitutes being-with-one-another (*FCM*, 67).[10] There can even be a fundamental cultural mood (*Grundstimmung*) that marks an era or time.[11] At any rate, mood is a pervasive and ever-present orientation that marks any comportment toward the world, ranging from intense extremes such as joy or grief to more subtle forms such as vague contentment and

slight apprehension. There is never an absence of mood, only changes of mood
(*FCM*, 68).

Since *Befindlichkeit* is primarily an emergent ambience that is not subject to conscious control (it is how one "finds oneself"), Heidegger introduces an important
concept here that will be crucial in much of his ontology, namely "thrownness"
(*Geworfenheit*). This concept can again be understood as a rhetorical counterstroke
to the modern conception of the subject as a self-grounding, self-originating, self-
directed agency. For Heidegger, Dasein is not and cannot be in complete control of
its being, because in various ways it is "thrown" into its world.

UNDERSTANDING

Understanding, in Heidegger's analysis, is different from the cognitive model of
beliefs about the world, and more analogous to the familiarity and know-how of
zuhanden involvement (*HCT*, 298). Understanding does not concern knowledge
of a particular being, but rather Dasein's potentiality-for-being (*BT*, 183). Dasein
is essentially possibility, always "more" than actuality, never a completed condition. Possibility here is not mere logical possibility but the existential meaning
and awareness of life's possibilities, with all their movements, uncertainties, and
concerns. Potentiality can also be taken in the performative sense of capability
(*HCT*, 298). Dasein, then, is able-to-be, a movement of actualizing potentialities
that never comes to rest.

Interpretation is the development and articulation of existential possibilities.
Understanding is the fore-structure of possibility that generates an interpretive as-
structure, where elements of the world are disclosed as pertinent to possibilities
(*BT*, 191). For instance, from my earlier example, the meaning and purpose of
restoring furniture is the fore-structure that animates the as-structure of certain
tools and supplies (for instance, a shaped piece of metal taken *as* a brace, as useful in reinforcing part of the furniture).

For Heidegger, every interpretation presupposes some prior understanding of
Dasein's existential possibilities (*BT*, 194–95). Even science—which sees the
world *as* a set of objects to be examined independent of use and involvement in
order to uncover causal explanations—presupposes modes of meaningful possibility: the interest in learning and discovery; the horizon of science as a quest to
uncover the secrets of nature and as an emancipation from superstition and ignorance. Heidegger makes the important point that even the most "exact" sciences,
such as mathematics, are not devoid of existential concerns and possibilities; they
simply reflect a *narrowing* of the scope of an existential base (*BT*, 195). This
implies a bridging of the supposed divide between the sciences and disciplines
such as history, philosophy, and ethics. The differences in disciplines simply
reflect the *extent* of existential concerns and how the different spheres open up
the world in view of these concerns. Accordingly, not even the "hard sciences"

are interest-free, and so the interest-laden character of, say, ethics, does not as such undermine its intellectual status.

From a philosophical standpoint, Heidegger's phenomenology does imply a certain ordering of disciplines. Since scientific objectivity and causal thinking do not as such articulate the existential meaning of such endeavors, then a language articulating meaning structures will have a certain priority owing to its comprehensiveness. This is simply a phenomenological point and not a denial of, or replacement for, causal thinking. The issue here is simply how to properly orchestrate thinking in response to philosophical questions such as the meaning of being. Causal thinking will have its place, but a limited philosophical role.

As I said earlier, the irreducible hermeneutic circle does not entail that knowledge is arbitrary or up for grabs. Heidegger clearly states that the circle of interpretation contains the possibility of a "primordial kind of knowing" that is attentive to the "things themselves" and not led astray by "fancies and popular conceptions" (*BT*, 195). Heidegger specifically connects interpretation with the notion of appropriateness (*BT*, 188–91), and so we can say that interpretation can and should be *appropriate* to phenomena.[12] But given the hermeneutic circle, the historical character of thinking, and the plurality of modes of disclosure, an interpretive model of thought must be more open than reductive models, such as a strict conception of causal explanation presumed to apply to any and all questions.

Consider the example of a tree. If the question concerns what the tree "is," we can say that the tree can be appropriately interpreted *as* a natural object of scientific study, a source of lumber, a shady spot for a picnic, an obstacle for a road builder, a dwelling for a treehouse, a historical site, a stimulation for artistic works, a thing of beauty, something in need of conservation or protection. Heidegger's phenomenology allows us to say that none of these disclosures is any more or less appropriate than others in an absolute sense, that each is properly disclosive in its own way. None of them represents "the real tree," measured against which the others can be called "mere interpretations" artificially projected onto the thing in question. It is important to stress here that the sense of *appropriate* differences in world-disclosure allows us to say that in a certain sense Heidegger is a pluralistic, phenomenological realist.[13]

Different contexts call for different disclosures. We can say that different modes of understanding—of *possibilities* that prompt different *questions*—provide the different backgrounds (fore-structures) that generate the different interpretations (as-structures). This is the key to Heidegger's ontological pluralism. If the question is, What makes the tree grow?, then a naturalistic causal model is appropriate, is more responsive to the question at hand than other perspectives. But different contexts and questions (Should the tree be preserved or harvested?) issue different accounts appropriately disclosing the different contexts. What is indicated here is a kind of lexical orchestration that shifts with different contexts. How Dasein's understanding is articulated in different ways brings us to the question of language.

LANGUAGE

The issue of language is crucial to Heidegger's phenomenology. Rather than a mere formal analysis of language, Heidegger explores the existential setting of speech-practice, exchanges of speech in Dasein's inhabited world. Affective attunement, understanding, and language can be distinguished in philosophical analysis, but in reality they are an indivisible whole, and a certain priority is given to language (*BT*, 172). For one thing, Heidegger points out that in arriving at language in the phenomenological analysis, we should not forget that language has already been operating throughout the text (*BT*, 203).

In stressing language as a practice, we come to findings very different from the philosophical tradition's emphasis on ideas in the mind. Language is essentially a public, communicative practice, a shared articulation of Dasein's dwelling in the world. Language should be understood more as something situated in the world, rather than as something originating in conscious thought and then launched out to others in the outside world. Indeed, like other modes of existence, language is ekstatically "there" in Dasein's world (*BT*, 205). In addition to communicative practice, an analysis of language should include sounds, movements, intonations, rhythms, nonverbal gestures, silences, hearing, listening, and responding (*BT*, 206). All this is much more complex than a science of linguistics that examines words as *vorhanden* entities and explores their verbal meanings, references, relations, structures, usages, and so on (*BT*, 209).

CARE AND ANXIETY

Heidegger's organizational term for the "whole" of Dasein's being-in-the-world is *Sorge*, or care (*BT*, 227). Care gathers in one term a complex of existential meanings: (1) caring about, a concernful mattering (*HCT*, 294), (2) taking care and caring for (*BT*, 157, 243), and (3) a negative sense of worries and burdens (as in the cares of the world). This last sense leads to Heidegger's emphasis on anxiety (*Angst*).

Mood has already been established as essential to Dasein's existence. Anxiety, for Heidegger, is a basic mood that opens up the general meaning of being-in-the-world. Anxiety is an experience in which meaning recedes and Dasein encounters a kind of "nothing." In anxiety, Dasein is *unheimlich*, no longer at home (*BT*, 233). Anxiety is ultimately associated with being-toward-death (*BT*, 310), the awareness of Dasein's ultimate possibility (which is its inevitable impossibility or absence).

The nothing experienced in anxiety is not the negation of the world per se, but the negation of its *meaning*, and thus its being in Heidegger's sense of the term. But Heidegger insists that this encounter with the nothing of meaninglessness is not the opposite of being or meaning, but rather the correlate of being and meaning, as the existential contrast that discloses meaning in the first place. We care about the world and our place in it *because* we are radically finite. Anxiety wrenches us out of familiar world-involvement and discloses the heretofore concealed meaning of that involvement, in a manner analogous to the disruption of *zuhanden* conditions. More on this in a moment.

AUTHENTICITY AND INAUTHENTICITY

For the most part, Dasein's existence is "fallen" (*BT*, 219ff), which does not connote a negative or deficient condition but simply Dasein's fascination with, and absorption in, its world of concerns and social relations, its familiar world of common practices and expectations shared with other Daseins. In its fallen condition of everyday concerns, however, Heidegger claims that Dasein is not "itself" (*BT*, 220). This brings us to the important notion of authenticity (*Eigentlichkeit*).

Here Heidegger is perpetuating a typical philosophical distinction between dimensions that are more and less "true" to the self's nature. But Heidegger's conception of authenticity is radically different from traditional models of the self, and inauthenticity does not indicate a mistaken or improper mode that must be given up or exchanged for something better. Ultimately Dasein "itself" as a "whole" is *not* a being or positive content, but a negative "transcendence" that is sheer possibility and finally the "impossibility" of death (*BT*, 294). Inauthenticity, then, involves a concealment of Dasein's radical finitude by way of a fallen immersion in the world of beings and a confinement to common, familiar modes of understanding, which are organized around the term *das Man*.[14]

The analysis of Dasein's authentic self is found in sections 54 to 60 of *Being and Time*, and it is cast in both ontological and ontical registers. On a more ontological level, authenticity involves the recognition of Dasein's radical finitude. The movement toward authenticity is attested to by the "voice of conscience" summoning Dasein to its "guilt," or "being the basis of a nullity," which is being-toward-death. Authenticity is indicated in "resoluteness," or wanting to hear the call of conscience, and in "anticipation" of death. So Dasein's authentic "self" is the radical negativity of being-toward-death, and hence completely different from traditional positive forms or groundings of selfhood. "Being a basis," the traditional implication of selfhood, is for Heidegger not a substantive foundation, but a radical, temporal thrownness (from birth toward the impossibility of death). Such thrownness "means *never* to have power over one's ownmost being from the ground up" (*BT*, 330). Here we find a conception of an ungrounded self that is "neither substance nor subject" (*BT*, 351). Authenticity involves the self coming to terms with its radical finitude that is usually concealed in its normal involvement with beings.

It is important to recognize the positive implications of such negativity. The nullity of the self is also an openness that is the precondition for freedom, for var-

ious countermovements to fixed conditions (*BT*, 331). The disruptive effect of
being-toward-death also opens up the possibility of ontical, existentiell authenticity by breaking the hold of common, established patterns and allowing an individual self to shape its own resolute existence, to discover modes of being that
are more appropriate to its particularity.

Authenticity, in both ontological and ontical senses, is marked by a double
movement that, again in typical Heideggerian fashion, involves a positive disclosure by virtue of a negative experience, or a process of disorientation and reorientation.[15] First there is the ontological double movement of being-toward-death
and care. The negativity of death discloses the existential meaning of the world
as care. The possibilities of loss, for example, show how and why things matter
to us. The nothing implicated in being-toward-death is that which discloses the
being of beings, that they are—that is, not nothing (*WM*, 103). A brush with death
can sharply open up the value of life in ways quite different from ordinary com-
portments.

> Just as every loss first really allows us to recognize and understand the value of
> something we possessed before, so too it is precisely death that illuminates the
> essence of life. (*FCM*, 266)

Heidegger sees in such a universally recognizable experience a primal phenomenological event that calls for philosophical mapping. The negativity of death,
then, generates the "throw" that opens up a world of meaning. The transcendence
of Dasein reveals an abyss (*Abgrund*) that each Dasein is for itself (*MFL*, 182).
But this is not a dimension apart from the world. Dasein is "held out into the nothing," but not as an empty nothingness. The nothing is a *power* that "constantly
thrusts us back into being," that lets beings be as beings (*FCM*, 299). What is
ingenious about Heidegger's analysis is that "unmeaning" (a limit to, or loss of,
meaning) is not an abnegation of meaning, but part of the very unfolding of
meaning.

Authenticity also involves an ontical double movement in that being-toward-
death disrupts the inauthentic familiarities, commonalities, and leveling tendencies
of *das Man* (*BT*, 321–22), which opens up the possibility of discovering one's own
and richer modes of care. It is important to establish that inauthentic *das Man* is
not a deficient or dispensable condition. Much of the analysis in *Being and Time*
carries the influence of Søren Kierkegaard's critique of bourgeois conformity, and
it gives the impression that authenticity would mean the liberation of the unique
individual from common social patterns. But we are told that authenticity is not a
departure from *das Man* but its modification, and that *das Man* is a "primordial
phenomenon" belonging to Dasein's "positive constitution" (*BT*, 167). *Das Man*
is even identified with the referential context of meaning through which the world
is initially understood (*BT*, 167). We can make sense of this if we interpret *das
Man* in a less pejorative manner as socialization, as the necessarily common ways
in which humans are initially enculturated into social practices, cognitive patterns,

and cultural norms. Some earlier texts make this clear: Everydayness and *das Man* are equated with tradition in the broadest sense (*CT*, 9); *das Man* is called the "common world," Dasein's *first* world *out of which* it can make its own way (*HCT*, 246). Authenticity, then, would refer to the *tension* between socialization and individuation, and not a break with the social world as such.

Authenticity can be understood as a confrontation with possibility in the midst of actuality and the fixation-tendencies of *das Man*. Anxiety and being-toward-death provide a certain distancing from the actual that shows cultural forms as finite *possibilities*, that is to say, as not eternal but historically emergent, as not self-evident but individually appropriable, as not inviolable but alterable. So authenticity can be both *creative*, as an innovative departure from established forms, and *elucidating*, as an apprehension of existing cultural forms that is clearer and sharper than the vague, flat commonplaces of ordinary understanding. In either case, authentic resoluteness is precipitated by an anxious estrangement from the comfort of secure, familiar renderings of the world. Such estrangement, for Heidegger, is always structurally linked to the possibility of an enhanced reorientation in the world, as opposed to some spiritual conception of detachment or intimation of another world, or some pessimistic denial of the world, or some romantic celebration of disintegration.[16]

In a general sense, the tension between authenticity and inauthenticity can be understood in terms of the role of language in Dasein's disclosure. Language allows the "preserving" of disclosure, the handing on and handing down of meanings that emerge in more direct experiences or in innovative discoveries. The synchronic and diachronic "distance" made possible by language allows both the preservation of disclosure and the problematic of inauthenticity. The tendency of inherited meanings to become secured as "tradition" can block the dynamic of new possibilities. Even with respect to traditional meanings, the handing down permits a remoteness from original environments that results in superficial distortions, simplifications, and commodifications of complex cultural notions (consider the easy talk of Americans about "freedom"). Authenticity, then, can be seen as a continuing struggle within language to open up space for new meanings and to plumb the depths of inherited meanings.

TEMPORALITY

The climax of Heidegger's analysis is the correlation of being with time, as opposed to the stable, fixed structures of the tradition, which had always seen time as problematic from an ontological standpoint. With being-in-the-world organized as care and based in the finitude of being-toward-death, the meaning of being is ultimately associated with temporality. Dasein and being in general can no longer be understood in strictly positive terms stemming from the *vorhanden* perspective. Possibility, death, care, and thrownness—which exhibit a confluence of presence and absence, uncovering and concealing—must be understood by way of the finite structure of temporality. For Heidegger, time cannot be understood as a series of (*vorhanden*) "now points," whereby future and past, as not-yet-now and no-longer-now, appear as modes of "nonbeing"—which gives rise to the various puzzles about the reality of time that have occupied philosophers. For Heidegger, Dasein *is* a presencing in the midst of future and past. In lived experience, future and past have a *presence* in anticipation and recollection. Dasein is ekstatically extended into future and past (respectively as possibility and being-thrown). Dasein exists in terms of what is to come and what has been; the present is a fluid, looping movement of these temporal dimensions.

Heidegger expressly gives priority to the dimension of the future (*BT*, 372), as *Zukunft*, coming-toward. The present cannot have primacy in expressing the movements of Dasein's existence. The future, as a coming-forth, has primacy, but always in the midst of the past as having-been (which is a formal way of expressing the hermeneutic circle). The future is not a separate sphere unto itself; possibility is always partly shaped by Dasein's inheritance. The crucial point is that the present is a *movement* that cannot be its own ground; it is always retentive and protentive (as recollection and anticipation), always laden with the past and pregnant with the future, always a "from" and a "toward." Accordingly, Dasein and being can never be understood as a constant presence (expressed as eternal truths or fixed conditions), because every present is saturated with the presence of absences: The "toward" of the future is the uncertain yet-to-be, and the "from" of the past is a thrownness not of one's own making (birth, inheritance, influences). Dasein's temporality involves the ekstatic dwelling in this fluid finitude.

Temporality is given a more concrete reference in the concept of *Geschichtlichkeit*, or historicality (*BT*, 434). Historicality involves the specific cultural forms that Dasein's temporality takes, as the actualizing of possibilities in the midst of inherited traditions. Like temporality, historicality cannot be fixed or grounded. The priority of the future disrupts all conservative foundationalism. At the same time, the essential role of the past disrupts any radical denial of tradition. Heidegger's conception of *Wiederholung*, or repetition (*BT*, 437), is nothing like a mechanical repeating of a past form or model, but rather a retrieving of the *possibilities* that have been handed down (*BT*, 437). Again, possibility is always paramount. As Heidegger writes, "within the ontological sphere the possible is higher than everything actual" (*BP*, 308). The past of one's tradition is better seen as a "launching" of potentialities, a complex intersection of temporal/historical dimensions that is essentially marked by an openness.

We should recall the phenomenon of being-in-question in its temporal structure to highlight Heidegger's sense of the historical openness of philosophy and being. To be in question is to be presently concerned with an inquiry into something which is already accessible by way of one's inheritance. But *as* questioned, inquiry is not bound by inheritance, but open to future possibilities. Questioning both surpasses the self-evident givenness of the past and exceeds past and present actualities in light of future possibilities. So questioning is a present openness toward the future through the past, and as such it is essentially excessive of actuality. For Heidegger, Dasein *is* this temporal openness that never comes to rest.

To summarize this overview of Heidegger's early thought, the meaning of being is to be understood as a temporal process. The being of beings is the emergence of meaning in the midst of limits, a movement that can never be purged of modes of absence. Heidegger, then, argues for the ultimate *finitude of being*, in the sense that there is always an "otherness" intrinsic to any moment or mode of being. We can understand the finitude of being in an *ontological* way, in terms of emergence from and amid negative dimensions, and in an *ontical* way, in terms of the fundamental relatedness and situatedness of beings. Since there is an intrinsic otherness in being, the "nature" of things will always exhibit an *ambiguity*, an ineluctable confluence of emergence and concealment, a constitutive contrast of sameness and difference, an absence that reverberates in every presence.

HEIDEGGER'S LATER THOUGHT

Heidegger's writings after *Being and Time* exhibit a number of shifts and alterations, but I am not one of those who think the later thought represents a radical break with, or repudiation of, the early phenomenological work. This is an enormously complex question, which would take me beyond my present aims. I will here only sketch some key elements in Heidegger's later texts that can bear on the issues in my analysis.

A central text in Heidegger's later work is the *Letter on Humanism*, in which he announces a "turning" (*Kehre*) in relation to the project of *Being and Time*. Such a turning has been interpreted as an admission of an early failure, and particularly as a movement away from the phenomenology of human Dasein as the basis of ontology toward "being itself" as an extrahuman basis of Dasein. Supposedly, Heidegger's later thought thus eclipses human existence in favor of a historical power or quasimystical force that envelops human beings and that calls for a kind of passive reception of being's transmissions.

It is true that Heidegger's later texts do exhibit a tone and rhetoric that can lend credence to such a reading, but I think it is mistaken for two reasons. First, I do not think that Heidegger ever surrendered a certain phenomenological approach that always implicates human modes of existence in the disclosure of being. Second, it is not true that *Being and Time* was engaged in a kind of philosophical anthropology or transcendental phenomenology that would ground the being of beings in Dasein, in a manner similar to modern projects that trace the structures of thought and reality to consciousness or subjectivity. *Being and Time* had always been conceived as a "preparatory" analysis that would move *through* the phenomenology of Dasein to the general question of being as such. But even the phenomenology of Dasein was not human-centered or subject-centered. Dasein, as being-in-the-world, was always conceived structurally as the ekstatic opening of the meaning of being, as responsive to, and disclosive of, being. As Heidegger says in *Letter on Humanism*, *Being and Time* was engaged in a thinking that "abandons subjectivity," and he reiterates the central notion of thrownness to stress this point (*LH*, 231).[17]

Letter on Humanism also establishes another central feature of Heidegger's later thought, the priority of language in the disclosure of being. In *Being and Time*, language is an essential element of being-in-the-world, as we have seen. Now Heidegger calls language the "house of being" and says that humans "dwell" in this home (*LH*, 217). Language is "the clearing-concealing advent of being itself" (*LH*, 230). Dasein's disclosive openness is now fully identified with language. I explore this further in the next chapter, but here I can mention the importance of poetical language for Heidegger. Poetry, in its creative, world-disclosing element, fits the emergent quality of being and marks an alternative to representational theories of language. In its meaning-disclosive element, poetry also offers an alternative to the dominant form of objective, disengaged, instrumental rationality that characterizes the modern technological era, an issue that came to preoccupy Heidegger in his later works.

The essence of modern technology, for Heidegger, is not simply identified with industrial production and machine technology. It is a mode of revealing being that is embodied in modern, disengaged, scientific reason, which discloses the world as a set of bare objects that operate according to mechanical laws and that accordingly are manipulable and controllable in the wake of reason's capacity to grasp these laws and their operative implications. Modern technology is a "challenging forth" (*Herausfordern*) that conceives nature as simply a "standing reserve" (*Bestand*), a store of energy and utility constantly on hand as a resource for technical projects and needs (*QCT*, 320–22). The essence of technology, for Heidegger, is expressed as an "enframing" (*Gestell*), the positing of nature and being itself as reducible to the grid of mathematical properties and serviceable to the dictates of the positing subject (*QCT*, 324ff).[18]

Heidegger offers an alternative comportment of *Gelassenheit* (*DT*), a releasement to the mystery of being, which is not subject to human control or reducible to scientific or instrumental properties. *Gelassenheit* opens up modes of "letting-be" that reveal other dimensions of the world, such as those a poet or artist would uncover. The central problem of technology is that it is the latest and most effective expression of the "oblivion of being," the absorption in beings that covers up the radical finitude of being. The danger of technology is not that it is evil or a violation of some pristine condition that needs restoring (see *BW*, 362, and *DT*, 53). The danger is that technology is so successful at controlling the world and offsetting negative limits that it might effectively obviate the ways in which these limits constitute the meaning and significance of being.

Heidegger claims that poetical thinking is needed in our time, not to banish, replace, or essentially change technology, but to protect and sustain a richer story of the world. Heidegger's later constellation of the "fourfold" is an example of such alternative thinking, where the world is portioned into sky, earth, mortals, and deities (*BW*, 351ff), each quarter with its elements of meaning and modes of concealment (night, ground, death, withdrawal)—taken all together, an image of "dwelling" to express being at home in a finite world. Much of Heidegger's later thought tries to evoke an alternative bearing to the detached, objective, reductive, instrumental, power-driven atmosphere of the modern world, an alternative bearing expressed in the notion of humanity as the "shepherd of being"—which, to come full circle, is directly connected to the concept of care in *Being and Time* (*LH*, 234).

NOTES

1. See Heidegger's analysis in the essay "Modern Science, Metaphysics, and Mathematics" (*BW*, 271–305).
2. *Discourse on Method*, Part VI, in *The Philosophical Works of Descartes*, vol. I, trans. Elizabeth S. Haldane and G. R. T. Ross (Cambridge: Cambridge University Press, 1969), 119. For a discussion of the mix of internalization, autonomy, objectification, and control in modern thought, see Charles Taylor, *Sources of the Self: The Making of Modern Identity* (Cambridge, Mass.: Harvard University Press, 1989), chs. 8–9.
3. Taylor draws the connection between modernism and traditional narratives of fall and return (*Sources of the Self*, 351).
4. See *PM*, 283–84. In my text I employ the spelling "ekstatic" in order to distinguish Heidegger's specific meaning from other possible connotations.
5. For Heidegger's most focused treatment of formal indication, see *FCM*, section 70. For helpful discussions, see Daniel O. Dahlstrom, "Heidegger's Method: Philosophical Concepts as Formal Indications," *Review of Metaphysics*, vol. 47, no. 4 (June 1994): 775–95; John van Buren, "The Ethics of *Formale Anzeige* in Heidegger," *American Catholic Philosophical Quarterly*, vol. 69, no. 2 (1995): 157–70; and Theodore Kisiel, *The Genesis of Heidegger's* Being and Time (Berkeley: University of California Press, 1993).
6. Because philosophy in this sense is both open to its prephilosophical milieu and more than simply an immersion in that milieu, the philosopher is a kind of double agent, who works both for and against reflection, both for and against prereflective practice.
7. I want to leave *Befindlichkeit* untranslated. "State of mind" has been recognized as inadequate; "disposition" is better but it too suggests a psychic state that misses the *world*-disclosive and ekstatic senses that Heidegger aims for in the connotation of "how one finds oneself."
8. Some examples of mood disclosure would be the world experienced as frightening, exciting, boring, intriguing, comforting, taxing, mysterious, and so on. Even science, then, can have its disclosive moods, in terms of how science matters and how it cultivates its interest in things (see *BT*, 177).
9. In *FCM* (64–66), Heidegger does not summarily reject the association of mood with the notion of "feeling"; he states only that such a category is freighted with subjectivity and therefore limited and not decisive in thinking through the nature and structure of

mood. For Heidegger, though an affect is certainly not "objective," it is not just "in us" but is disclosive of the world in some way. An insightful analysis of this question is David Weberman, "Heidegger and the Disclosive Character of the Emotions," *Southern Journal of Philosophy*, vol. 34, no. 3 (Fall 1996): 379–410. The only drawback in this essay is some restriction to traditional connotations of subjectivity, objectivity, and emotion.

10. Here Heidegger talks about how a mood can be "infectious," how a certain bearing in a person can have a direct effect on the "atmosphere" of a social gathering.

11. See *FCM*, sections 16–18; *GA* 39, 140–41; and *GA* 45, 197.

12. Appropriateness is related to an important term in Heidegger's later thinking, *Ereignis*, understood as "event of appropriation."

13. See Hubert L. Dreyfus, *Being-in-the-World: A Commentary on Heidegger's* Being and Time (Cambridge, Mass.: MIT Press, 1991), 253ff.

14. I prefer to leave *das Man* untranslated. Translations such as the "they-self" or "the one" do not do justice to the meaning of this term, which I hope to make clear shortly.

15. Lawrence Vogel, *The Fragile "We": Ethical Implications of Heidegger's* Being and Time (Evanston, Ill.: Northwestern University Press, 1994), 74.

16. Of course, this enhanced reorientation can only be called a possibility, because anxious estrangement could certainly prompt otherworldly interests or a reassertion of fallen immersion as a refuge from anxiety.

17. On the question of subjectivity, see the important study by François Raffoul, *Heidegger and the Subject*, trans. David Pettigrew and Gregory Recco (Atlantic Highlands, N.J.: Humanities, 1998).

18. It is important to recognize that Heidegger is not calling for a rebellion against technology, but only against its predominance in thinking and in life. Modern science and technology are legitimate modes of revealing; in their way they permit "correct determinations"; indeed they stand as the destiny of our time (*QCT*, 329–31). The danger of modern technology is that its very mastery and success will (1) crowd other modes of revealing and (2) seduce us into further concealing the "thrown finitude" of existence, even with respect to how technology's own mode of revealing is not simply a human product (*QCT*, 332–33).

Chapter Two

Language, Pluralism, and Truth

As I have shown, Heidegger came to correlate the emergence of being with the world-disclosive function of language. For Heidegger, language cannot be understood simply as forms of object designation, as significations for, or as representations of things in the world, because such theories bank on modes of disclosure already presented in language. To think that the world is a set of prelinguistic things that are designated by words is to overlook the fact that "thing" is a word (as are "world," "is," "a," and so on). This is why Heidegger correlates language and being, since any disclosure will unfold by way of already inherited linguistic meanings and uses. Consequently, Heidegger calls language "saying as showing" (*OWL*, 123), as the very manifestation of the world's meaning, and thus of being.

The philosophical climax of this analysis is that the disclosure of being cannot be reduced to the human mind or objects in the world, since "mind" and "object" are linguistic presentations. Accordingly, answers to philosophical questions about the nature of things cannot be found in some explanatory reduction to a cause, entity, or faculty, since such reductions would postdate the presence of language. Here we can better understand Heidegger's emphasis on the element of concealment or mystery at the heart of being. Any attempt to explain language must employ language (for example, taking words as "expressions" of "ideas"). From this standpoint, there is "nothing" outside of language, or better, there is an irreducible concealment intrinsic to the question of language. What could one *say* about a nonlinguistic foundation of language, or something prior to language? Phenomenologically speaking, the world is disclosed or unconcealed through language.

One might object: Are there not experiences and activities in which language is not operating? For example, consider the silent witnessing of a dancer silently performing sophisticated, expressive movements. There are two ways to address this objection on behalf of Heidegger's position. The first is a contextual point. Once we *inquire* into the question at hand and perhaps bring up the above example as part of the inquiry, we are inescapably enveloped in linguistic operations.

Philosophy cannot proceed without language. When Heidegger calls language the "house of being," he is not suggesting some kind of linguistic idealism, but simply that language is the irreducible element of thinking. Fine, but what about when we are not practicing philosophy, as in the example of simply witnessing the dancer? First, we should remember that language, for Heidegger, even in *Being and Time*, is not simply words and their employment. Language involves disclosure of the world, which can involve nonverbal elements. It still can be said, however, that the learning of verbal language has a certain priority by orienting a person in disclosive modes of understanding that prepare and allow the meaningful engagement of supposedly nonverbal experiences. To have an "experience" of a dancer is to presuppose a host of preceding understandings that go all the way back to childhood and the learning of language.

It is no wonder that a child's first words are such a momentous event. When a child learns to speak, the world begins to open up, and the child begins to develop in ways that far exceed prelinguistic conditions. And the setting of child rearing shows that language should not be understood simply as the employment of words, but as a symbiotic development of the child's capacities for understanding and behavior in the midst of a prompting linguistic environment. In fact, it is clear that language is a multifaceted environmental influence on children from their first moments of life. If language were simply the speaking of words, then all the verbal behaviors that parents naturally engage in with infants before they learn to speak would seem to be a wasted activity. But research has shown that the parental instinct here is appropriate and crucial for the child's full development later on. This suggests that infants are exposed to a preverbal "rehearsal" of a complex linguistic environing-world from the very start—in terms of touch, physical interactions, gestures, sounds, rhythms, intonations, emotional cues, and a host of behavioral contexts.[1] In more advanced stages before speech, parents are constantly engaging the child's activities by way of the above complex together with more focused and deliberate verbal associations, especially in terms of purposive behavior. This continues, of course, as the child begins to speak and goes on to develop linguistic competence. But what happens *before* a child learns to speak shows that language is a complex constellation of practices and is from the beginning an active, performative, affective, embodied, purposeful environing-world that is (in Heideggerian terms) *there* shaping the child's sense of things.[2] Both Heidegger's views on language and his phenomenology of being-in-the-world are given added strength when considering child development. This will become important later in discussing a child's development of an ethical sense.

PLURALISM

The phenomenological priority of language opens the way to ontological pluralism. Language gathers and in fact embodies the disclosive process of unconcealment that is bounded by concealment and thus not traceable to "entities." The priority of concealment precludes reductionistic groundings that would exclude or colonize different (and differing) modes of disclosure. The coexistence of multiple presentations in language is protected in principle. For example, the language of "values" need not be undermined or problematized by the language of "facts," since an ontological grounding in empirical facts can be subverted by a more complex and open phenomenological array of disclosures. It is important to stress that, for Heidegger, language differences are not simply different ways of talking, but different ways in which the *world* is disclosed. We are simply asked to surrender the assumption that the disclosure of being can only be properly comprehended if it is reduced to a single governing form. Heidegger gives a pointed account of ontological pluralism in the following passages:

> There is no such thing as *the one* phenomenology, and if there could be such a thing it would never become anything like a philosophical technique. For implicit in the essential nature of all genuine method as a path toward the disclosure of objects is the tendency to order itself always toward that which it discloses. (*BP*, 328)

> All real thinking has its theme, and thus relates itself to a definite object, i.e., to a definite being which in each case confronts us, a physical thing, a geometrical object, a historical event, a "linguistic phenomenon." These objects (of nature, of space, of history) belong to different domains. They differ in their subject-matters, each differing completely in the kind of thing it is. Plants are something other than geometrical objects, while the latter are completely different from, say, a literary work. But these things are also different in the way they are, as things existing either naturally or historically. The determinative thinking which is to measure up to the particular being in question must also take into account a corresponding diversity regarding what and how the being in each case (*jeweils*) is. The thought determination, i.e., the concept formation, will differ in different domains. Scientific investigation of this thinking is in each case correspondingly different: the logic of thinking in physics, the logic of mathematical thinking, of historical, theological, and even more so, philosophical thinking. The logic of these disciplines is related to a subject-matter. It is a *material logic*. (*MFL*, 2–3)

Heidegger's main point is that formal, theoretical structures can be disclosive in their way, but the error lies in colonizing the lived world by presuming to govern all thought and experience by way of a single ruling model—thus concealing the specificity, plurality, fluidity, and finitude of Dasein's existential world. Different contexts of meaning can exhibit their own structure and shape, and so a certain emergent material "logic" can be uncovered in considering each sphere (more on this shortly). The error lies in the overly formal logic of a theoretical construction, which *abstracts* from context and poses as a sufficient account or measure of an experiential field that eludes systematic organization.

In general terms we can say that Heidegger's sense of ontological "appropriation" allows us to talk of different ontical modes of appropriate disclosure, wherein Dasein can properly uncover various facets of the world. In this regard Heidegger specifically mentions the disciplines of psychology, anthropology, ethics, politics, poetry, and history (*BT*, 37). But because of the radical finitude and temporality of being, such modes of disclosure cannot presume to be fixed, exact, or universally applicable. This ambiguous correlation of disclosure and limits brings us to the question of truth.

TRUTH AND UNCONCEALMENT[3]

From early on in his thinking, Heidegger was engaged in thinking the word truth (*Wahrheit*) in terms of the notion of unconcealment.[4] Such thinking stemmed from a twofold analysis: (1) an etymological analysis of the Greek word for truth, *alētheia*, stressing the alpha-privative—literally unhiddenness; and (2) a phenomenological analysis of the priority of disclosure in Dasein's being-in-the-world, something implicit but unthematized in ordinary conceptions of truth. The correspondence theory of truth, for example, holds that truth is the "agreement" or matching of a statement with a state of affairs in the world. The statement "the cat is on the mat" is true if in fact there is a cat on the mat, and false if not. Heidegger argues that *before* this supposed matching could be accomplished, a wide array of meanings and understandings first must be disclosed to Dasein in its being-in-the-world: the meaning of "cat" and "mat," disclosure of something *as* cat and mat, the "on" relation, the context of relations into which the cat and mat fit, statements, the relatedness of statements and states of affairs, and finally the primal meaning of being as finite presencing named in the "is" (*BT*, 260–61). For Heidegger, the "is" names the "open" region of being that allows the "traversing" relation implied by the notion of "agreement" in the correspondence theory.

This open region that cannot be identified with either the self or things in the world involves both the opening of being and Dasein's openness *to* being. This ontological openness is the setting for Heidegger's distinctive conception of freedom. Dasein's freedom is not the property of the self (*GA* 31, 133); it is the openness that allows any disclosure (including self-disclosure) to unfold in the first place. Such openness is the deepest sense of truth as letting-be, which is neither an objective condition nor a construction of the subject, but a primal process of unconcealment "between," so to speak, Dasein and the world (*ET*, 123–30).

Heidegger does not reject the notion of truth as correspondence; rather, he argues that correspondence is not adequate to capture the full meaning of truth, and that the theoretical assumptions underwriting correspondence are caught in the subject–object dichotomy that existential phenomenology has aimed to surmount. Heidegger claims that given the environmental character of Dasein's being-in-the-world and its prepredicative sense of appropriate disclosure, it was inevitable that the correspondence theory took shape in the tradition, since it derived from an original relatedness of Dasein and its world articulated through language (*BT*, 262). One way to understand this is as follows: In immediate experiences and language uses, the theoretical problem of truth as a "matching" of statements with states of affairs might not arise. Language can be immediately world-disclosive. Think of me frantically searching for my cat, and someone says, "Look, your cat is on the mat." Here is an utterance directly disclosive and saturated with my concernful being-in-the-world. But then we can see that Dasein's temporality and the capacity of language to sustain meanings separated from immediate experiences can bring about contexts in which the problem of a statement's proper disclosive function can and does arise ("He says he saw your cat on the mat an hour ago")—hence the problem of a statement's according or not according with a now distant original experience (*PS*, 18).

The correspondence theory of truth, however, in its own instructional or discursive context, deals abstractly with statements yanked out of everyday contexts and situations, as exercises in the abstract question of how we can be correct or incorrect in our statements. Here the theory's reliance on formal constructions of ideas, beliefs, and statements in relation to things, facts, and states of affairs encourages the abstract model of mental subjects in relation to external objects, which then conjures up the problem of how, or even if, these two spheres can be "joined" (*BT*, 267). Heidegger's point is that both the theory and its performative setting miss and distort a good deal of Dasein's modes of being-in-the-world. In the cat context cited above, such problems and questions would not arise—or better put, if they did ("Is that my cat?"), they would not be framed in terms of theoretical constructions of mental representations matching external entities, but simply in terms of appropriate uncovering of phenomena.

> To say that an assertion "*is true*" signifies that it uncovers the entity as it is in itself. Such an assertion speaks out, points out, 'lets' the entity 'be seen' (*apophansis*) in its uncoveredness. The *being-true (truth)* of the assertion must be understood as *being-uncovering (Entdeckend-sein)*. Thus truth has by no means the structure of an agreement between knowing and the object in the sense of a likening of one entity (the subject) to another (the object). (*BT*, 261)

In addition, the correspondence theory is restricted to positive conceptions of formed beliefs and actual objects, which conceal the radical finitude of being (the correlation of being and nothing, presence and absence). Truth conceived as unconcealment is better able to express this primal emergent sense of being, which Heidegger came to call the "truth of being" as distinct from the truth of beings (*ET*, 135). In an early essay, Heidegger provides a helpful summary by distinguishing between propositional truth (the kind operating in the correspondence theory) and a more original truth of unconcealment, which itself is divided into ontological unconcealment (the openness of being as such) and ontical unconcealment (the manifesting of regions of beings in their appropriate and different ways).[5] For Heidegger, traditional theories of truth are simply stuck in propositional forms and miss the richer, less exact, and thoroughly finite atmos-

Chapter Two

phere of world-disclosure implicit within propositional judgments. In general terms, ordinary conceptions of truth block entry to the coordination of truth with the question of finite being (*BT*, 272). Propositional truth "is indeed necessary in a certain respect, yet it is not *originary*" (*FCM*, 290).

Truth as unconcealment is prior to "what" is disclosed by naming the *process* of disclosure itself. That process as such cannot be disclosed since any disclosure presupposes the process. The only thing prior to unconcealment is not some other condition or state of affairs, but, as the word suggests (as a double negative), concealment. Here Heidegger claims that we must acknowledge and be open to a "mystery" at the heart of being (*ET*, 130, 134), a mystery that subverts any claims to foundational truth. The mystery of being is not a yet-to-be-discovered truth or a condition of confusion or obscurity. Nor is it a denial of various positive findings. It simply gives voice to ineluctable limits at certain levels of exploration, limits that should restrain the impulse to subject the world to an ultimate explanation and to govern human endeavors solely by rational procedures and arguments. At certain levels, for Heidegger, we are engaged with sheer "happenings" that cannot be fully controlled or grasped by the human subject, and that call simply for a more perspicuous reception rather than rational explanation or demonstration. This atmosphere of thinking and experience will figure prominently in subsequent discussions of ethics.

The advantage of Heidegger's notion of truth as unconcealment over truth as correspondence is again its comprehensiveness. Disclosing–concealing has a wider and richer application than true–false in the sense of correct or incorrect "matching" of statements with states of affairs. Heidegger does not deny the notion of true and false propositions, but rather the exclusivity of the correspondence model and its theoretical baggage, which conceals pretheoretical contexts of use that exhibit the disclosive function of language.

Would anything be lost if "true" and "untrue" were simply redescribed as disclosing and concealing rather than as correct and incorrect? The former dyad could encompass the latter ("untrue" could mean "covers up") as well as apply to a wider extension of uses. Truth as disclosure in the context of concernful being-in-the-world can apply not only to descriptive truth (knowing-that), but also to pragmatic truth (knowing-how, familiarity-with), and prescriptive/normative truth, which is notoriously problematic for theories restricted to matching mental representations with external objects. World-disclosive truth can also apply to various performative utterances such as announcing, appointing, commanding, promising, commending, condoling, and apologizing.[6] Finally, disclosive truth can apply, without pause or qualification, to probable and partial truths.

UNCONCEALMENT AND TRUTH

The most important implication of truth construed as unconcealment has already been broached in this chapter. Unconcealment delivered from foundationalism allows us to articulate and orchestrate different accounts of the world that are properly disclosive, but that are limited and thus not universally applicable; in other words, we find here a pluralistic conception of truth, in the sense that there are different kinds of truth (*WT*, 26–27). Before I explore this question, an important matter in Heidegger's later thought must be addressed. Near the end of his thinking, Heidegger spoke less of the correlational, disclosive character of unconcealment and came to stress the mystery of concealment itself, distinct from metaphysical advents of being. His interest was to think that which withdraws in the process of disclosing the being of beings. With this shift, the terms "being" and "truth" are now reserved for positive metaphysical forms of thought. In pursuing the negative background of withdrawal, metaphysics is now "left to itself" (*TB*, 24). Consequently, the word truth (*Wahrheit*) is no longer thought in terms of unconcealment (*alētheia*) and is delivered back to the notion of correctness (*TB*, 70). Alētheia is now thought in its own right as a unique word, in terms of the essential hiddenness (*lēthē*) concealed in all disclosure, and the hiding of *alētheia* itself in the history of being. The association with the word truth is thus put aside.

In my view it is important to resist Heidegger here and retrieve the connection between truth and unconcealment. I do not think truth should be segregated from unconcealment and thus reserved solely for the realm of beings (as correctness). I have two reasons.

(1) Thinking truth as *unconcealment* shows that the disclosure of beings is not some stable realm with simply a hidden origin or background. Metaphysics "left to itself" gives the impression that metaphysical thinking simply is what it is, somehow distinct from the "negativity" of a mysterious origin. Truth-as-unconcealment alerts us to the fact that all forms of disclosure, including the so-called hard sciences, show *in their activity* elements of unconcealment. The process–character of unconcealment speaks to and fosters the dynamic, open element in all thinking, which despite metaphysical pretenses has never been fixed, certain, or closed, either diachronically or synchronically.

(2) Thinking unconcealment as *truth* gathers the notion that unconcealment is more than hiddenness, mystery, and negativity; it is disclosure. As Heidegger puts it in an early work:

What is first required is an appreciation of the "positive" in the "privative" essence of *alētheia*. The positive must first be experienced as the fundamental trait of being itself. (*PM*, 182)

But more: Unconcealment is not sheer groundless, chaotic, or arbitrary disclosure. Unconcealment can and should be integrated with the positive, "authoritative" sense of the word truth — not in the same way the word was taken in the tradition, but in some way.

Following this line of thinking produces a twofold effect: Truth-as-unconcealment "loosens" all forms of thinking from the constraints and reductions found in

traditional assumptions about truth. Unconcealment-as-truth "tightens" unconcealment in the midst of world-disclosure and allows some connection to the
authoritative implications of the word truth—something which, as we have seen,
Heidegger's early writings did not in fact ignore. Unfortunately, the same cannot
be said for certain movements in continental philosophy inspired by Heidegger
that have taken his critique of metaphysics as an antimetaphysical suspicion of
any talk of truth. There should be a thinking "in between" unconcealment and
ordinary truth, which articulates the "aletheic" element in all thinking and yet still
permits an authoritative sense of truth.[7]

Taking a lead from Heidegger's contention that disclosure of being happens in
language, we can take up this question in terms of how the word truth works and
what it shows. Can the word truth exhibit a meaning of unconcealment? The
Greek word *alētheia*, of course, clearly shows such a meaning. The German *wahr*
has a connection to *wesen* in the sense of unfolding, and in English there is a
sense of movement indicated in the phrase "to true up." There is also something
suggestive in the phrase "the moment of truth," which does not connote correspondence or correctness or even a vague conception of a ground for knowledge,
but rather a situation of uncertain anticipation of an important occurrence soon to
be disclosed. So the word truth can show a connection with a process of disclosure prior to correctness, and accordingly the word can operate in areas that have
more to do with coming-forth than with accuracy, one example being art.[8]

Unconcealment is not enough, however. Once truth is related to unconcealment, we should perform the return gesture and relate unconcealment to the
authoritative sense of the word truth, but always in view of the loosening effect
of truth-as-unconcealment. Truth is needed to prevent unconcealment from being
let loose as a random, chaotic, arbitrary emergence. The word truth can display a
number of existential meanings that fit this connotation without any theoretical
sense of correctness or certainty: for example, steady and faithful staying (being
true to someone), what properly belongs to something (a true friend), to fit properly, loyalty, a mutual pledge.[9] To speak of unconcealment-as-truth is to suggest
some kind of fitting disclosure that can persist in some way and thus support the
possibility of various kinds of judgment.

SETTINGS OF TRUTH

At this point I am shifting from giving an exposition of Heidegger's thought to
advancing my own reflections on the nature of truth. My aim is to provide some
preparation for addressing the complex questions of whether and how truth can
function in the sphere of ethics.

In general terms, I want to define truth as *a process of disclosing different settings that open up regions of beings*. This shows itself to be a three-dimensional
correlation of disclosure, settings, and beings: (1) disclosure in the Heideggerian

sense of unconcealment; (2) settings in the sense of a background or environment, such as a scene setting in the theater; in other words, various paradigmatic assumptions, models, patterns, orientations, or narratives that set the stage for thinking, stemming from the different possibilities of Dasein's understanding (for instance, settings in science, art, ethics, politics, and religion); and (3) beings, or the specific ways in which the world is disclosed in the light of the different settings.

Even with elements of negativity and openness in unconcealment, truth in some positive sense can still happen and work. Unconcealment-as-truth can indicate the appropriateness of the settings and their manner of opening up the world; it can speak to the "authority" of these disclosures and the ways in which they claim us, making our commitment to them something more than arbitrary. Though always working in a nonfoundational process of unconcealment, the disclosure of settings and their results can give us the right to talk of truth, and hence of the viability of judgments in some way.

Why is this important? Because the lived world, the analysis of which generated Heidegger's insights into the negativity of being, also exhibits and requires some sense of the positive, decisive tone ringing in the word truth. Without restricting truth to correctness and without slipping back into metaphysical constructions, we still need to be able to say that scientific and ethical settings, for example, exhibit some sense of truth, so that we can give a robust response to radical versions of skepticism, subjectivism, relativism, conventionalism, or anarchism that continue to circulate in philosophy.

We can make some headway in this discussion and go further in clarifying the realist character of Heidegger's thought by considering the question of objectivity. There are many senses in which the word "objective" can be used. Consider *responsive*, which indicates the most basic and far-reaching sense that can simply be put in negative terms: not subjective, not based merely in an individual mind (psychological subjectivity) or merely in cognitive faculties of the human mind (transcendental subjectivity); *unbiased*, an open-minded disposition that does not presuppose the validity of one's own viewpoint; *detached*, a disconnected absence of interest in something; *value-free*, devoid of value designations; *public*, sharable knowledge and experience, rather than private introspection; *observable*, witnessable in the world by others, rather than merely imagined; *real*, in the sense of ordinary realism, that which exists outside of us in the world and may not always accord with our thoughts and desires; and *really-real*, in the sense of metaphysical realism, that which exists in the way it is "independent" of any human thought, desire, feeling, awareness, or response.

From what I have shown, existential phenomenology can be thoroughly conversant with the senses of responsive, unbiased, public, and real, not always with observable, and in a strict ontological sense not at all with detached, value-free, and really-real. This helps us understand that Heidegger's conceptions of being and truth involve Dasein's disclosive response *to* the world, but the implication of Dasein in any disclosure disrupts certain pure conceptions of "objective reality."

As Heidegger says, both traditional realism and idealism contain a "kernel of genuine inquiry," since realism suggests that beings are "there" in the world and idealism suggests that disclosure cannot occur without Dasein (*BT*, 250–51). The mistake is that, owing to the contours of modern philosophy, the two theories are forced to choose sides between the object and the subject in their arguments. The point is that Heidegger's phenomenology of Dasein does not amount to a subjectivism or a denial of all senses of objectivity. He clearly states that the "objectivity" of a science is given in terms of how it *uncovers* beings in its sphere of questioning, and therefore it is nothing "subjective" (*BT*, 447). The same is said with respect to truth (*BT*, 270). Indeed, Heidegger indicates that disclosure does not "create" truth, as though it did not exist in any sense prior to its discovery.

> Once entities have been uncovered, they show themselves precisely as entities which beforehand already were. Such uncovering is the kind of being which belongs to truth. (*BT*, 269)

The "beforehand" indicates a clear kind of realism, but the "uncovering" that only occurs by way of Dasein's being-in-the-world undercuts the strict sense of "independence" from Dasein suggested in metaphysical realism.

Heidegger even goes as far as saying that the existence of Dasein is dependent on the extant presence of physical nature (*MFL*, 156). From a *philosophical* standpoint, however, the meaning of being cannot be grounded in an objective ontology of nature, because the disclosure of such a setting presupposes Dasein's concernful being-in-the-world. In any case, Heidegger allows for a certain independence of beings as entities other than Dasein, although their being (the disclosure of finite meaning) cannot be understood as strictly independent of Dasein (*MFL*, 153).

It must be added that Heidegger's pluralism is to be distinguished from standard conceptions of realism and objectivism in that it confers "reality" on modes of disclosure that are often denied an "objective" status owing to a physicalistic or naturalistic ontological bias.

> [T]he existence of the material things of nature is not the only existence; there are also history and art works. Nature has diverse modes: space and number, life, human existence itself. There is a multiplicity of *modi existendi,* and each of these is a mode belonging to a being with a specific content, a definite quiddity. The term "being" is meant to include the span of all possible regions. (*MFL*, 151)

As we have seen, Heidegger's phenomenology does not deny or seek to replace scientific objectivity, but rather "order" it among other modes of disclosure, according to different kinds of questions arising in Dasein's understanding-as-possibility. Such ordering will give a certain priority to meaning structures, since scientific objectivity too is a form of being-in-the-world permeated with existential meaning (*BT*, 417). Conceptual ordering, both within and between various settings of disclosure, suggests an expanded and enriched "logic." Such a logic follows Heidegger's retrieval of the Greek word *logos* and its connection to *legein*, which has connotations of "gathering." For Heidegger, *logos* involves the multiple ways in which the sense of the world comes forth in selective gatherings of language (*AM*, 120–26; *PM*, 212–13).

SIGNS OF TRUTH

In my proposal, truths in different settings would be shown in their responsiveness and appropriateness to phenomena, in the sense that they are not mere fabrications, inventions, or conventions. This does not eliminate process, negativity, and limits. Truth can be understood as dynamic "moments of truth" that emerge, change, struggle between and within settings, shift between settings and overlap settings— because this is what always *has* happened and *does* happen in our thinking about the world. But at the same time, in lived experience we also "take hold" in certain ways, which is an essential manner of dwelling that must involve something more than mystery, groundlessness, or undecidability. Truth is not some kind of master name, but rather a working word that gives us bearings. I want to propose a sense of truth that is both expressive of the negativity of unconcealment and responsive to the possibility of judgments. In keeping with Heidegger's image of thinking as a "way," I will suggest a set of "signs" for truth—in the sense of road signs—that is, ways in which the language of truth can give direction in a finite process of world-disclosure without metaphysical guarantees.

I should establish two points at the outset. First, I am focusing primarily on how these signs can work at the level of settings that open up various regions of the world. Different forms of truth would be shown in the extent to which and the way in which the signs work in the different settings. The concept of settings is quite important in elucidating the meaning of pluralism. Different truths organized around different settings undermine indiscriminate, anarchic claims that *anything* can be advanced or challenged; that is, a kind of generalized relativism, subjectivism, or skepticism. What should matter is the *context* of a particular inquiry or endeavor that might privilege one setting over others and allow its specific mode of disclosure to deliver truth in that context. Accordingly, questions about the meaning of life are more properly addressed in religious, philosophical, or literary settings than in a scientific setting. Questions about how to live are more appropriate for ethical and political settings. Questions about the workings of nature are more properly addressed in a scientific setting. As specific settings, such disclosures have a certain *logos* that can prevent someone from advancing just anything (either within a setting or from another setting).[10]

Second, nothing in what follows is meant to reflect a closed structure or even an aggregate of different closed structures. The open atmosphere of disclosure applies to both the unconcealment *of* a setting (how science as a mode of disclosing unfolds in the midst of other modes) and unconcealment *within* a setting (how science operates). The notion of unconcealment prompts an acknowledgment of alterity, because disclosure will always involve a tension with otherness: Scientific findings screen out emotional states, religious belief surpasses an account of ordinary events, an ethical "ought" differs from claims of fact, order contests disorder, and so on. Movements of thought exhibit an alterity that is essential not only for understanding the meaning of a truth, but also for appreciating the way in which a truth unfolds or changes. Truth is not the elimination of otherness but an emergence saturated with tension (*P*, 17).[11] The signs of truth simply show that in the midst of unconcealment and limits, truth can still happen and work—there are moments of truth.

The signs of truth fall in two groups: The first (inhabitive signs) has to do with world-disclosure, the second (aletheic signs) has to do with the limits of disclosure. The two groups are correlated and modify each other, and all the elements in the two groups make up an indivisible complex.

(1) *Inhabitive* signs point to modes of "dwelling," or ways in which we are situated and find a place in the world:

(a) *Appropriateness*. Truth is fitting for phenomena, there is a sense of responsive, appropriate showing, and the world responds back to our saying. This is not to be taken as a strict objectivism. It does, however, call on us to be "faithful" (true) to phenomena by attending carefully and thoroughly to matters at hand, and to avoid omissions, distortions, or confusions with different kinds of phenomena.

(b) *Reliability*. Truth has a steadiness, a kind of continuity that is not utterly unstable or instantaneous or unrepeatable; we can "go on" with it. This is not to be confused with eternal truth, strict certainty, or constant universals.

(c) *Workability*. Truth is effective, it permits us to engage the world, and the world responds back to that engagement. Truth has a pragmatic element, which is not to say that truth is only a matter of practical utility.

(d) *Agreement*. Truth is sharable, communicable. Agreement is an indication that something is displayed *to* us and is not simply a subjective opinion. This is not to say that agreement is sufficient for truth (the first three signs show that truth cannot be merely conventional), or that seamless unanimity could or should be the aim of thought.

(e) *Sociality*. Given the importance of upbringing, inheritance, testimony, trust, and corroboration, truth is a cooperative, intersubjective endeavor rather than a monological discovery.

(f) *Sense*. Truth gathers experience into a shape that gives a kind of coherence to particulars. This has nothing to do with a rigid, systematic structure or a single overarching order.

(g) *Elucidation*. Truth is a clarifying process of explicating and articulating the tacit background of inherited sense.

These inhabitive signs provide truth in the sense of exhibiting an *appropriate responsiveness*; in other words, what is said is not arbitrary, not mere opinion, and not merely subjective (in either a psychological or a transcendental sense). Truth involves ways in which the *world* shows itself.

(2) *Aletheic* signs address the limits of disclosure in an ungrounded atmosphere of unconcealment. As with some road signs that tell us what we *cannot* do, aletheic signs tell us that truth is:

(a) *Nonfoundational*. Truth involves elements of mystery; it does not stem from or refer to a fixed source or determinate ground; there are no ultimate explanations.

(b) *Nonreductive*. Truth is contextual, pluralistic, and inclusive. No one setting can stand as a measure for all other settings.

(c) *Nonuniform*. Truth is multidimensional. No setting is fixed in one form internally (the idea of a single method in science) or sealed off from other settings. There is interpenetration and overlap among the settings (certain values indigenous to science, and factual considerations in ethics).

(d) *Nonimperial*. Truth is a letting-be. No setting can crowd out, absorb, or banish other settings that are appropriate in their fashion.

(e) *Nondefinitive*. Truth is not closed off or complete in any particular setting or its findings. Disclosure is always revisable or revisitable.

Inhabitive signs point to disclosing regions of beings, and they permit affirmative statements. Aletheic signs indicate the limits of these statements, an ontological openness, and a pluralistic openness to different regions and their settings. In this way another kind of truth is expressed that can permit negative judgments, so that a reductionistic claim can be called "untrue" in an aletheic sense. With a material setting, for example, where physical and empirical descriptions are the issue at hand, all the inhabitive signs can be followed (thus there is much world-disclosing truth here). But if aletheic signs are "disobeyed"—in other words, if a material setting becomes metaphysical material*ism*—the inhabitive signs cannot be followed, because such a reduction cannot make sense of certain significant phenomena (for instance, neurological descriptions of my brain states at the time of composing this sentence would not be able to convey its meaning). Accordingly, both from an aletheic and inhabitive standpoint, we can say that materialistic propositions are not true.

With respect to any statement, we can ask about its truth in terms of the following questions: Is it appropriate, reliable, and workable? Is there agreement and sense? Is it foundational, reductive, or imperial? We can then work at various answers regarding truth and untruth. It should be added that since the signs are an indivisible complex, being true will always be a complex matter. Even the simplest empirical statement can be traced throughout the entire complex. And the aletheic signs show that "being true" refers not only to what can particularly be said of something; it also includes the limits of what can be said, as well as the need for and relation to other kinds of saying. Truth, then, will not ultimately involve one statement, but a constellation of many statements, a lexical ordering that gathers disclosive, delimiting, and relational elements.

We need an open sense of truth that also carries some authority, because there are times when something calls for and receives our *commitment*.[12] Although in an ultimate sense nothing "holds" (given temporality and death), sometimes we "take hold." The word truth functions at these times, when something calls for, and can receive, an affirmation. As we have seen, such an analysis of truth accords well with Heidegger's early considerations of language and truth.

> [A]ssertion, as communicative-determinative exhibition, is a mode in which Dasein *appropriates* for itself the uncovered being as uncovered. This appropriation of a being in a true assertion about it is not . . . a merely subjectivistic apprehending and investing of things with determinations which we cull from the subject and assign to the things. . . . Assertion is exhibitive letting-be-seen of beings. (*BP*, 219)

APPLICATIONS

Here I will sketch some ways in which this conception of truth can work in particular settings and in response to classic philosophical problems. First, consider the problem of the underivability of first principles. How can the correspondence theory of truth itself be said to be true? To what does it correspond? The standards of empirical verification in science cannot themselves be verified. What is their justification? How can any principle of justification itself be justified? In the tradition, the underivability of first principles was usually expressed in terms of "self-evidency," meaning immediately certain, beyond question, a fundamental starting point or reference point. But if a principle does not follow from anything, this can imply an "abyss." Aletheic truth allows us to talk of the truth of baseline assumptions (in settings) in a special way, as simply disclosed. The problem of a background abyss is dissolved because aletheic truth *affirms* conditions of mystery, emergence, and limits. Unconcealment can express a sheer "givenness" at certain levels of thought, but it insists on naming the negativity here as well, so that "given" will not mean something like self-evidence.

Aletheic truth amounts to a positive transformation of what would be a flaw by traditional standards; in other words, the dilemma of circularity posed by self-reference problems can be converted from vicious circles to virtuous ones. Recall Heidegger on the hermeneutic circle, which renounces the search for foundational starting points and affirms the condition of Dasein's thrownness into modes of understanding that cannot be scanned with some panoptical metaphysical vision. But beyond simply saying that certain principles of thought are "groundless," my analysis would *add in* inhabitive signs of truth to show that such modes of thought are not simply arbitrary constructions or fictions.

Here we locate the most decisive defense of pluralism, because we can affirm the truth of settings besides science that are likewise ultimately groundless, but also no less "evident" in an aletheic manner. We find a way around familiar critiques of ethical, aesthetic, and religious claims—for instance, that these claims cannot satisfy conditions of truth, such as correspondence with empirical facts or consistency with conceptual principles. An aletheic element opens up truth for these settings too, since the supposedly more "exact" settings are no more secure at their deepest levels. From an aletheic standpoint, reductionistic exclusions or demotions of various settings lose their warrant. But again, if we add in the inhabitive signs, then ethical claims, for example, can also be more than simply "disclosed." They can in their way exhibit a comparable sense of inhabitive truth, which has a kind of authority and claim, which is not simply arbitrary or a matter of subjective preference or human projection. Phenomenologically speaking, when we *practice* science or *commit* to moral values or *respond* to beauty or *engage* in philosophical inquiry, such activities are not taken to be simply projections upon a neutral or unknowable world. The direction is not taken to be coming solely from *us*, but also from the environment in which we are engaged. A certain claim upon us is the catalyst for the language of truth.

The phenomenology of ethics explored in this book assumes that there can be truth in ethics, that moral settings permit (finite) judgments. A moral setting can follow both the aletheic and inhabitive signs of truth. The elusiveness of "justifying" moral claims, which typically has been considered a frustration or obstacle for moral philosophy, now exhibits aletheic truth. Indeed, this groundlessness helps us overcome theories that presume to ground ethics in "subjective preferences," and thus we open ethics to its environing-world, its inhabitive truth. Are my objections to torture simply a matter of subjective preference? If my objections are shared, is the agreement simply a matter of collusion or a collection of preferences? Are objections to fraud in scientific research simply a function of interior estimations superimposed upon value-free practices?

Disagreement and lack of settlement shown in moral matters have often been cited as reasons for turning to inner attitudes: If the same act can be considered moral by one person and immoral by another, how can the moral "property" inhere in the act or in the world? It must, then, stem from a subjective state. The assumption here, however, is that limits and disagreement are decisive threats to truth, which would follow only from traditional standards of strict objectivity and certainty. Such an assumption, though, has not been in line with the actual course and practice of human thinking anyway, in any form. Scientific inquiry, both diachronically and synchronically, is marked by limits, disagreement, controversies, and dissettlement at certain levels.[13] We could distinguish between science and ethics in terms of the *degree* of agreement and uncertainty, but one need not divorce truth from ethics simply because of disagreement and uncertainty.

As we will see in this investigation, finding truth in ethics will not mean that moral claims can be justified by a purely objective, rational, or fixed standard. Nor will it eliminate limits, disagreement, and alteric tensions from the moral sphere. In an existential sense, a moral life is never free from the tension of certain counterforces in ourselves and in the world; it is pervaded with an alterity

that makes it a continual *achieving*. Ethics also cannot avoid dilemmas and conflicts between different contexts, agents, groups, and principles. All this does not
preclude, however, use of the word truth in the domain of ethics. Even though
ethics involves uncertainty and tension, we can (1) affirm the elements of aletheic
truth here, (2) take account of inhibitive truth, and (3) factor in that ethics at a
certain point demands deliberation, decision, and commitment. One of the things
that emerges in the pages to come is that a phenomenology of decision and commitment in ethics tends to cast doubt on strictly objective moral frameworks (one
does not "decide" that objective conditions obtain) and subjective models as well
(one does not "commit" to mere opinions).[14]

To conclude, truth-as-unconcealment and unconcealment-as-truth together
express an ungrounded, dynamic, pluralistic "family" of settings for disclosing
the world, settings that are variously appropriate at different times, in different
contexts, to different degrees. There are times when verification is to be preferred
over intuition (and vice versa), facts over mystery (and vice versa), reason over
emotion (and vice versa), clarity over ambiguity (and vice versa), order over
freedom (and vice versa), and the group over the individual (and vice versa).
There are also times when settings such as these overlap and interpenetrate each
other in various ways. Moments of truth are shown in judgments of appropriateness and inappropriateness at these times. The art of thinking is to orchestrate
these movements, but also to acknowledge their indigenous limits and tensions.
But along this pathway, signs of truth can be guides to places that can best be
called sojourns, or momentary stays along the way.

NOTES

1. See "New Insights into How Babies Learn," *Science* (August 1997): 641, for how
early "baby talk" to neonates and various interactive behaviors actually contribute to brain
development. See also Jerome Bruner, *Child's Talk* (New York: Norton, 1983).

2. This discussion borders on the important question of embodiment, something to
which Heidegger gives little attention but that is implicit in his conception of being-
in-the-world. He does in fact acknowledge Dasein's "bodily nature" (*Leiblichkeit*) and link
care with the body (*BT*, 143, 242). The classic source for a phenomenology of embodiment
is Maurice Merleau-Ponty. See *The Phenomenology of Perception*, trans. Colin Smith
(London: Routledge & Kegan Paul, 1962), and *The Primacy of Perception and Other
Essays*, ed. James E. Edie (Evanston, Ill.: Northwestern University Press, 1964). The latter work contains an important essay on child development, "The Child's Relations with
Others." For a rich trilogy of works that explore embodied existence, particularly as it
relates to social development, see David M. Levin, *The Body's Recollection of Being* (London: Routledge & Kegan Paul, 1985); *The Opening of Vision* (New York: Routledge,
1988); and *The Listening Self* (New York: Routledge, 1989).

3. Some of the following is taken from my essay "Rejoining *Alētheia* and Truth,"
International Philosophical Quarterly, vol. 30, no. 4 (December 1990): 431–47.

4. The significant texts are *BT*, section 44; *BP*, sections 17–18; *ET*; and "Plato's Doctrine of Truth" (*PM*, 155–82).

5. "On the Essence of Ground" (*PM*, 103–4).

6. See J. L. Austin, *How to Do Things with Words* (Cambridge, Mass.: Harvard University Press, 1975), 151ff.

7. My approach here is compatible in many respects with the hermeneutics of Hans-Georg Gadamer and Paul Ricoeur. Both thinkers try to strike a balance between modernist foundationalism and postmodern contingency, by articulating a pluralist–realist account of multiple avenues of interpretive practices and truth that are appropriate to phenomena and sensitive to limits. See Gadamer, *Truth and Method*, trans. G. Barden and J. Cumming (New York: Seabury, 1975), and *Philosophical Hermeneutics*, trans. David E. Linge (Berkeley: University of California Press, 1976). See also Ricoeur, *Hermeneutics and the Human Sciences: Essays on Action, Language, and Interpretation*, trans. John B. Thompson (Cambridge: Cambridge University Press, 1981). Both thinkers are greatly indebted to Heidegger, yet I think more attention to finitude in terms of what I am calling aletheic truth should be incorporated into their findings.

8. For an insightful discussion, see Charles Guignon, "Truth as Disclosure: Art, Language, History," *Southern Journal of Philosophy*, supplement to vol. 28 (1989): 105–20.

9. See the *Oxford English Dictionary* entries for "true" and "truth." The German *Treue* means loyalty, and Heidegger uses this word in reference to Dasein's authentic resoluteness (*BT*, 443).

10. In certain circles of philosophy and literary theory there is a lot of interrogation of science on a number of fronts. I should say, though, that such critiques of science should not engage in, or be read as, a dismissal of scientific findings or their appropriate status. That would be silly. The issue is rather the hegemonic notion that the *setting* of science is paramount or the exclusive province of truth in all matters. In Heideggerian terms, the problem of science does not pertain to its ontical discoveries but to its ontological reach.

11. Consider Heidegger's use of rift and strife in *BW* (174ff) and *polemos* in *IM* (61–63). For an extended treatment of how rationality emerged and took shape in tension with nonrational elements of culture in the Greek world, see my *Myth and Philosophy: A Contest of Truths* (Chicago: Open Court, 1990).

12. See Heidegger's use of the term commitment (*Bindung*) in *MFL*, 192.

13. As I have said, scientific thinking should not be segregated from the implications of unconcealment. Science has its own process character, social practices, and historical dimension, and its modes of thinking are not divorced from creative, imaginative, intuitive, even aesthetic features. Philosophy of science inspired by the work of Thomas Kuhn can find much in common with phenomenological hermeneutics. See Richard Bernstein, *Beyond Objectivity and Relativism: Science, Hermeneutics, Praxis* (Philadelphia: University of Pennsylvania Press, 1983); Theodore Kisiel, "Heidegger and the New Images of Science," *Research in Phenomenology* 7 (1977): 162–81; and Joseph Rouse, "Kuhn, Heidegger, and Scientific Realism," *Man and World* 14 (1981): 269–90.

14. The approach I am taking might be able to hold off the specter of relativism that haunts moral philosophy. Radical relativism is simply the reversal of absolutism. If the latter is put in question, the former can lose its force. As I will suggest, judging individuals or

groups against their own preferences need not require an absolute standard or the vantage point of strict objectivity. Some moral conflicts can be understood in a pluralistic rather than a relativistic way by including a responsive element, as opposed to a sheer reduction to different preferences. Moreover, moral commitment is impossible with the egalitarian implications of relativism (that different ethical positions have equal standing). I cannot commit to an ethical decision and at the same time affirm the equal validity of opposing views. That would make ethical decisions completely vacuous. See my discussion in *A Nietzschean Defense of Democracy: An Experiment in Postmodern Politics* (Chicago: Open Court, 1995), 182–84. For an insightful work that addresses dubious charges of relativism leveled against nonfoundationalist philosophies, see Barbara Herrnstein Smith, *Belief and Resistance: Dynamics of Contemporary Intellectual Controversy* (Cambridge, Mass.: Harvard University Press, 1997), especially ch. 5. Peter Railton argues for an ethical pluralism that, while issuing dilemmas, need not be incompatible with a kind of moral realism. See his "Pluralism, Determinacy, and Dilemma," *Ethics* 102 (July 1992): 720–42. Heidegger's multiple interpretive as-structures show that conflicted viewpoints can be taken as disclosive of the *objective complexity* of the world, rather than as an inconsistency calling for rectification.

Chapter Three

Being-Ethical-in-the-World

The aim of this chapter is to apply the elements of Heidegger's thought discussed in the preceding chapters to questions in ethics. I will proceed by outlining general features of modern moral philosophy and then surveying how Heideggerian phenomenology can open up alternative paths in ethics in ways analogous to Heidegger's alternative path in ontology.

MODERN MORAL PHILOSOPHY

Modern moral theories reflected the general intellectual developments in modern philosophy sketched in chapter 1. The model of the free rational individual took shape in ethics as the promotion of free inquiry and individual autonomy in determining what is right and wrong, as opposed to defining the good or norms of behavior by the unexamined dictates of religion, custom, habit, or various traditional authorities.[1] Modern moral theory turns to the reflective subject as the self-grounding basis of moral inquiry and decision methods.[2]

We have seen how the modern disengagement of the rational subject prompted the disenchantment of nature. With priority given to objectification, mathematization, and mechanization, then notions of meaning, value, and purpose were stripped from the environing-world in deference to nature understood as a set of causal forces and verifiable, predictable facts. Whatever space could be found for moral values or notions of right and wrong would have to be located in the human subject and not in any objective condition; that is, not in the world itself. Usually the turn to the subject intended to retain elements of rationality, but in the subject's practical reason rather than the scientific execution of theoretical reason.

The modern bifurcation of subject and object, value and fact, prompted various problems for moral philosophy and generated different moral theories to respond to these problems and to secure moral constructs consistent with the

contours of modern thought. A significant problem that has endured since the
modern period is moral skepticism. Since the subject–object split prompted
skepticism even about the possibility of knowledge in general, it was easy for
some to claim skepticism about any form of moral knowledge. Since values
vary and are not susceptible to objective verification and conformity, it was
short work to deny knowledge and truth conditions in the realm of ethics. Taking a cue from David Hume's famous division of values and facts, it was maintained that what "ought" to be the case can never be derived from, or located
in, what "is" the case. An influential later development in this vein was logical positivism's emotivist theory of ethics, which held that moral notions are
nothing more than emotional responses and preferences that have no status as
truth claims.[3] Although most modern moral theories shared the view that ethical notions cannot measure up to standards of scientific objectivity, several
approaches tried to surmount skepticism and articulate reliable principles that
could answer decisively the philosophical question of what makes actions
right or wrong. In other words, several theories aimed to provide foundational
guidance for ethical questions, but in keeping with the modern profile, any
such foundation would be subject-based.

Ethical egoism holds that what is right and wrong is based on individual self-
interest. The right thing to do is whatever individuals conceive to be in their own
self-interest, as opposed to being compelled to act in the interest of others or by
way of externally imposed moral constraints. Ethical egoism usually is derived
from psychological egoism, a theory of human nature arguing that we cannot
help but act in our own self-interest: Human beings are atomic, individual organisms that by necessity perceive and interpret everything through the lens of self-
interest, of what is beneficial or harmful to each organism. Based on this supposed fact of human nature, ethical egoism argues for a moral theory that is
consistent with this fact, and that can prompt honesty in ethical dealings, rather
than various poses of altruism that other moral schemes ask us to adopt. Ethical
egoism need not be wanton hedonism or narcissism; an egoist can delay gratifi-
cation, help others, and avoid harming others out of a rational analysis of long-
term self-interest. Nevertheless, critics claim that the theory has weak, if any,
resources to check recalcitrant behavior of the wanton variety, and that it cannot
resolve moral conflicts stemming from two or more ethical egoists confronting
each other with clashing interests.

Utilitarianism is a moral theory that can improve upon egoism by constructing a socially based normative framework. Utilitarianism is often called
consequentialism, in that the right thing to do is what produces the best consequences for the greatest number of people. Utilitarianism is not entirely different from egoism in assuming that human beings are individual subjects
moved by self-interest and preferences regarding what brings pleasure and
pain, benefit and harm. In its classic form designed by Jeremy Bentham, the
good for human beings is happiness, or the utility of what maximizes pleasure

and minimizes pain. The defects of egoism are addressed in utilitarianism by defining moral right as happiness for the greatest number.

The theory of utilitarianism was originally geared primarily toward public policy questions, and for many adherents this remains its strength. In considering an action or policy, a utilitarian must weigh the utility for all persons concerned and do what produces more happiness in the aggregate than other alternatives. Subsequent versions of utilitarianism have tended to define happiness in broader and richer ways than simply pleasure and pain, with notions such as well-being, preference satisfaction, or interest satisfaction. In any case, the theory operates by way of quantifying units of utility, and then performing a disinterested calculation of the aggregate that will provide the measure of right and wrong actions. In this way, utilitarianism aims to provide a kind of moral science that offers a precise technique for ethical adjudication. The strengths of the theory include its accommodation of both self-interest and social constraints, its flexibility in adjusting to varying conditions, and its decisiveness in complex cases. In utilitarianism, what is right and wrong is not predetermined or constructed independently of actual outcomes for actual communities.

One of the great legacies of modern thought is the moral philosophy of Immanuel Kant. Kant's ethics is called nonconsequentialist because it critiques both the egoist and the utilitarian emphasis on consequences and happiness, whether in an individual or a collective sense. What brings pleasure and pain, happiness and unhappiness, varies between and within individuals or groups. Moreover, consequences are uncertain. Basing ethics in happiness and consequences, therefore, produces an unstable, malleable directive that can permit heinous acts or counterintuitive justifications. Not only can egoism permit injurious acts, utilitarianism can permit injury to, or exploitation of, individuals if the calculus produces enough utility for the well-being of the community. For Kant, morality should be deontological, or duty-based, independent of good or bad consequences or the interests of individuals or groups. Just as in the military, where doing one's duty is independent of, and usually contrary to, one's normal inclinations, Kant thinks that ethics requires a principle that can define what is right in a way that commands the will's compliance, regardless of gains or losses in life.

Kant thinks that the abstract universality characteristic of reason can supply such a principle and a kind of necessity that can command the will to act out of duty rather than inclination. Egoism and utilitarianism define what is right on the basis of what individuals or groups value as good or desirable. Kant turns the tables and insists on the priority of an abstract principle of right over the good, because of the variability and inconstancy of conceptions of the good. Kant shapes a principle of right in the categorical imperative, which dictates that one act in such a way that one could consistently will one's rule for action as a universal law. In other words, one should only do what could universally bind all rational agents. The categorical imperative is a thought experiment conducted by the rational subject independent of circumstances or particular features of life,

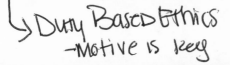

→ Duty Based Ethics
  —Motive is key

and its measure is rational consistency or inconsistency rather than outcomes or preferences. For instance, false promising is morally wrong because it cannot be universalized. If every promise were false, false promising would deconstruct, because no promise would be believed and yet the aim of the liar is to be believed.

The most influential version of Kant's categorical imperative is the principle of respect for persons, which can directly intercept possible injustices in egoism or utilitarianism by dictating that one should never treat persons solely as a means to one's own ends, but should allow them the freedom of being ends in themselves. Exploiting persons for one's own purposes violates the baseline freedom of persons as rational agents, as end-seeking, self-directing beings.

In terms of what actions are right and wrong, Kant's ethics turns out to be not much different from moral precepts found in the Western tradition, particularly the Judeo-Christian moral tradition. Kant (and many other modern moral theorists) did not actually reject moral tradition as much as aim to give it a rational grounding and reconstruction. In this way, the individual subject could truly "own" its moral compass by discovering its own self-grounded rationale for moral action. For Kant, freedom is not license but *self*-legislation by way of reason. The universality of rational constructs provides a constraint on the will, but as self-generated in the process of rational construction, it is autonomous rather than "heteronomous," or directed from external forces or prompted by natural impulses. For Kant, genuine moral worth requires such an autonomous, self-imposed rational ground. And presumably a self-imposed moral directive would produce the strongest force of obligation.

The preceding represents only the barest sketch of some typical modern moral theories. In due course, I will expand upon this sketch in various ways. Presently we can summarize four basic characteristics that mark the philosophical paths outlined above. Modern moral theories are (1) *foundational*, in claiming to find a unified explanation for what is moral and immoral, and a grounding principle for determining what is right and wrong; (2) *decisive*, in that the theoretical principle supplies a decision procedure for arriving at a moral judgment, where the principle applied to a particular case delivers an answer in a conclusive chain of reasoning; (3) *action-guiding*, in that moral philosophy is confined mostly to rules and principles for judging right and wrong actions, rather than broader conceptions such as the nature and quality of persons, forms of life, or comprisals of meaning; and (4) *subject-based*, in that moral analysis is centered in the human subject, its faculties, procedures, and decisions.

HEIDEGGERIAN ALTERNATIVES TO MODERN MORAL THEORY

Despite Heidegger's demurral on ethical questions and dismissal of certain basic conceptions of moral philosophy, I aim to draw out some possible resources for ethics from the elements of Heidegger's thought covered in the first two chapters. Heidegger was preoccupied with extraordinary dimensions of thought and experience—for example, the finite openness of being, authenticity, and poetical thinking—yet as we have seen, the path to such dimensions passes within and through the quotidian life-world, Dasein's everyday familiarities, practices, and prereflective bearings. The problem with the everyday world is not that it represents some discrete dimension that fosters a mistaken outlook on reality, but that it tends to conceal the radical finitude of being that is *immanent* in lived existence. Herein lies an important point. The modern disengagement of reflective reason from the lived world can be understood as a consummated refuge from the finitude of being. Modern thinkers championed detached reflection because it opened up secure structures of thought that could surmount the contingencies of the quotidian world—its affective, practical, habitual, embodied, temporal, historical elements. Prior to Heidegger's lofty ontological adventures, his mundane construction of being-in-the-world provides an important challenge to the disengaged reason of modern thought. Dasein is already engaged with the world before it is subjected to reflection, and so there is good reason to presume a certain aptness in that prereflective bearing. The modern project can certainly attest to certain limits or restrictions in that initial bearing and disclose modifications and new horizons, but the tendency toward wholesale dismissal or segregation of the life-world can be diagnosed as a *flight* from the finite complexity of existence.

My suggestion is that modern moral philosophy in certain respects follows the same problematic disengagement from finite being-in-the-world, and that ethics can benefit from Heideggerian phenomenology and its divergence from the modern project.[4] Heidegger included ethics in ontic domains that conceal in their positive disclosures the radical finitude of being. This was not a dismissal of ethics but rather a postponement of its proper treatment until the general question of Dasein's mode of being could be explored (*BT*, 37).

Ethics as a mere doctrine and imperative is helpless unless man first comes to have a different fundamental relation to being. (*WCT*, 89) **importance of being**

I am here trying to make good on Heidegger's intimations about rethinking ethics in the light of his ontological discoveries. As I said in the introduction, I want to modify a classic Heideggerian take on finitude in the following way: Rather than simply saying that ethics as an ontical sphere conceals the finitude of being, I want to argue that traditional moral philosophy has concealed the finitude of ethics. Although much of moral philosophy has been rich in its disclosure of important ethical concerns, it has been poor in its attention to being-ethical-in-the-world, in the sense of a situated finitude.

We have established that the setting of ethics is concerned with matters of existential weal and woe in social life, with matters of welfare, help and harm, justice, freedom, responsibility, and virtue. In this setting, we have said that ethics

→ Denial of mortality.

unfolds as action-guiding, action-judging, value-disclosing, and life-shaping. My proposal is that, contrary to the theoretical tendencies of modern moral philosophy, ethics should be understood as the contingent, heuristic, interactive engagement of basic practical questions: How should human beings live? How should we live together? How should we treat each other? What do we owe each other? What are better and worse ways of conducting our lives?

At the same time, we should balance such interrogative openness with Heidegger's notion of a *situated* openness. Ethics must acknowledge prephilosophical, traditional inheritances that shape the self and that present a degree of consensus "already" regarding better and worse ways of living. Considering our own culture, we tend to agree already in a rough fashion and to a certain extent that lying, stealing, and killing are unacceptable, and that violence, cruelty, and indifference are worse than kindness and concern. Such estimations are not unique to our culture and time. The philosophical task of ethics would not be to put our entire moral outlook into question from the ground up, or to discover some brand new set of norms and values (nothing so radical has ever happened in history). Rather, moral philosophy should be an engaged openness that pursues the following five tasks.

(1) A contextual examination of moral values and conceptions of the good as cultural phenomena. What does it mean to value something, to conceive of life or persons as good or bad? Here ethics takes up much more than simply rules for living or the modern emphasis on obligatory or permissible actions and piecemeal moral problems. Ethics must consider questions of meaning and importance, patterns and narratives that shape a sense of a life well lived—in other words, not just what we do, but how we live and who we are.[5] Here I side with those who take the good as prior to moral right in ethics. What is meaningful, worthwhile, desirable, and important will always register in ethical considerations and cannot be subordinated to abstract principles of right.[6]

(2) An examination of the meaning of inherited values, norms, and narratives. In view of Heidegger's notion of inauthenticity, we can say that familiar ethical notions are not as clear, straightforward, and unambiguous as they seem. Philosophical examination can provide both elucidation and disruption of a distorting complacency.

(3) An engagement of the question, Why should people be ethical in the way their culture bids? This question is not a call for demonstration or proof to banish doubt or disagreement, but rather an existential, addressive question that takes up the developments, conflicts, tensions, and burdens that mark an ethical life. In this way, moral philosophy should be inseparable from moral education. Critical reasoning and arguments are certainly a part of ethics; such operations arise naturally in circumstances of doubt, disagreement, and disorientation. Criticism and defense of moral notions, however, are better rendered as contextual responses to actual doubts, conflicts, and challenges, rather than the Cartesian legacy of "justification" that mandates doubt as an a priori methodological requirement, and

' whys instead of hows.
- examination of old instead of
developing news

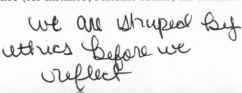

Origins

that accordingly measures interrogative outcomes by a standard of indefeasible certainty. We should begin by sorting out areas of agreement and disagreement before we assume what needs defending.

(4) An exploration of developmental questions. How do people become ethical or unethical? What conditions, attributes, or processes are involved in actualizing or blocking ethical potential? A developmental analysis is essential to ethics, especially with regard to child rearing and education.

(5) An interrogation of moral tradition in the face of actual doubts, challenges, or conflicts, with an eye toward uncovering possible inconsistencies or failures, and considering innovations that might be needed to revive or alter tradition.

My contention is that many perennial problems and controversies in moral philosophy can be effectively addressed with the adoption of the profile of ethics sketched above. I believe that ethics can benefit from Heidegger's thought in a manner comparable to his revisioning of traditional ontology. Heidegger never claimed that rational or metaphysical models of thought are false or dispensable (see *LH*, 233), only that they are not primordial enough, that their disclosures conceal the finitude of being, and that such finitude must be addressed to reorient our thinking about the world. I am suggesting an analogy between Heidegger's approach to traditional ontology and my venture into ethics. Traditional moral theories are not false or dispensable; they disclose much that is important for ethics. But the tradition is saddled with certain metaphysical presuppositions that cover up the prereflective life-world and the radical finitude of existence, attention to which can reorient ethical thinking for the better. So the ethics that is put in question is not moral life as such, but rather traditional theoretical and metaphysical presumptions in moral philosophy. If we attend in a Heideggerian manner to the existential environment in which and out of which the moral life arises, such a metaethical analysis can give us clues for a more adequate ethics in terms of the fivefold task described above.

The task for ethics should not be the search for a theory or principle that can survive rational scrutiny, that can satisfy objective cognitive standards inherited from traditional logic and the sciences, or that can provide clear and certain criteria to guide adjudication. Such an orientation shows that ethics has been distorted from the start. We already *are* shaped by ethics, before we reflect on it. Given a situated, socialized self, we are ethically *thrown*. An ethical bearing in one way or another goes all the way down. The question is not *whether* to be ethical but *how* to be ethical. Attention to this prereflective ethical world will provide a better understanding of how values and norms function in human existence, and will better open up ethical life with all its existential conditions, limits, and difficulties. In my view, the main features of Heidegger's configuration of being-in-the-world can be effectively translated to prepare such an approach to ethics; the result would be a comparable structure of being-ethical-in-the-world.

Many moral theories have searched for an objective, rational standard that could operate as nearly decisively in ethics as in the domains of mathematics, logic, and science (for instance, Platonic forms, the Kantian categorical impera-

we are shaped by ethics before we reflect

tive, the utilitarian calculus). One way or another, the hope has been that we can discover a measure to govern the existential conflicts and empirical contingencies of the ethical field. From a Heideggerian perspective, the futility of such a search is forcefully shown in the fact that even the most "objective" disciplines are deconstructed into the dynamics of the lived world. Since no form of thought can claim a purely objective, fixed warrant, it is short work to show that objective certainty is a chimera in ethics. Being-ethical-in-the-world can be drawn along the same lines as Heidegger's ontological constellation. Everyday ethical involvement gives access to a prereflective environment that opens up the following conditions. With radical finitude as the existential thrust of care, we understand the urgency of concern for our possibilities that can bear us in, and in which we can bear, our finitude. Values and norms are intelligible in such an environment as modes of "shelter" and "release" for beings that are continually vulnerable to conditions of finitude: death, loss, pain, failure, humiliation, domination, and so on. But ethical values and norms as such are no less finite that the environment in which they arise, and so "being ethical" must be understood in terms of the same limit conditions uncovered in Heidegger's phenomenological analysis: thrownness, particularity, plurality, unconcealment, temporality, and historicality, which altogether undermine the search for a purely objective standard.

FINITUDE AND THE OUGHT

There are a number of ways in which Heideggerian phenomenology can apply to a basic question in moral philosophy: the nature and status of the "ought." In ordinary terms, the difference between what ought to be the case and what is the case has always been recognized: The ought involves values as distinct from facts, preferences as distinct from objective conditions, possibilities as distinct from actualities, and decisions as distinct from causal necessities. Many ontologies have privileged the latter term in each of the above distinctions, and so the ought has been suspect in its ontological and cognitive status. Values have not measured up to the standards of objective facts because of their variable, decisional nature. The best we can say, perhaps, is that the ought reflects subjective interests rather than objective being.

I have shown, however, that Heidegger offers a very different conception of being that need not conflict with the evaluative nature of the ought. With being-in-the-world, being is associated with meaning. The interest-laden character of being then allows values to have a kind of being. Heidegger clearly objects to the contraposition of being and the ought, since this implies a delimitation of being, as though the ought does not belong to being. The ought, however, *does* belong to being (*PM*, 285). In a certain respect, Hume was right about the *difference* between the ought and (some senses of) the is; but for Heidegger, this difference is still part of being, and so only a certain ontological ideology threatens the status of values.

The finitude of being and Dasein's finite transcendence can deepen our understanding of the ought and how it is disclosed. Dasein's transcendence, which exceeds conditions of actuality, makes possible a wide range of cultural forms that are animated by wonder, curiosity, and questioning, and that proceed in the light of possibilities that exceed an immediate perceptual encounter with the brute present—an excess operating in settings such as art, religion, and science. Likewise, the very nature of ethics involves the difference between actualities and possibilities, in terms of a differential relation between oughts and extant conditions, a relation made possible by the negativity of Dasein's transcendence. Both the "ought" and the "ought not" pertain to negation, in recommending something different from what can be, is, or has been the case. The temporal structure of prescriptive ought-utterances thus exhibits an excess of actuality. Such excess is fully consonant with Heidegger's sense of being and does not prompt any automatic suspicions about legitimacy or warrant.[7]

ETHICAL HERMENEUTICS AND INTERROGATION

Heidegger's sense of the hermeneutic circle precludes any sense of a purely objective ground for thinking. Dasein's interpretive nature is indicated in both the situated givenness of its traditional inheritance and the responsive adjustment to circumstances in its environment. Regarding ethics we can say that Dasein is "always already" ethical in some way, that traditional heritage, upbringing, habits, social practices, linguistic competence, and predisposed interests shape Dasein as an evaluating being, in terms of disclosing better and worse, important and unimportant modes of life. Values, then, go all the way down, there is no baseline value-free dimension to juxtapose against dimensions of meaning and interest. Even modern schemes of objectivity are constituted by their own modes of value—the importance of certainty, simplicity, uniformity, predictability, and truth telling—and so the value realm is a condition of understanding as such and therefore cannot be bracketed or placed before the gaze of objective examination.

As we have seen, Heidegger's hermeneutic circle is not a conservative closure since it is consistent with the openness of being-in-question. Heidegger suggests a mode of questioning that is a responsive, engaged openness, which means being interested in possibilities intrinsic to an already familiar realm of meaning. So to inquire into something is to be already concerned with it in some way. Accordingly, to ask about the good or ethical possibilities is to already be *interested* in ethics, as opposed to mechanical obedience, resistance, or a thoughtless indifference. To be-in-question ethically, then, is to already *be* ethical in some broad sense.[8]

Socrates' famous question—How should one live?—reflects broad, rich, complex issues regarding the weal and woe of one's self in relation to others, and generalized narratives of life.[9] As a question, however, it reflects a philosophical venture beyond the mere dictates of tradition, custom, habit, authority, and law. It is not merely reflective and elucidative, it is also open. And since it presupposes a social framework, its searchings tend toward widely applicable generalities rather than sheer idiosyncrasies. Being-in-question exhibits itself in moods of wonder, curiosity, fascination, unrest, or perplexity, and it is prompted when values or norms are taught, doubted, or challenged, and when we confront alternatives, ambiguities, disruptions, conflicts, or times of crisis (all of which are more likely in complex, developed, mobile societies).

In a general sense, the openness of ethical questioning is balanced by a thrown situatedness. There are a number of ways in which ethical interrogation is balanced by responsive results. In everyday practice, coordinated rituals of questioning, answering, and reason-giving are an intrinsic part of social life. (Why did you do that? Don't you think that was wrong?) Here we expect at least the possibility of forthcoming answers that might persuade or prepare consolidation. But rationalistic moral theories—which move from models of convergence and generality toward a realm of universality by searching for an overall regulation of this social field by way of presumed or accomplished principles that will be acceptable to any rational being—may not fit the different ways in which much social interaction proceeds or resolves itself (or does not resolve itself). For instance, ethical questions in conversation might be satisfied by a personal narrative or an emotional appeal. Ethics does not originally exhibit some kind of demonstrative or axiomatic logic, and sometimes not much of any logic. But a certain addressive, dialectical logic (of the kind portrayed in Platonic dialogues) can have, and often does play, an important role in ethical exchanges—in the sense of following what a conversant presents in conversation, with an eye toward discovering intrinsic implications, inconsistencies, or modifications that might inhabit professed beliefs. So a certain dialogic can be affirmed in the midst of ethical questioning, although the limits of discursive reason need acknowledging as well (as I show later in the thought of Aristotle).[10]

Another way in which ethical openness is balanced by responsive results is in decision making. Ethical existence involves a confluence of enculturation, interrogation, and selection, in that it mixes a situated being-in-question with the task of coming to a decision, of choosing one path over others.[11] Even with the determinate character of decisions, however, we can say that being-in-question can still saturate ethical life in the sense of an open excess that precludes even our deepest commitments from ossifying into secure truths without remainder. In other words, being ethical sustains, and is even fostered by, a sense of fragility and cognitive humility. More on this in later discussions.

DECONSTRUCTING THE MORAL TRADITION

As we have stressed, Heidegger does not dismiss traditional philosophical models, or reason and truth, or even certain modes of objectivity. He argues against the predominance of certain metaphysical conceptions in the tradition, diagnoses their limits, and suggests richer, more complex registers of thought. In ethics, we need not jettison standard moral theories or orientations (for example, egoism, consequentialism, deontology, sentiment theory, the care ethic, value theory, virtue theory, liberalism, and communitarianism). We can acknowledge what is disclosive (what is inhabitively true) in such accounts, especially in terms of their historicality, their emergence in response to an era's problems and conflicts or to the limits and omissions apparent in extant moral frameworks. In this way, we can survey various norms and values that have taken shape and found a voice in ethical discourse. Nevertheless, questions about the reach of these notions—given the intrinsic tensions between them, how they tend to mutually check each other, suggesting an open, unregulable dynamic—will point to the inevitable limits of these constructs (their aletheic truth).

Consider various intersecting complexities that emerge regarding modern moral theories we have mentioned so far. Emotivism is disclosive in pointing to the role and importance of affect in ethics, but the reduction to mere subjective preference cannot suffice for inhabitive signs of truth that might well operate in ethical thinking and practice (appropriateness, workability, agreement, sociality). Affect, as we have seen, can be world-disclosive (more on this shortly). And the reduction to subjective feeling is philosophically impotent if a certain desirable moral feeling is absent or diminished.

Moral egoism is disclosive of the ethical importance of self-interest, which often needs protection from consuming social forces. But the reduction to self-interest seems to champion the kind of bearing that prompts most ethical problems in the first place. People pursuing only their own interests are what usually cue moral constructions in human societies. Egoism's confinement within individual subjectivity cannot suffice to articulate the familiar moral sense of obligation and responsibility, that one is "called" to expand one's horizons beyond mere self-regard. With egoism it is hard to fathom any sense of an ethical *claim*.

Utilitarianism is an improvement in asking individuals to adjust their actions to the overall well-being of the community. But the community is simply the aggregate of individual subjectivities, so it does not therefore supersede the assumption that the good is an internal preference having no external claim. Given utilitarian psychology, it is hard to account for why one should or would adopt the disinterested perspective of calculating the well-being of all concerned. Or given the disinterested perspective, where is the force of moral motivation?[12] Nevertheless, utilitarianism does contribute attention to actual consequences for actual agents and communities, and therefore grants a concrete regard that is missing in more abstract, formal theories. And it gives systematic organization to a familiar and widespread ethical habit, namely the balancing of interests and outcomes in a differentiated social field. Nevertheless, the theoretical technique of quantifying utility raises the problem of how effectively or even whether one can measure the qualitative experiences of life-goods, and how one can draw

comparative measurements across different goods and different persons. Read as
an obligation to maximize collective well-being, the theory can also be seen as
requiring too much of people. The criterion of collective utility also contains the
danger of majoritarian tyranny that has often plagued utilitarianism. The emphasis on instrumental reason seems to leave little room for the dignity of persons,
the notion that there are some things that should not be done to persons regardless of possible beneficial consequences for the aggregate.[13]

The modern moral theory that best addresses the need for an ethical claim is
the kind of deontological theory inspired by Kant. Here the rational subject dis-
covers universal principles solely through the use of abstract constructions that
are independent of inclinations, interests, consequences, and empirical conditions, and that should command ethical thinking in the same way that other
rational truths claim the mind's assent. Here possible abuses in egoism and utilitarianism are overruled in principle, and the inviolable dignity of persons that
commands respect is given a powerful voice in ethics to stand against injustices
of all kinds. But there are a number of difficulties that confront Kantian ethics.
First of all, from a technical standpoint, the universalization procedure might justify unexpected outcomes.[14] And we can detect in Kant's disengaged, abstract
route to universal consistency something akin to the metaphysical subjectivism
critiqued by Heidegger. The strict segregation of moral right from existential
interests and the contingencies of experience produces a kind of imperial formalism that can be blind to actual life conditions and outcomes.[15] Even if one accepts
the warrant of Kantian principles, the theory does not seem to provide much
guidance concerning when, whether, or how to apply principles to concrete cases.
Kantian formalism can also become dangerously inflexible, mandating what is
right at any cost. Finally, Kant not only disregarded the contingencies of experience in determining moral duty, he gave little attention to the obvious problem
that a moral situation can involve a conflict of duties. For instance, the abortion
debate seems intractable because, for one thing, it pits different duties against
each other (preserving life and respecting freedom).[16] It is the perceived formal-
istic defects of Kantian ethics that prompt the counterreaction of consequentialist
theories, affect-based theories, and virtue ethics.[17]

A main problem with traditional moral theories is that each has striven to provide a rule or principle that can ground and govern the entire ethical life-world.
But many moral situations are complex, variegated, and constrained by contextual, temporal, and cognitive limits. Isolated moral theories will likely fail to provide clear, decisive guidance in such situations. We might understand their limits
in terms of Heidegger's notion of formal indication, in the sense of being reflective bearings that are disclosive but that nevertheless must defer to the finitude of
concrete performance. This would indicate the intrinsic limits of abstract theoretical formulas and point to a kind of practical discernment and finesse in negotiating a complex ethical environment.[18]

BEING-IN-THE-WORLD AS AN ETHICAL ENVIRONMENT

The structure of being-in-the-world exhibits a general sense of finite dwelling; a performative sense of prereflective involvement and practice; a temporal, situational contextuality; an intrinsic sociality; and an ekstatic disclosure of meaning. Applied to ethics, such a structure can help overcome certain problems and bifurcations that have vexed moral philosophy (for instance, skepticism and the divisions of fact and value, theory and practice, and individuality and community) which arise out of the modern subject–object binary. Elements of being-in-the-world can provide different philosophical routes to the disclosure of ethical meanings, bearings, values, and norms, in ways that can enrich moral discourse by (1) salvaging ethical notions from various demotions, distortions, dismissals, and confinements stemming from modern philosophical biases, and (2) opening ethics to a finite complexity that displaces the reductive blind spots of most moral theories. Construing ethics as an *engaged responsive openness* allows an articulation of its inhabitive truth (as engaged and responsive) and its aletheic truth (as open), and both modes of truth can be presented as the province of a robust moral philosophy.

Recalling the threefold sense of the world in Heidegger's phenomenological treatment, we can begin with the self-world. The concept of mineness captures the first-person particularity of meaning and mattering. Mineness can apply to the importance of individual interests as a source of ethical concern, in claiming the freedom to lead one's life and in granting the same to others. Mineness can also apply to an individual's responsiveness to, and involvement with, other selves in an ethical relation—in other words, it can apply to caring, commitment, and motivation in the ethical sphere. Far from simply an ego-state or an internal subjectivity, mineness as a self-*world* can be seen as both disclosive of, and engaged with, what is *there* in Dasein's environment.[19]

The environing-world might not seem relevant to ethics, especially since the analysis in *Being and Time* is restricted largely to instrumental, productive, practical dealings with a work environment. But I think there are some helpful elements in this conception that can bear fruit in ethics. First of all, the analysis of the practical environing-world establishes that Dasein is essentially an active, performative self. For Heidegger, Dasein *is* what it *does* (*BT*, 155, 163); it is nothing other than its living dealings and movements (*GA* 21, 146); and being a self is its *process* of realization (*MFL*, 139). Even one's own Dasein is originally perceived in terms of what one does, uses, or performs, not as an inward subject as the "center" of action (*BT*, 155). The practical discipline of ethics, therefore, would not pertain to a mere facet of the self, but to its very being, and ethical performance would be the true proving ground for moral philosophy, rather than theoretical governance.[20]

Second, the prereflective familiarity exhibited in Dasein's practical dealings with the environing-world can find an analogical application as a kind of ethical inhabitance. Our everyday social interactions, habits, competencies, and expectations are permeated with and reflect a host of values, norms, and preferences, ranging from common courtesy and etiquette to basic social customs and ethical routines. Say I walk into a shop, exchange greetings with the clerk, carefully browse the merchandise, choose an item, take my place in line to purchase it, move aside as someone needs to get by, stumble on something, and fall, injuring myself. People immediately come to my aid, someone says, "I'm a doctor, let me help," and I let her. This episode is filled with spontaneous performances of various social values and norms—concerning manners, decorum, respect for property, fairness, unobtrusiveness, heedfulness, beneficence, truthfulness, and trust. And such routines play out without reflection or some procedure of theoretical application of rules to cases. And the aptness of the behaviors can well illustrate certain inhabitive signs of truth, namely appropriateness, workability, reliability, and sense. Such unreflective ethical capacities can trace back to child rearing and educational training, in that how we are raised enculturates and incorporates values and norms into a habitual, performative competence. This important question is explored further in the next section.

The with-world rounds out this discussion and is clearly applicable to ethics. Dasein is always already social in its dealings and activities, and its sociality involves an ekstatic in/there/with structure that entails responsive disclosure, rather than an inside-out movement that takes social relations as secondary to the primacy of self-consciousness. This is an important contribution to ethics, because we do not have to argue for the legitimacy of social spheres conceived as extrinsic to the self. Dasein *is* social from the start, and inhabitive signs of agreement and sociality would point to the possibility of ethical truth in this respect. The question would concern not whether Dasein is or can be social, but how sociality is shaped.

As distinct from the environing-world, Heidegger indicates that Dasein's being-with-others is ontologically different from relations with things in the world (*BT*, 162). Other Daseins are not things but likewise concernful being-in-the-world (*BT*, 156). In other words, other Daseins are likewise needful; they too experience the radical finitude and possibility that marks existence (*BT*, 159). Where Dasein's involvement with things *(zuhanden)* is characterized as *Besorgen*, Mitsein involvement is characterized as *Fürsorge* (*BT*, 157).[21] *Fürsorge* is said to be essential to Mitsein: "as Mitsein, Dasein is essentially for the sake of others" (*BT*, 160). Later I explore further the obvious ethical implications of *Fürsorge*. For now, let me say that *Fürsorge* is essentially different from *vorhanden* and *zuhanden* relations, which suggests an ethically robust contrast with modes of objectification and instrumentality. Yet despite this important contrast, what I want to suggest and work with in this study is an analogical treatment of ethical Mitsein compared with other modes of ekstatic being-in-the-world, particularly regarding how the *vorhanden* perspective unfolds out of disruptions in the *zuhanden* perspective.

Heidegger did little to explore the ethical implications of *Fürsorge*. Indeed, it can be said that Heidegger's important treatment of Dasein's practical dealings leaves almost untouched the significant sphere of *social practice*, the ways in which human beings engage each other in interpersonal relations and the province of values. Nevertheless, certain parallels can be drawn between *zuhanden* relations and social practice. Heidegger does indicate the social implications of *Zuhandenheit*, in that productive activity presupposes and discloses a public, shareable, co-produced world (*BT*, 100). He also intimates an analogy between Mitsein involvement and the circumspection of *Zuhandenheit* (*BT*, 159). Social practice, as I have suggested, can be understood as prereflective, engaged, environmental, interactive performance patterns—which, like productive practices, are more modes of competency (knowing-how) than of cognition (knowing-that) or of the theoretical formula of beliefs applied to circumstances. The fluid field-concept of social practice helps us avoid ethical reductions to individuality, reflection, or fixed constructions.

It is possible to explore ways in which social values and norms are ekstatically *there* in Dasein's practical world, rather than superimposed on some value-free field of action. Heidegger directly says that values and the "being of goods" cannot be understood as "added on" to the world (*BT*, 132). This suggests that values can be understood as immediate disclosures of the life-world. Social and ethical competencies are a significant way in which the ekstatic in/there/with structure of values can be exemplified. The importance of everyday familiarity in Heideggerian phenomenology can help articulate how human beings are normally and usually "ethical," as contrasted with standard theoretical constructions and applications in moral philosophy.

The beauty of Heidegger's analysis of the *zuhanden–vorhanden* dynamic is that it can help account for how ethical questions, problems, and reflections arise, and consequently how moral philosophy and its familiar constructions take shape. Just as disruptions in practical familiarity both disclose the meaning of Dasein's circumspective concern and open up an attentive gaze on *vorhanden* properties of things in experience, so too, certain breakdowns, disruptions, or novelties occurring in familiar social/normative practices disclose the meaning, characteristics, and possibilities of the ethical world, and hence open up the various reflective elements of moral philosophy.

For Heidegger, disruptions of familiarity are an essential part of encountering the world, because they show the unpredictability of things and the world as "mostly always somehow other" (*GA* 63, 100). Even though familiar social patterns have a certain priority (children could not be raised without being socialized into common practices), nevertheless both the maintenance and the breakdown of familiar practices are two facets of the same phenomenon for Heidegger, because disruption figures in the illumination of the meaning of practices (*BP*, 305). With respect to the normative sphere, ethics can be called a focused disclosure of the meaning and elements of social goods, stemming from various breaches, disturbances, or disorientations in familiar ethical habits and expectations.[22]

We can recognize different levels of ethical competence, ranging from somewhat automatic customs to a kind of proficient facility in responding to moral situations without much reflective effort.[23] Then there are many ways in which such familiar competencies can be interrupted. We can confront novel situations that do not fit expected patterns: for example, the prospect of gay marriage or animal rights. We can come across disparate patterns, as in the case of different customs from other cultures. We can experience the unexpected contravention of a pattern: for instance, questions do not arise about being thanked for a gift, but about not being thanked. We can confront situations marked by a conflict of different patterns: for instance, if a friend asks me about something that will hurt him, my loyalty, honesty, and beneficence all collide. In times of historical crisis, new patterns can emerge as critical forces when old patterns are no longer experienced as fitting or workable, as in the women's movement; and familiar conceptions can reveal their ambiguity and contestability, as in the Vietnam era, when the meaning of "patriotism" was claimed by both hawks and doves. Finally, the sphere of moral instruction contains intrinsic elements of resistance: for instance, the young commonly tend to contest what they are taught.

Disruptive confrontations such as these prompt the questions, analyses, and deliberations that characterize the discipline of ethics: What is patriotism? What are its features and possible conflicts? What is citizenship and what do citizens owe their country? Can we formulate definitions or generalities that can guide deliberation in these matters? Yet since disruption-of-prereflective-ethical-bearings is an indivisible package, both moral philosophy and a prephilosophical milieu must be thought together. One way to put this is as follows: There is much in human ethical bearings that does *not* prompt "ethics." A Heideggerian analysis allows both the disclosures of moral philosophy and a recognition of the background and limits of philosophical constructions.

ETHICS AND CHILD REARING

Childhood and child rearing have not been given much consideration in philosophy, most likely because philosophy engages in complex conceptual reflections and articulations that are not indicated in a child's abilities and experiences. Childhood has either been ignored or retrospectively described as some kind of primitive precedent to mature rational competence. The predominance of rational, reflective models in philosophy has produced much distortion of the child's world and its relation to adult experience. Even in granting the importance of advanced rational constructions, the fact that such constructions have a history in an individual's life, that they emerged out of, and often in tension with, other quite different modes of being, suggests that child development should be of pressing interest to philosophy.

Heidegger, too, gave little attention to childhood, but his philosophical emphasis on prereflective practice and understanding seems uniquely qualified to help make sense of a child's experience and development. Moreover, it seems to me that many central Heideggerian concepts are best defended, exemplified, and articulated by bringing child development into the discussion. Consider how potentiality, temporality, and historical transmission of tradition mark child rearing as the beginning of Dasein's situated emergence; consider also how the hermeneutic circle (the "always already" givenness of Dasein's understanding) and especially Dasein's thrownness are perfectly intelligible in terms of having been reared.

Heidegger does offer some occasional remarks about childhood that are of interest. He says that the child's world, too, is laden and charged with Dasein's meaning structures (*BP*, 171). He also grants that being-toward-death is a one-sided phenomenon, that a full articulation of temporality must include birth, and that care is a stretching between birth and death (*BT*, 425ff). It would do well, I think, to explore further this temporal stretching with respect to child development. Heidegger says very little in this regard, except for some tantalizing passages in the 1928–29 lecture course *Einleitung in die Philosophie* (*GA* 27). The child is no less a human Dasein than an adult is (*GA* 27, 123), but the child exists in a kind of "twilight" condition and as a "helpless deliverance in the world" (*GA* 27, 125–26). Our birth and early experiences are not just a temporal beginning; they are the early manifestation of being-in-the-world that "does not simply lie behind us," that is still close to us in some way (*GA* 27, 124). The twilight character of the child is described as rest, warmth, nourishment, sleep, and a kind of nontelic directedness of movements toward and away from elements in the environment (*GA* 27, 125). The child comes into the world crying, and negative experiences of shock and fright continue to shape the child's comportment (*GA* 27, 125). Heidegger here is able to draw on his phenomenology to show that such comportment belies the notion that an infant is "closed in on itself." The spontaneous disturbances in a child's experience are disclosive modes of *Befindlichkeit*. The child is not an enclosed subject, but is ekstatically "outside among" its world (*GA* 27, 125). The child's modes of turning-toward and turning-away, of approach and resistance in its world, are an early version of Dasein's being-in-the-world, charged with limit experiences such as fright, shock, and disturbance. The child, then, exists in a twilight condition of ekstatic finitude.

The Heideggerian notion that negative experiences such as anxiety are implicated in the disclosure of being and meaning receives strong reinforcement in considering child development, especially with regard to the universal experience of separation anxiety.[24] Human attachments and negative experiences of separation from attachments occur throughout human life in various forms and contexts: for example, losses of or threats to possessions, things, people, habits, beliefs, possibilities, environments, or roles; and encounters with something different, novel, strange, or unfamiliar. Despite the difficulties and traumas accompanying such experiences, human growth and development are impossible without separating from certain attachments and confronting new situations, so facing anxieties is essential to human development.[25] Particularly important is the role of separation anxiety in early child development. Acute separation anxiety usually occurs around eight to ten months of age, typically in the context of caregiver separation and object loss. Separation anxiety alters an earlier, more undifferentiated relation to caregivers and things. For this reason, separation experiences are correlated with the course of individuation.[26] In true Heideggerian fashion, then, it can be said that separation anxiety is a double movement; it is not a fully negative phenomenon because its affective force helps sharpen a child's experience of itself and things in the world, thus enriching experience and fostering development.[27] Again consistent with Heidegger, it appears that the process of early separation and individuation is less a cognitive–perceptual phenomenon and more an emotional–motivational–developmental phenomenon.[28]

Healthy child rearing involves a balance of love and limit setting, which on the child's side is experienced as a fluctuation between the satisfaction and the frustration of its interests. Individuation prompted by separation will then involve a certain internalization of the fluctuating balance initially shaped in the care environment.[29] In other words, part of human growth and development involves confronting finite limits in the environment, learning to tolerate such limits, and negotiating various balances between self and others, interests and frustrations, presences and absences.[30]

A look at childhood and social development shows that such early stages of life are neither amoral nor premoral, but saturated with a host of norms, values, and goods.[31] Such spheres of ethical development can be roughly organized around the importance of freedom, responsiveness to others, and situated limits—a triad that can approximate somewhat Heidegger's constructions of self-world, with-world, and environing-world.

Freedom can be understood as a good in the child's world, in terms of many different bearings and movements expressing the child's needs, interests, and activities. Most such movements, however, are only partially supported by the environment and social milieu; from early on children experience indigenous limits and obstacles to their freedom. In this regard, a wide range of alternating elements are ethically relevant with respect to a child's actualization of potentials in a finite world: alternations of pleasure and pain, satisfaction and frustration, gain and loss, success and failure, safety and risk, excitement and boredom, familiarity and strangeness.

The most ethically significant limit to a child's freedom is presented in the social world. Manifestations of freedom encounter tensions with the freedom of others and with various role and power relations in the social milieu, particularly child–parent, sibling, and peer relations. Here children learn the complex ethical permutations of socialization juxtaposed with individual freedom: such things as sharing, cooperating, turn-taking, reciprocity, fairness, and respecting property. On a more affective level, children are continually exposed to ethical scenarios of cruelty and kindness, hurting and helping, self-interest and empathy. I have more to say on this matter in a later discussion.

A consideration of ethical elements in a child's environing-world certainly overlaps significantly with the with-world, and it allows us to modulate the discussion in various ways, one example being the value and importance of the child's *zuhanden* relations in its practical, behavioral milieu: the cultivation of skills, habits, and performances in a host of making, doing, and playing scenarios. We can also consider how correlations of the child's behavior and the environment exhibit the well-known dyad of nature and nurture with respect to ethical development. I will have more to say on this later, but two things should be mentioned here. First, the relation between a child's nature and its environment seems to be a fluid, reciprocal, intersectional correlation that reflects well the kind of dynamic, holistic structure of being-in-the-world. Second, the important role of imitation—especially motor mimicry—in various linguistic, social, and behavioral developments in a child's life is a perfect illustration of Heideggerian ekstatics. Mimetic development shows that what is ekstatically *there* in the child's environment precedes a fully formed self that is "inside," so to speak. Children may need to be shown what to imitate, but not how to imitate. An intrinsic mimetic capacity in children suggests that the direction toward self-formation is first cued by ekstatic absorption in environmental prompts.[32]

The environing-world and with-world are clearly relevant to ethical development as a web of enculturating forces such as reward and punishment, praise and blame, modeling, prompting, and exhortation. As evidence of this formative nexus, children exhibit spontaneous "social referencing" by looking to others to get their bearings in social practices.[33] Children also become oriented to various arenas of power and authority in the social world, and concurrently with occasions of obedience and disobedience, compliance and resistance.

The three ethical spheres described above become more variegated, complex, and intricate as the child becomes more individuated, especially in the midst of language development. In line with what I have said before about language generally, the learning of language begins the opening and articulating of a child's ethical world, beginning with such basic utterances as "yes" and "no," "nice" and "mean," "good" and "bad," in the context of early behaviors. The child's linguistic development permits giving a presence to the absences of past and future, thus enriching the capacities of memory, anticipation, and imagining different possibilities. Such temporal alterability is essential to the possibility of moral instruction, of initiating a sense of the differential element in every ought and ought not. At the same time, to the chagrin of most parents, the cultivation of linguistic ability and alterability also enhances the child's resources for resistance (the verbal creativity of a child in trouble is often astounding). So language development permits both the convergences of socialization and the divergences of individuation.

Language development, individuation, and socialization also exhibit early manifestations of social practices that have always been the lifeblood of moral philosophy. Children display what seems to be an intrinsic capacity for rituals of question and answer, reason giving, negotiation, reciprocation, and modification in the context of ethical situations involving parents, siblings, and peers. Role playing, pretend play, and storytelling also are important parts of developing a child's ethical sense.[34] All such practices suggest an early capacity for ethical appropriation in a social setting, as opposed to sheer rote learning or mechanical conditioning. Children seem to be budding moral thinkers from early on (unless we drill it out of them).[35]

The point of this section has been to spotlight the complex web of goods, values, and norms that are intrinsic to a child's environment and development from the start, the array of meanings, practices, and relations that shape an ethical bearing from the beginning of life in a prereflective manner. Moral theories can be seen to draw on such a milieu in a more reflective manner. But the modern bias of subject-centered reason is challenged by a Heidegger-inspired look at early human development, which shows that we are always already ethically situated and thrown in a way. Since various ethical forces come to shape the self in the first place, the modern theoretical tendency to ground ethics in self-reflection requires an originating "self" that in many respects is a fictional object.

The different permutations within and between the three ethical spheres in a child's world also open up and illustrate the complexities and tensions that are intrinsic to an ethical environment. Both parents and children are readily aware of the commingling of diverse and competing goods that are not amenable to neat organization or clear resolution. Parents, for instance, experience the tension between permitting, even encouraging a child's freedom to explore its world and conduct its life, and worrying about the dangers, risks, and sufferings that the world can visit upon an advancing child. There is also the tension of wanting a child to develop both a healthy self-regard and a concern for others. There is no formula or guidebook that can suffice in such settings. Raising a child is at best an attentive experiment marked by a blend of encouragement, protection, joy, hope, and anxiety.

Children, too, come to experience the difficult confluence of goods in their world. For instance, children have a natural interest in the value of freedom and desire satisfaction. They also need no help in recognizing unfair treatment—for instance, when another child might get a larger piece of cake. But they also see that fairness should be reciprocal, yet fairness to others might block or limit their own freedom or desire satisfaction. Children readily experience this tension as a perplexing yet compelling feature of the social world that is simply there and that cannot be outstripped.

Consider the tension between individuation and socialization in another register. Children display natural tendencies toward assertiveness, resistance, aggressiveness, pride, and possessiveness that certainly can be problematic for the cultivation of prosocial dispositions. Norms in the social world continually check such tendencies in different ways and to varying degrees. Even with the force of such norms, however, a child exhibits a natural interest in testing their limits, often with a sense of excitement. Despite the difficulties here, it is important to recognize the significant role that a child's resistance plays in individuation and development. An utterly obedient child would likely develop into a feeble adult, if at all. Child resistance, especially in the infamous "no" stage, is an essential ingredient in a child's growth. As Hegel and Nietzsche have indicated on a larger scale, there is no individuation without some degree of conflicted differentiation from others. The child's "no" is in part a scoping out of its own space.

Both parents and children learn that the complex tensions of an ethical environment cannot be fully managed or regulated from the standpoint of rigid guidelines or systematic order. The best that can be achieved is an ongoing balancing act of negotiation, orchestration, and experimentation. Such contingent modes of coping with the fluid intricacy of the social world continue to mark ethical bearings beyond the milieu of child rearing as well. Mature ethical life involves refinements and modulations of its original milieu, especially concerning correlations of self-regard and responsiveness to others, freedom and responsibility, appropriation and authority, development and limits—all of which exceed the strict taxonomies and directives that have animated many moral theories.

MOOD AND AFFECT IN ETHICS

Heidegger gives a certain priority to *Befindlichkeit*, or mood as an ambient attunement, over a strict sense of cognition counterposed to feeling and emotion. Prior to "knowing," Dasein is *moved* by interest, involvement, and mattering, disclosed through mood. In this vein, Heidegger's thought to some extent can be related to so-called noncognitivist ethical theories, which take moral life to stem more from feeling and emotion than from rational constructions or inferences. Hume is an important figure in this regard, and in certain ways he represents a significant alternative to mainstream modern moral philosophy. Hume's division between facts and values stems from partitioning empirical descriptions from moral prescriptions, and logical inferences from moral motivation. No propositional relation between the act of killing and its moral reprobation will dictate that one refrain from killing, unless one is repulsed by a certain feeling. For Hume, the province of ethics is attention to moral sentiments such as benevolence, revulsion, and sympathy.[36]

One advantage of considering affect in ethics is that it speaks well to questions of moral constitution and moral motivation. For example, if I witness the wanton beating of a child, I take this *as* an ethical situation not by way of some classification technique but by way of affective reactions of revulsion and compassion, which also motivate me to condemn the act and do something about it. In other words, we can consider certain feelings and emotions as modes of "moral perception" that first give access to the moral sphere and to a kind of interest and mattering that prompts involvement and commitment.[37]

There are significant advantages in bringing a Heideggerian perspective on mood into this discussion of ethical affects. First of all, we would not be bound by a strict fact–value binary that segregates an ethical sphere of feeling from a cognitive sphere of knowledge and truth. We have seen that Heidegger locates elements of interest, disposition, and mood in all areas of thought, science included. We can bridge ethical and cognitive domains not simply by valorizing ethical interests and dispositions, but also by attending to dispositions like wonder, curiosity, and excitement in science. If we might resist calling curiosity in science a "mere feeling," we might be able to do the same with ethical dispositions. We can notice other bridging effects by considering certain "values" in science, such as truthfulness, and certain "virtues" that mark critical thinking, such as open-mindedness, courage, and attentiveness.

A second related advantage in turning to Heidegger is that we are released from the subject–object binary that prompts an account of affects as merely subjective phenomena. For Heidegger, affect can be *world-disclosive*, as an ekstatic openness rather than a mere subjective state. For Heidegger, a mood "is not itself an inner condition that reaches forth in an enigmatic way and puts its mark on things and persons." Mood is disclosive of the world and other persons (*BT*, 176).

Where the tradition tended to stress the "passivity" of emotion, largely in contraposition to the supposed active mastery of reason, a Heideggerian sense of "thrown affect" is a much more complicated and ambiguous notion. Being thrown is not simply something that happens *to* me; I *am* thrown. Moreover, thrownness suggests being thrust *out* to the world, and not simply an inner condition. Consequently, advancing the role of feeling and emotion in ethics need not face certain problems of subjectivism that have haunted noncognitivist ethical theories. So it is possible to address philosophical questions of moral constitution and moral motivation without being pressed into some subjective or internal sphere as distinct from some world-disclosive sphere. Recalling the many senses of "objective" discussed in chapter 2, it is possible to suggest an objective character in certain affective responses, in the sense that they can be called appropriate disclosures of some ethical import in the world, and not simply subjective states. Regarding the example cited previously, it is possible to talk of appropriate revulsion to the beating of an innocent child. We might even say that someone who takes an indifferent or detached stance toward such an act is not responding appropriately, is in a way not being morally objective.[38]

Another angle on the nonsubjective character of affect would be found in Heidegger's sense of collective mood. Although it is difficult to articulate, there is such a thing as a group's palpable mood, or a mood of an era (think of the 1920s or 1960s). One way to gain entry into such a notion is to think of an intimate relationship and the vague but pressing intimation about a tension or difficulty that can arise between partners. It can begin with a bodily sense of apprehension, sharpen with certain nonverbal cues or tones of voice, and proceed to a cautious venture into what is the matter. Often the source of difficulty is not simply a fact or belief to be uncovered, as much as a more visceral disturbance that can run deep into one's being. That is why it often matters how partners engage each other dispositionally, rather than simply whether relevant facts are revealed. The point here is that there are comparable examples on a larger scale that are relevant to ethical and political concerns. Often social problems inhabit an atmosphere of collective or historical moods that are palpable yet elusive of clear articulation (think of the very different attitudes toward the poor in the 1930s and the 1990s). That is why moral influence and affecting moral change are often not a matter of constructing the right arguments or policies, but at best of tapping into these moods to better understand them and perhaps stimulate different or altered moods, or at worst of admitting the limits of influence and bearing with patience the resistance of history to acts of will and rational design.

As I will show later, it is important to stress that the role of affect and mood cannot be sufficient for an ethics. We cannot dismiss the role of reason or principles in the moral sphere. The problem with most modern moral theories, however, is that they have either minimized the role of emotion in ethics or even taken emotion as a counterethical force. A Heideggerian approach would insist on recognizing the ontogenetic role of moods and feelings in ethical comportment.

UNDERSTANDING AND ETHICS

For Heidegger, understanding is connected with potentiality-for-being, with Dasein's tacit awareness of possibility animating its care. Accordingly, being is understood in terms of a temporal towards-which and not-yet, which undermines the dominance of actuality and constant presence in traditional ontology. In ethics, instead of reductions to rational universals, essences, calculations, conventions, preferences, or needs—all taken as actualities and objective references to ground and guide moral thought—a Heideggerian approach can highlight the lived experiences of possibility in ethical life. Ethics can be seen as pertaining to human possibilities and as itself a possibility in human life.

In a general sense, ethics can involve a wide range of human social dealings that find us implicated in each other's possibilities. How we experience such situations, engage their effects, and come to decisions, can be quite different from following rules or applying principles to particular cases. Think of the wrenching complexities in deciding whether to get a divorce or fire an employee. Some might call such situations merely existential problems that are not the province of ethics, but surely we wrestle with "what should be done" in such cases.

Moreover, focusing on potentiality can be associated with more familiar ethical themes if we consider that so many human values and norms relate to supports for, and obstacles to, human development: in child rearing, home life, work, social relationships, cultural pursuits, and so on. Even on a political level, social programs can be understood as animated by ethical questions: What are desirable ends of human activity? What are ways in which a human life can flourish and turn out well? What material, environmental, social, and educational conditions make such flourishing more likely? If we consider such things as nutrition, upbringing, opportunity, and the like, in terms of human potential and development, then such social questions as public education, welfare, health care, and civil rights can at least be addressed with more clarity and attentive public discourse if we trace them to fundamental existential concerns we all tend to recognize and value.

Human possibility and potentiality also carry a performative sense of capability, which applies to ethics itself as a human potential, as the possibility of becoming a person who is capable of living well with others. Attention to the human condition in all its facets would be an essential ingredient in moral education and cultivating an ethical life. Heidegger's rich analysis of temporal existence is useful because it can help us understand what *becoming* ethical involves or requires—not simply education in the right values, but how values shape our very being-in-the-world, and what it takes to enact values in a complex, finite world. Attention to our very sense of existence and to the existential demands and difficulties of an ethical life have usually not been the focus of moral philosophy—literature has been more prone to explore such matters. The temporal structure of finite being-in-the-world helps open up a narrative sense of living well, of leading a good life, with all its movements, complexities, uncertainties, concerns, demands, and risks.[39]

An emphasis on Dasein as a being of possibility contributes an important register of finitude to ethical bearings. Dasein's finitude means that it is an essentially vulnerable being, not simply in being subject to forces of change and destruction, which is true of any entity, but in *being aware* of the possibility and meaning of its end; and not simply in terms of world forces that can bring about ruin, but in terms of the indwelling vulnerability of existing *as* possibility, since possibility means "can be," which also entails the possibility of failure, incapacity, obstruction, or loss. Human strivings and achievements are fragile things, and important levels of ethical sensitivity are often triggered by heedfulness to the fragility of the human condition. Such heedfulness is needed to counter the sanctimonious rectitude of certain ranges of moral condemnation and presumptions about individual responsibility or self-mastery. More on this in due course.

TRUTH IN ETHICS

We can follow Heidegger's sequence of mood, understanding, interpretation, and language to raise again the question of truth in ethics. The fore-structure of understanding intrinsic to the as-structure of interpretation can be located in the example of child beating. My prereflective understanding of human possibility and affective disclosure of its fragility constitute my interpreting this situation *as* an ethical one, as a situation prompting a response to the ethical worth of the act or agent, unlike other human endeavors such as technical skill or cognitive investigation. The understanding of human possibility is implicated in the ethical disclosure of various modes of care and neglect, help and harm, *as* matters that are appropriately weighable as better and worse performances in the context of existential weal and woe. The ethical sphere, then, is hermeneutically distinct from other spheres of life. And then within the ethical sphere itself there is a hermeneutical element that issues interpretive variations and disagreements as to what counts as better or worse performances and to what degree. For instance, the scenario cited above might be different if it involved simply a parent spanking a disobedient child.[40]

From a Heideggerian standpoint, ethics is an essentially hermeneutic endeavor. In fact, ethics is a good example of a "double hermeneutic," in that the matter being interpreted—human activity—involves an already interpret*ed* being (having been reared) and an already interpret*ing* being (as existing); and *in* ethical interpretation, human beings engage in self-alteration. It is important to reiterate, however, that hermeneutics does not entail something arbitrary or unhinged. The sequence of understanding and interpretation includes language and truth, which are marked by Dasein's *responsive* openness, by the appropriateness of disclosure. The language of ethics involves evaluative, social, addressive, and performative modes of disclosure that can have their truth, as varying sorts of appropriate disclosure along the lines of the signs of truth sketched in chapter 2.[41]

If we consider questions of child neglect, for example, which often prompt drastic interventions into families and abrogation of parental rights, we can recognize inhabitive signs of truth that show such judgments and responses to be hardly arbitrary: Judgments about the immorality of child abuse are certainly *appropriate*, given the suffering involved and what is known about a child's developmental needs. There is also widespread *agreement* about such judgments, and the ethical norms involved are certainly *reliable* and *workable* with respect to child-rearing practices in general terms.

Truth in ethics is certainly different from truth in science, but it can be truth nonetheless. Aletheic signs also operate in those many instances of indigenous disagreement, conflict, and limits that mark the ethical sphere. Here we run up against the perennial problem of moral knowledge, of whether morality can have any cognitive status comparable to other forms of knowing. Many debates in moral philosophy about truth in ethics have concerned whether or not there are any "moral facts" that are not simply a function of individual or cultural construction. Affirmative or negative answers here have corresponded to whether or not a kind of constant presence could be located to secure the "being" of moral facts from conditions of variation, mutability, or contingency. Measured against scientific or metaphysical warrants, it has been difficult to argue for moral knowledge, since ethics inhabits a realm of affectivity, uncertainty, and disagreement. We have seen, however, that Heidegger offers a different sense of being that permits a sense of truth that is not bound by a model of constant presence drawn from scientific methodologies or conceptual abstractions. So the finite complexity of an ethical world can admit being and truth in Heideggerian terms. Indeed, all modes of knowing, for Heidegger, are situated in the finite dwelling of being-in-the-world. The difference between science and ethics is simply the *degree* to which existential concerns are implicated in, or screened from, their disclosures. Given this continuum, then ethics, in being simply *more* animated by finite existential concerns, cannot on that account alone be cast outside the realm of truth. For Heidegger, the disclosure of being is a finite, dynamic, pluralized process that subverts traditional philosophical confidences. The irony is—and this is a major contribution to moral philosophy—that the limit conditions of ethical life that had typically weakened its claims to knowledge and truth, can now be seen to strengthen those claims, as long as knowledge and truth are given proper post-metaphysical adjustments.

It is important, however, to spotlight inhabitive modes of ethical truth so as not to overestimate the contingency of ethical existence. Just as we should not overstate the extent of agreement and stability in scientific thinking, we should not overstate the degree of disagreement in ethics, despite the obvious range of variations and disputes in the moral sphere. From a pedagogical standpoint, although ethical controversies are an excellent setting for cultivating critical thinking skills, and although there is certainly much disagreement and controversy in ethical matters, students are misled when we concentrate primarily on dilemmas and disputes in moral considerations or on the shortcomings of moral paradigms. We should at least start with areas of agreement (for example, all students agree that they should be graded fairly) before we take up controversies, so as to avoid the impression (very common among students) that moral values are completely undecidable. Stressing "lifeboat" scenarios, for example, is like beginning physics instruction with the uncertainty principle or the wave-particle paradox. Moral disagreements often turn on the extent of a norm (Is it always right to tell the truth?) rather than on its status *as* a norm.[42]

Many moral cases do not arouse interrogation because they do not disrupt basic ethical bearings. There is little controversy in cases of indiscriminate or wanton killing, for instance. We might be interested, say, in questions concerning why someone goes on a killing spree for thrills; yet who would question the wrongness of such an action? Of course one might ask such a question as a theoretical exercise, and someone who commits such an action might honestly claim to be in the right. Certain Heideggerian notions we have been considering could be brought into play in such a discussion. Indiscriminate or wanton killing violates the primal meaningfulness of living, of care for being. Moreover, such an act can be seen as a violation of thrown finitude: a finite being cannot take command of the full being of another without disowning its finitude. This might appear to mirror a theoretical technique of justification. Yet a Heideggerian approach would be more along the lines of simply recognizing and articulating primal meanings and dispositions as appropriate to being-in-the-world. An addressive approach to ethics would turn on concrete modes of *being*-in-the-world, rather than some demonstrative or justificatory project. I can simply stand for the importance of life and stand against the offense of annihilation. If someone actually were to defend killing for thrills, there is very little that philosophical debate can contribute, anyway. Such a person is really not interested in ethics as a question.

CARE AND ETHICS

The overall structure of care as Dasein's situated being-in-the-world is clearly relevant to ethics, especially in the connotations of caring-about and caring-for that mark Dasein's concern. Indeed, the care structure can be connected with two trends in moral philosophy that have emerged in recent years, care ethics and communitarian ethics, both of which have challenged modern moral theory's emphasis on disengaged, impartial reason, abstract principles of justice, and individual rights. The care ethic has grown out of feminist thought, counterposing the situation of women as responsive caregivers to the male-based ideal of respecting freedom and individual interests.[43] Communitarianism has argued for a situated, social self that is shaped by tradition, to counter the modern ideal of autonomous, self-directed reason.

I have more to say on some of these matters in due course. Presently I can say that Heidegger's notion of care can make important contributions to the questions at hand. For one thing, Heideggerian phenomenology offers a richer and deeper understanding of care, especially in terms of its ekstatic, thrown character that is not reducible simply to human bearings, feelings, roles, or cultural constructs. Second, the finitude of care addresses how disclosure is caught up in limits and disruptions, and so is not so stable as to coalesce in some secure conception of social relations. Third, the notion of a detached, reflective standpoint is not ruled out in Heideggerian phenomenology. Finally, the situated sociality of the self must be tempered by authentic individuation, to protect the self against being consumed by social forces and prosocial dispositions.

AUTHENTICITY AND ETHICS

Heidegger's notion of authenticity—understood as the tension between socialization and individuation, animated by an anxious disorientation and reorientation— has much to contribute to ethics. I want to explore two questions in this section: How can Heidegger's own conception of authenticity be taken as ethical in a broad sense? and How does ethical life more narrowly construed exhibit elements of authenticity?

In the broadest terms it is possible to notice a certain ethical register in Heidegger's ontological narrative of Dasein's authenticity, since it surely implies a preference for authentic individuation as a better mode of existence than the concealments of everyday *das Man*. Heidegger admits that the ontological inter- pretation of Dasein presupposes "a definite ontical way of taking authentic exis- tence, a factical ideal of Dasein" (*BT*, 358). Beyond this, it is also possible to articulate a range of applications of authenticity to more specific ethical topics. To begin with, there are two basic dimensions in an ethical world: (1) the social and cultural *formation* of norms, values, and goods, which can take shape in insti- tutions (political, legal, and educational structures) or in more informal civil asso- ciations (family, religious, and social organizations); and (2) an individual per- son's *engagement* with these orders, in terms of obedience, appropriation, modification, or resistance. Both dimensions are covered in Heidegger's thought.[44] Moreover, the historical character of the formation dimension and the decisional character of the engagement dimension indicate an ungrounded open- ness in an ethical world, an element of finitude that can prompt an anxious estrangement from the everyday familiarity and security of social patterns, but that can also prepare an authentically individuated modification of one's ethical endowment.

The disruption of inherited ethical patterns can be a much more far-reaching and traumatic experience than the disturbances to *zuhanden* practices sketched in *Being and Time*; indeed, ethical estrangement can approximate the force of anx- ious being-toward-death because of the depth to which ethical bearings shape human life. In many ways we can recognize the early modern European period as a time of anxious estrangement, since long-standing religious and moral tradi- tions were being dislocated and unsettled owing to the cognitive dissonance cre- ated by new scientific, political, and economic developments. As I have shown, much of modern moral theory can be understood as attempting a rational recon- struction of ethical norms in the midst of the cultural vertigo of the period.

What makes a Heideggerian approach different is that cultural vertigo does not prompt a reflective separation from inherited social patterns. The everyday social world is Dasein's *first* world. Anxiety opens up the possibility of authentic appro- priation, illumination, and modification of one's social world. Indeed, anxious estrangement helps overcome the kind of thoughtless complacency and comfort that keeps Dasein from seeing its ethical bearings more clearly *as* possibilities to be ascertained and chosen. As Heidegger says, what is "good" for Dasein is something both inherited and chosen (*BT*, 435), and authentic choice is made pos- sible in an anxious finitude that sharpens Dasein's vision, by wrenching it out of the clutter, dissimulation, and facile shirking of responsibility and seriousness that can characterize the everyday social world (*BT*, 435).

Another way in which a Heideggerian approach would differ from modern the- ories is that it would want to retain the educative influence of anxiety and hold onto the finitude of ethical experience. The problem with everyday ethical *das Man* is not so much its content as its problematic self-evidence and comfort, its evasion of the finitude of its field of disclosure. Modern moral theories can be seen as pushing this evasion even further in a sense. We have suggested that the disengagement of modern subject-based reason can be taken as a refuge from the contingencies of the life-world. Modern moral theories might then be diagnosed as overdetermined by vertigo, as a hyperbolic response to the traumatic displacement of traditional warrants, perhaps even as a rational reconstitution of old theological scripts of governance from a transcendent standpoint. A Heideggerian approach to ethics, then, would challenge both everyday familiarities and traditional philosophical constructions by recommending a cultivated bearing of finitude. Citing the finitude of ethics in no way entails a rejection or dissolution of moral values. From a Heideggerian standpoint, experiencing the *unheimlich* character of one's ethical world can open up the possibility of a richer, more perspicacious dwelling in that world. The unease of losing ethical bearings can elicit a concentration on the crucial importance of ethical concerns in human life, which can prompt an articulation of this importance, perhaps now with more attention to its fragility, intricacy, and limits. This might be an improvement over erstwhile securities that can distort and even disfigure the contours of ethical existence. Such education by anxiety can occur in the atmosphere of any moral groundwork, whether the reference point is religion, reason, nature, feeling, self-interest, chauvinism, habit, and so forth.

Heidegger's notion of authenticity fits in quite well with Charles Taylor's challenges to modern moral theory. Taylor wants to broaden the scope of ethics beyond the modern fixation on rules for action and obligatory principles to include wider and deeper questions such as How should I live my life? and What is the meaning of life?[45] These questions are particularly urgent in the wake of modernity's displacement of tradition and disenchantment of the world. Authenticity is clearly applicable to the narrative sense of the first question and it provides important depth and force to the second. In fact, both questions are well addressed *in terms of* the loss of, or threat to, human meaning that has characterized the modern era. With Heidegger we can attend more to the positive potential in the unsettlements of modern life. As I have shown, unmeaning (in the sense of losses or threats) is not simply a void to be filled in by some newly secured construction of meaning; unmeaning in fact is *productive* of meaning in the dynamic of being-toward-limits that animates authentic disclosure. Moreover, unmeaning retains its resonance in the open finitude of authentic existence.

The double movement of authentic care is portrayed in *Being and Time* by way of ontological conceptions of guilt, conscience, and resoluteness, conceptions which Heidegger expressly does not want to be taken in their ethical (ontical) sense.[46] Nevertheless it would be a mistake to assume that these ontological notions have nothing whatsoever to do with ethical meanings. First of all, the ontological terms draw some of their sense analogically from ethical meanings: The ontological nullity of being-guilty is drawn from the sense of being the basis of a moral lack (*BT*, 327–28), and conscience is drawn from the ethical sense of being called or reproached (*BT*, 336ff). What makes ontological guilt and conscience different from ethical connotations is that they disclose Dasein's radical negativity of being-toward-death, and so do not refer to any particular deeds, prospects, or directives (*BT*, 340). However, the ontological analysis is not separated from ontical practice. As I have indicated, authentic being-toward-death opens up Dasein's authentic care and taking action in an existentiell sense. Consider a passage regarding the call of conscience in relation to ethical guidelines. Since the call is connected to being-toward-death and not any ontic state, conscience here gives no practical injunction. And yet:

> On the other hand, when the call is rightly understood, it gives us that which in the existential sense is the "most positive" of all—namely, the ownmost possibility which Dasein can present to itself, as a calling-back which calls it forth into its factical potentiality-for-being-its-self at the time. To hear the call authentically, signifies bringing oneself into a factical taking-action. But only by setting forth the existential structure implied in our understanding of the appeal when we *hear it authentically,* shall we obtain a fully adequate interpretation of what is called in the call. (*BT*, 341)

It is possible to construe ontological notions of guilt and conscience as background structures for ethical existence. Consider a passage where Dasein's essential being-guilty is called "the existential condition for the possibility of the 'morally' good and for the 'morally' evil—that is, for morality in general and for the possible forms which this may take factically." (*BT*, 332) Indeed, the negativity of Dasein's ontological being-guilty is called the condition for Dasein's capacity for factical guilt, for experiencing the lack implicit in owing something to someone (*BT*, 332). It seems as though there is some kind of reciprocal relation between ontological and ethical concepts in Heidegger's analysis.

In this regard, I want to explore a more specific ethical application of Heideggerian senses of guilt, conscience, and resoluteness, an application that can benefit from sharing the ekstatic, thrown structure of the ontological configurations.[47] A combination of Dasein's in/there/with structure, mineness, authentic care, and resoluteness would capture both the sense of appropriated decision and the sense of obligation and responsibility that are so important for ethics. I am struck by the fact that Heidegger chose terms such as guilt and conscience to shape his ontological investigation. I want to suggest a certain feedback loop between ethics and ontology, where ethical terms imply a situated involvement that keeps ontology in concrete existential territory, and where ontological terms drawn from, and pointing back to, ethical senses can "ontologize" ethics in such a way as to surmount certain doubts, restrictions, or demotions that have been part of modern moral philosophy.

Ethics should involve something of a "call," something having a claim on us, something that draws us and motivates a commitment in the midst of counterimpulses. Such a call need not reflect the traditional force of a command, but since normative matters imply the human potential to alter one's behavior in the face of other (likely more ready) inclinations, then some sense of a "self-transcendence" is needed to capture the tone of obligation that seems so indigenous to ethics. Here Heidegger's ontological critique of subjectivity can bear fruit in moral philosophy.[48] I have noted that many problems in ethical theory can be traced to the modern tendency to ground values in a subject, variously conceived in individual, collective, or cognitive terms. I have sketched how emotivism, egoism, and utilitarianism are liable to the charge that responsiveness to, and responsibility for, others might be unintelligible in their orientations. We also indicated how Kantian ethics purchases responsibility and obligation at the cost of an impartial universalism that may not be responsive enough to situated finitude. In different ways then, the orientation toward the subject in modern moral theory can be implicated in various problems that have continued to frustrate ethical discourse.

Without claiming that Heidegger's thought can solve all these problems, I think his critique of subjectivity can give a good start in addressing the underlying assumptions that foster these difficulties. With Heidegger we can say that "grounding" ethics in the subject is as problematic as grounding any region of being. Rather than annulling ethics, this opens it into the overall configuration of finite being-in-the-world. As with other concerns of Dasein, values can be understood as uncovered in Dasein's *world*, and not simply in some inner subjective zone. As part of the world, values can be seen to have as much a *claim* on Dasein's understanding as other factical conditions into which it is thrown. Here there is some relief from individualistic and subjectivistic conceptions of values, as well as from a hyperbolic conception of existential freedom that in the end sees values as arbitrary choices or sheer creations. And regarding difficulties attaching to utilitarianism and Kantian theory, Dasein's in/there/with structure overcomes the subject–object bifurcation and opens up the ekstatic situatedness of world involvement, which is richer than simply the rational calculation of human interests or the pure abstraction of universal consistency.

Since Dasein *is* at bottom an ekstatically thrown engagement with the world and other Daseins, then ethical concerns and involvements pertain to Dasein's very being, and thus not to some extrinsic or rationalized sphere that somehow must be incorporated into an initially self-absorbed existence, with all the philosophical difficulties that go with advancing such a bifurcated scenario. In Heideggerian terms, Dasein always already is a responsive openness to the world, and so certain ethical relations and bearings are possibilities that are intrinsic to human existence. There is some relief here from a certain skepticism or cynicism about experiences of guilt, conscience, and responsibility that have been inspired by egocentric conceptions of human nature. We need not buy the notion that such experiences are simply an internalization of external conditioning regimes by force of social norms superimposed upon the self, or perhaps simply a slavish surrender of freedom owing to fear of social retribution.

In addition to finding ethical registers in Heidegger's notion of authenticity, I want to suggest an analogical sense of authenticity *in* ethical life by way of the familiar phenomena of guilt and conscience. In other words, experiences of guilt and conscience can be indicative of an authentic ethical bearing, of an appropriated responsiveness to the claim of ethical responsibility. To begin with, we should take notice of Heidegger's remarks about ordinary ethical connotations of guilt and conscience in sections 58 and 59 of *Being and Time*. Guilt is a phenomenon that exposes a full sense of the self's being, as indicated in the utterance "I am guilty" (*BT*, 326). But guilt is also essentially a function of being-with, since it discloses a lack or failure in oneself with regard to important social relations (*BT*, 328), where one owes something to others or is responsible for having caused some harm to others (*BT*, 327). Guilt is also connected to the call of care (*BT*, 332) and with thrownness (*BT*, 330), in other words, with a sense of *not* being fully self-grounding—or put in positive terms, of essentially being in/there/with others. Conscience, for Heidegger, in an ontological sense is a calling-forth of Dasein to embrace its finitude. Ethical conscience, too, is a calling-forth, in that it is not simply backward-looking in terms of a past deed, but also forward-looking in terms of guilt, responsibility, and debt (*BT*, 337). In other words, guilt and conscience contain a responsive element, both toward a past deed and toward some recompense, some modification of future behavior, or some spur to social action. In general terms, guilt and conscience allow Dasein to be *verantwortlich*, or answerable to, and responsible for, others in social life (*BT*, 334).

Although Heidegger is clearly interested primarily in ontological senses of guilt and conscience, and although a fallen immersion in public rules and norms can block entry to ontological conscience (*BT*, 334), Heidegger says that ethical connotations of conscience should not be disregarded (*BT*, 336).[49] Indeed, he says the ontological analysis should not be cut off from ontical, ethical experience; not only can ontological analysis help make ethical senses more intelligible, it can also open up possibilities of a more primordial existentiell understanding of these ethical experiences (*BT*, 336, 341).[50] It is such possibilities that I am trying to explore here. If I correlate Dasein's ekstatic in/there/with/ structure, mineness, and authentic resolve, it can be said that guilt and conscience are ethically authentic in disclosing my own concern for my ethical bearing and involvement with others (as opposed to mere mechanical obedience or compliance from fear of retribution), and my own sense of responsibility to others and for my ethical possibilities. Moreover, Dasein's ekstatic structure indicates that such responsibility is consonant with Dasein's fundamental openness *to* the world, and so ethical responsibility and obligation need not be construed as something foisted upon the self or as something constructed only *from* the self's reflective reason. Dasein's situated and responsive selfhood allows for a more robust conception of ethical responsibility that is intrinsic to human existence, as socially engaged all the way down. Here one can avoid certain philosophical difficulties that have haunted modern moral theory in its various attempts to think ethical responsibility from the starting point of a disengaged self. Situated selfhood, of course, does not mean that human beings *are* ethically responsive in some way all the time, or that ethics is only about responsibility to others. It simply allows that some central features of ethical life, such as responsibility and obligation, are not *alien* but rather structurally intrinsic to the human condition.

Say I experience guilt at having been cruel to someone and feel pressed to apologize and make amends. Phenomenologically, such an experience is a blend of self-reproach, regret, sympathy, and being claimed or called to resolve things. My guilt, then, is a mixture of a lack and a responsiveness to an Other. Here I experience a claim *upon* me *from* and *toward* an Other, and yet the claim is not external to me; it is intrinsic to me as *my* being claimed.[51] The "source" of the claim can be multifaceted and can be articulated well with the help of terms that have run through the discussion in this chapter: Here is an experience that is mine, that matters to me, and yet that is a thrown, ekstatic, disclosive response within an environment wider than myself; the thrown response is strongly affective and expressive of a with-world exceeding my self-regard; and it is likely implicated with my upbringing and a narrative sense of how I envision my life. The point is that here an ethical "norm" regarding cruelty is fleshed out existentially in terms of an expansive horizon of the self, its ekstatic in/there/with structure disclosing an immediately felt sense of Other-regarding concern.[52] In other words, conscience here displays a responsive responsibility that is ethically world-disclosive and not simply something in or of the self. With Heidegger one can say that ethical phenomena such as care and responsibility are simultaneously an Other-relation and a self-relation, as a bearing-toward-others-that-matters.[53]

The ekstatic thrownness of Dasein's with-world can be cashed out ethically as a kind of presumptive responsibility and obligation in certain human relations, which can show themselves as immediate *claims* upon and in the self, which therefore would not be intelligible as ethical "options" facing a discrete, reflective subject that proceeds to reason out justifications for choices, whether it be in terms of reckoning self-interest, calculating consequences for all concerned, or applying a principle drawn from a universalization test.

Not all human endeavors can be explained by dreary "rational choice" models that measure actions in terms of maximizing the utility of an agent's aims. A clear example would be parent–child relations. Parental obligations to children can be seen as simply *given* in a situation that calls for appropriate responses. This is not to say that individual interests of parents are ethically irrelevant, or that complications or dilemmas could never qualify obligations, or that reasoning procedures never figure in such settings. It is simply to say that at a certain level, being a parent is being *thrown* in and amidst a situation that *calls* for care (or cries for care). Why should parents care for their children? Of course a host of reasons can be articulated, yet most parents do not need guidance from some moral theory and do not *base* their care for their children in some inferential reasoning. Heideggerian phenomenology is able to articulate the ekstatic, situational, affective, environmental responsiveness that marks most parents' experience. The ethical force is simply *there* in the child's cry and fragile need, and parents dwell *in* that need. A parent is certainly "free" to neglect, abuse, or abandon a child, but such freedom can easily be deemed unethical, even inauthentic, as the fracturing and disowning of a thrown responsibility.

The possibility of ethical truth (in the sense of appropriate disclosure) can be fathomed here if we revisit certain traditional dismissals of truth in moral propositions: "All children are born of biological parents" can be seen as conceptually true; "The child is in the crib" can be seen as empirically true; "Parents should care for their children" is neither conceptually nor empirically true and so it might simply be a subjective matter having no warrant beyond emotional forces or social constructions. But if we shift bearings a little and consider propositions like "The child is crying for help" or "The child is hungry," and consider these in their situational presence (not simply as abstract examples in a philosophical analysis), then what might seem merely like other instances of empirical claims turn out to have an existential "claim" intrinsic to their disclosive effect; they *call* for certain appropriate responses that expand their truth to include (inhabitive) ethical senses. The cry of a child is a thrown disclosure of an ethical claim.[54]

The notion of thrownness, I think, can provide an important ethical configuration for moral philosophy, which has been dominated by subject-based reason even in theories that aim to construct compelling obligations. Thrownness suggests certain situations that exhibit a presumption of ethical obligation, there in the existential environment, claiming the self, not rationally (re)constructed by the self. The task would be to identify situations that might exhibit intrinsic obligations—being a parent, a spouse, a friend, a teacher, an employer, and so on—that are contextually appropriate and that claim a person simply by virtue of inhabiting the situation. The obligations appropriate to such situations can be illuminated by considering the intrinsic elements of trust granted us by others in these circumstances. Being a parent, a teacher, or a spouse elicits presumptive expectations and therefore trust from others that we will treat them in a certain way. When such trust is violated there is commonly an automatic disappointment that opens the space for moral assessment and lays out the social structure of obligations intrinsic to these circumstances.[55] Presumptive obligations, however, can be qualified or even overridden in the face of certain complications, conflicting obligations, or extreme conditions. But we can at least identify an ethical base in many situations that offers provisional bearings and that arises out of an existential sense of being-in-a-situation, rather than mere reflective agency.

The argument is not that choice and reason do not or should not operate in ethics, but that moral philosophy should not be confined to theories that base ethics ontogenetically in subject-based reason, whether in terms of self-interest, calculations of the greater good, or autonomous duties. Kant's ethics certainly allows a strong sense of obligation (too strong perhaps), which can fit in with the above discussion. But the question is how ethical obligation arises and activates in human experience. Would Kant claim that parental duties, to be truly autonomous and hence moral, must stem from constructing a categorical imperative? At the very least, this would not fit the phenomenology of parent–child relations. A Heideggerian approach presents, I think, a more fitting ontogenetic account of certain dimensions of ethical life. With Heidegger, we can attend more to affect, thrownness, sociality, and environmental claims—a setting which, unlike Kantian moral agency, can show ethical responsibility to be existentially responsive to concrete persons and situations, and not just to reason.[56]

I have suggested an ethical take on Heidegger's sense of authenticity that can be applicable to a host of issues in moral philosophy. The advantage is that the ekstatic structure of authentic care and being-in-the-world implies an ethical bearing of responsive appropriation, a bearing that is not grounded in individual agency or in a wholly extra-individual sphere, but that is situated in an environmental mattering. In addition, as I will consider in a later chapter, the individuating elements of authenticity are important not only to open up ethical appropriation, but to counterbalance certain forces in the ethical with-world that tend to consume or suppress individuality.

THE TEMPORALITY OF ETHICS

Dasein is essentially temporal and not some kind of fixed or stable essence. The futurial openness of Dasein becomes important later in discussions of human nature and selfhood. Here I note how temporality connects with ethics as a practical discipline. Heidegger's temporal ontology does not subordinate practice to theory, doing to knowing, or acting to completed states. The performative movements intrinsic to ethics-as-practice are intrinsic to Dasein's being. As we have seen, Dasein is nothing other than living dealings and movements (*GA* 21, 146). In our social dealings we encounter others as they are, and "they *are* what they do" (*BT*, 163). Dasein is originally a performance rather than a knowing subject. Accordingly, action is not subordinated to the supposedly more stable sphere of cognition.

Temporality figures in ethical disclosure in a number of ways. Particularly significant is the temporal structure of desire and its role in ethics, something I develop further in upcoming discussions of Aristotle. Desire shows itself to be a "towards-which," an affective, dynamic, futurial impetus drawing the self's movements. Heidegger is clear in claiming that such existential temporality is primarily a function of *Befindlichkeit*, mood, and affect. The movements of life are less a cognitive matter and more a conative matter. The advantage of Heidegger's analysis is that it can address questions of motivation in ethics in a robust manner, as we have seen. Pure reason—construed in the tradition as clear and distinct ideas fixed in the mind and condensed into stable presences by abstraction from lived experience—not only does not as such "move," it does not usually move *us* either.[57] The motivation, animation, and "charge" of ethical existence, then, would have to manifest as a mode of desire and interest, as a towards-which moved by a perceived absence. One problem with modern moral philosophy is that it has underplayed, ignored, or even disparaged the force of desire in ethical life.

A temporal ontology also provides another angle on overcoming the is–ought binary, if we consider the ought as a temporally structured possibility. Part of the opening of ethical disclosure is sensing and wanting something "more" than given actualities, and oughts take shape in this excess. An ought as a possibility in the context of human action has an essentially temporal structure, either as a temporal revisioning of a past action, or as a possibility looming in the future. Indeed, the phenomena of guilt and conscience discussed earlier display a temporal structure in terms of the looping dimensions of past, present, and future that constitute the calling, claiming element concerning things that have been done or are to be done.

Temporal finitude is also indicated in the structure of ethical decisions, where the openness of the future is given shape through the present in the midst of the past. Ethical decisions are more a creative bringing-forth compared with other kinds of thinking and acting. In deciding what to do ethically, I shape a scenario out of possibilities, a scenario that remains permeated by possibilities and uncertainties. If I decide to tell the truth to a friend about a delicate matter, I set in motion a course of events that otherwise would not happen and that is marked by uncertain outcomes. This creative element is what distinguishes ethical "acts" from causal "effects" or fact-based inferences.[58] Such temporal openness accounts for the existential stress that often accompanies ethical decisions, owing to the perceived tensions, limits, complexities, and uncertainties attached to moral situations. Ethical action is more a *task* than an "event," and it is fundamentally different from certain other sequences in experience and thought. Here is where the perennial association of ethical action with freedom is given an existential orientation. Not only is freedom seemingly intrinsic to moral responsibility, it is phenomenologically evident in the unsettled and unsettling *experience* of moral performance.[59]

THE HISTORICALITY OF ETHICS

A Heideggerian sense of historicality can be distinguished from much of standard moral philosophy, especially in the analytic tradition, which has tended to see ethics as a set of typical, freestanding moral problems to be resolved by way of guiding principles. A historical approach to ethics would insist on examining moral life as a complex inheritance, which opens up questions of historical sources of current moral concerns, the particular historical contexts of these sources, and any alterations of these sources that may have occurred over time. It is not enough, for example, to examine the moral significance of freedom. We must understand the concrete history of notions of freedom and the complex forces that came to shape these notions. Historical understanding will open up the contextual tensions that generate the unfolding of ethical ideas: For instance, how modern freedom was a resistance to certain social forces (aristocratic exclusions, religious confinements of thought, cultural biases against quotidian life) and how the assertion of modern freedom excited counterresistances (owing to concerns about social fragmentation, disenchantment, new economic exclusions, and loss of traditional excellences).

I would like to stress the complexity of moral inheritance as a way of spotlighting the tensions and difficulties of ethical finitude. Our own ethical environment is a confluence of many different historical sources and influences that are manifested in different ways in various contexts of upbringing, education, and socialization. We value a sense of heroic achievement, adventure, courage, and honor that found voice in Homeric poetry. We also value a more internalized sense of virtue (in contrast to outward modes of achievement and power) that took shape in Plato. Also a generalized sense of benevolence and compassion (in contrast to selective interests and hierarchies) that took shape in Judaism and Christianity. Also the value of various group allegiances. Also a host of individual-based ideals that have marked so much of modern identity (the autonomous individual, the self-controlled individual, the creative individual). Also the affirmation of market freedom and contractual relations, and yet a humanistic concern for the welfare of dispossessed persons. Also the importance of sentiment in ethical relations, and yet the need for principles and obligations that exceed emotional capacity.

This complex environment is an accumulation of historical influences that continue to circulate in our social world, and in such a way as to embody the complex variances of ethical existence. Some of these moral elements are at odds with each other in the social environment. In fact the historical emergence of these moral sources was usually generated by perceived limitations or excesses in existing sources. Yet such emergences were prone to a foundationalism that was not able to tolerate otherness. In other words, many of these moral sources were presented or taken as replacements for the "errors" of other models: Consider the attitude of Platonism toward the traditional heroic ideal, of Christianity toward paganism, of modernism toward traditional authorities and religious sources, of deontology toward consequentialism, of socialism toward capitalism, and so on.[60] Historicality, on the other hand, would suggest that none of these sources is "eternal," or stable enough to warrant calling the other sources baseline errors. Each source can be seen as world-disclosive, as having taken hold in history owing to a certain appropriateness. But since part of this disclosiveness involves conflicted relations with other existing sources, there is an ineluctable tension here that calls for coexistence with otherness.

Historicality also shows ethical life to be the engaged openness of being-in-question, construed as a present concern with future possibilities in the midst of past inheritances. As we have seen, Heidegger's sense of historical repetition is not a return to some original content that has been lost or distorted, but an appropriation of a historical source that is a *potentiality*, a revisitable launch of possibilities rather than a "ground." Repetition in this sense opposes both conservatism, which sees possibility only as the development toward presumed norms and which therefore closes off the future by a reduction to the past, and radicalism, which denies tradition on behalf of a revolutionary beginning, a utopian future, or a hyperbolic openness. In Heideggerian terms, ethical tradition is the ambiguity of situated possibility, which is both backward-looking and forward-looking.

THE FINITUDE OF ETHICS

In looking back over the course of this chapter, it would be hard to dismiss outright the elements that a Heideggerian phenomenology can bring to an analysis of ethical life. Indeed, defenders of modern moral theories might easily concede the effects of tradition, upbringing, history, temporality, concrete involvement, and such, but insist that moral philosophy should take shape independently of these elements or at least at their margins. Here is the crux of the philosophical matter at the heart of this investigation. I would insist on not simply acknowledging these existential elements, but thematizing them in such a way that alters moral philosophy. I suggest that a main reason why modern moral theory has sidestepped the existential environment stems from an implicit recognition of, and perhaps anxiety over, the intrinsic finitude of this environment: its limits, ambiguities, complexities, tensions, flux, and encumbrances, all of which can be taken as a disruption of the subject-centered reason at the core of modern thought.

As I hope I have been able to show so far, thematizing the finite existential environment of ethics does not entail a wholesale rejection of traditional moral conceptions. Rather, the question involves lifting the theoretical anchors of these conceptions and discerning the extent to which, and the contexts in which, they are relevant and defensible, but at the same time limiting them in a temporal, contextual, diversified environment. Both the modern and the postmodern periods have been characterized as a confrontation with the loss of moral universals: the modern period with the loss of traditional universals, the postmodern period with the loss of modern rational universals. Such experiences of loss can engender anxiety, and in response perhaps a dogmatic refuge in threatened universals. At the other extreme, loss of universals can suggest that ethical norms are simply arbitrary, conventional, indefensible, or infinitely open—some of this perhaps even taken as an exhilarating emancipation. It is important to realize, however, that the second extreme implicitly shares the traditional notion that secured universals are the measure of ethical truth, so that we are faced with the following (false) choice: Either ethics is securely grounded in objective universals or it is arbitrary, merely subjective, or infinitely open.

Heidegger's thought permits a middle ground in this scenario of anxiety and loss that can be quite productive. First of all, anxiety figures in the very generation of meaning and so it is not an experience of sheer loss. The finitude of meaning, though, does alter how cultural constructions are to be understood. In the light of a temporal/historical analysis, it is not traditional ethical notions that are lost but their tendencies toward exclusivity or dogmatic closure. The familiar tendency to demote ethical norms as arbitrary or outside the realm of truth is in fact an overreaction to the eclipse of traditional constructs. With Heidegger, we can retrieve the finite meaning of traditional ethical notions and affirm the ways in which they operate in human life—and do so without either demonstrative certainty or its evil twin, radical skepticism.

HEIDEGGER AND THE QUESTION OF VALUE

In *Letter on Humanism*, Heidegger directly addresses the question of ethics. In particular he voices his concerns about "value theory." As I have shown, in general terms Heidegger considers ethics to be an ontical discipline that can stand in the way of his ontological investigation. For Heidegger, the standard term "ethics" seems to be restricted to moral theory and its search for a regulatory measure of right action. He thus takes appeals for him to write an ethics as a charge to offer rules and directives for living (*LH*, 255). In resisting this, Heidegger is distancing himself from the modern tendency toward abstract principles and formal structures that reduce and confine human comportment to calculable orders.

The deepest issue that Heidegger raises in this regard stems from his critique of the senses of being and value governing modern approaches to ethics. As I have indicated, the subject–object binary generated a value–fact binary that confined values to the sphere of the subject. Value theory took shape as an attempt to rescue values from being demoted to "mere" subjective occasions, but it was still in the thrall of the modern subject–object delineation. Value theory involved attempts to construct "objective" (noncontingent) notions of value in ethics, art, and religion, but grounded *in* the subject in a manner distinct from scientific constructions of objectivity geared toward the natural world (see *IM*, 197–98). For Heidegger, the attempt to ground the "validity" (*Geltung*) of values in some necessary condition of the subject is in a double sense a reduction of being to actuality: first to a *vorhanden* property that conceals lived involvement (*BT*, 132–33), and second to something simply from and for the subject (*LH*, 251). For Heidegger, seeing the world in terms of values is confining it to human estimations, preferences, uses, and needs—which strips the world of its own modes of presencing on its own terms.[61]

Heidegger's objections to values, then, stem from his critique of value theory and constant attempt to protect being from a reduction to fixed, discrete constructs grounded in the human subject and human interests. In addition to ontological considerations, I am convinced that the same can be said for ethics, that rejecting the value paradigm is not a rejection of ethical concerns but a protection of their authentic meaning from the distortion of reducing them to merely human, subject-based estimations.[62] Consider the following passage from *Letter on Humanism*:

> To think against "values" is not to maintain that everything interpreted as "a value"—"culture," "art," "science," "human dignity," "world," "God,"—is value-less. Rather, it is important finally to realize that precisely through the characterization of something as "a value" what is so valued is robbed of its worth. That is to say, by the assessment of something as a value what is valued is admitted only as an object for man's estimation. But what a thing is in its being is not exhausted by its being an object, particularly when objectivity takes the form of value. Every valuing, even when it values positively, is a subjectivizing. It does not let beings: be. Rather, valuing lets beings: be valid—solely as objects of its doing. The bizarre effort to prove the objectivity of values does not know what it is doing. When one proclaims "God" the altogether "highest value," this is a degradation of God's essence. Here as elsewhere thinking in values is the greatest blasphemy imaginable against being. To think against values therefore does not mean to beat the drum for the valuelessness and nullity of beings. It means rather to bring the clearing of the truth of being before thinking, as against subjectivizing beings into mere objects. (*LH,* 251)

As I have noted before, Heidegger's critiques are usually directed at certain philosophical *theories* rather than at the phenomena such theories are trying to think. Regarding ethics, Heidegger suggests an alternative to subjective and objective orientations by retrieving the Greek word *ēthos*, which means abode or dwelling place (*LH,* 256).[63] If *ēthos* can suggest Dasein's ekstatic openness to being, then it can be called an "original ethics" (*LH,* 258). So for Heidegger, ethics should be thought in an ontological register as the finite dwelling of being-in-the-world.[64] He seems to have been concerned that the ordinary sphere of ethics and moral philosophy closes off an openness to such an original ethics.

Heidegger never denied the importance of ethics or the need for ethics, especially in the current critical era of modern technology.

> The desire for an ethics presses ever more ardently for fulfillment as the obvious no less than the hidden perplexity of man soars to immeasurable heights. The greatest care must be fostered upon the ethical bond at a time when technological man, delivered over to mass society, can be kept reliably on call only by gathering and ordering all his plans and activities in a way that corresponds to technology. (*LH,* 255)

But he was preoccupied with a thinking of being, which he presumed would have to *precede* any venture into ethics (*LH,* 255). What I am attempting in this study is just such a venture, one that does not rest with an "ontological ethics" of original openness to being and finite dwelling, but that proceeds to think about ethics as it is normally construed, yet animated by Heideggerian phenomenology.

Heidegger himself acknowledged more familiar ethical senses in the Greek word *ēthos* before philosophical systems and disciplines turned ethics into a theoretical enterprise. For the Greeks, *ēthos* referred to human comportment (*Haltung*), human doing and letting (*Tun* and *Lassen*), the self-conduct of human beings as distinct from *phusis*, or nature in the narrow sense (*FCM*, 35–36). I even think it is possible to work with the term "value" in a Heideggerian manner, as long as it is not restricted to subject-based connotations or the constructions of value theory. If we associate value with meaning, importance, and interest, it is fully consonant with Heidegger's sense of being-in-the-world. In Heideggerian terms, the world cannot be comprehended as valueless or value-neutral; owing to Dasein's original involvement as care, the world is originally value-laden.[65]

Accordingly, I suggest that we can examine ethics as a sphere of valuing, of disclosing and discerning what is good and bad in human existence, in terms of what is worth doing, having, desiring, or aspiring to in life. The "worth" element implies a certain scalar preference for, and choice of, some paths over others. The "-ing" element points to the temporal finitude that pervades ethical existence. In addition, a Heidegger-inspired phenomenology of language and truth allows a specific articulation of ethical experience in terms appropriate to its world-disclosive dimension, rather than measuring ethics against scientific objectivity or retreating to spheres of subjectivity.

NOTES

1. See J. P. Schneewind, *The Invention of Autonomy: A History of Modern Moral Philosophy* (Cambridge: Cambridge University Press, 1998).

2. This turn is the source of the emancipatory legacy of the Enlightenment in ethical, social, and political thought. The idea that people can discover for themselves the grounds of right and wrong, rather than passively submit to traditional civil and political domains, opened space for democratic movements and contract theories of government—inspired by the general belief in human persons as self-governing, autonomous agents.

3. See A. J. Ayer, *Language, Truth, and Logic* (Mineola, N.Y.: Dover, 1952). Then there is the "error theory," which grants that moral claims can be assessed as true or false, but concludes that they are false. See John L. Mackie, *Ethics: Inventing Right and Wrong* (New York: Penguin, 1977).

4. In the analytic tradition, the work of Bernard Williams advances a critique of modern moral theory that fits my orientation in several ways, especially in terms of pluralism and the limits of rationality. See his *Ethics and the Limits of Philosophy* (Cambridge, Mass.: Harvard University Press, 1985). Williams seems to identify moral philosophy with moral theory (p. 74), which I would question. He does intimate that a phenomenology of ethical life might be good philosophy (p. 93). I agree. Another relevant work is Stuart Hampshire, *Morality and Conflict* (Cambridge, Mass.: Harvard University Press, 1983), which argues that morality at all levels is inseparable from conflict.

5. An important work in this vein is Charles Taylor's *Sources of the Self: The Making of Modern Identity* (Cambridge, Mass.: Harvard University Press, 1989). For Taylor, modern moral theory emphasizes what it is right to do, rather than what it is good to be (p. 3). He wants to emphasize "strong evaluations" and "moral sources" that animate the full

story of how one exists. In this way he wants to retrieve a kind of moral ontology. Taylor underplays finitude, however, and I think Heidegger's thought improves upon his efforts to overcome subjectivism in ethics (ch. 4).

6. In referring to values in this paragraph, I run up against the problem of Heidegger's objections to the term "value" and to value theory. I will address this matter in the last section of this chapter.

7. Here I might be able to avoid certain versions of the naturalistic fallacy. It might be possible to "derive" an ought from an enriched "is," although with Heidegger's inclusion of possibility, transcendence, temporality, and freedom, such derivation will be quite different from other naturalistic groundings that have been proposed and that have their own ontological blind spots. To be precise, I should not say here that an ought is logically derived from a nonmoral fact (in which case the naturalistic fallacy might be an apt charge), but that an ought is *disclosed* out of an enriched "is," that ethical meanings are *there* in Dasein's world and have an irreducible and underivable *being*.

8. Williams makes a comparable point in *Ethics and the Limits of Philosophy*, 27.

9. See Williams, *Ethics and the Limits of Philosophy*, ch. 1.

10. As in the discussion of objectivity in chapter 2, it is possible to lay out a range of meanings for rationality, in order to avoid the false choice between modernist rationality and postmodern irrationality. What is meant by "being rational"? The following senses of what I would call *existential* rationality are amenable to the orientation taken in this study. To be rational in this sense is to be *explicative*, as in ordinary reason-giving and the capacity to articulate reasons for acting; *dialogical*, in that one's reasons can make sense to, and might persuade, others; *realistic*, in that one is responsive and attentive to how things are; *discerning*, in that one can make appropriate practical judgments; *well disposed* to thinking, in that one is interested in truth, open-minded, curious, fair, attentive, and so on; *consistent*, in that one follows through on the implications of professed beliefs; and *organized*, in that one's thinking is not sporadic or chaotic. From these meanings can be distinguished elements of *modernist* rationality, which push existential rationality in the direction of foundationalist guarantees. Modernist rationality is *disengaged*, in terms of cognition fashioned apart from interests, desires, customs, and traditions; *apodictic*, as measured by universality and necessity, by way of principles no rational person could dispute; and *demonstrative*, in establishing conclusions solely by the logical force of a reasoning process. My contention is that existential rationality can and should operate in ethics, but that modernist rationality is at least inappropriate for most of ethical life. For an important study of the possibilities of rationality beyond modernist models, see Calvin O. Schrag, *The Resources of Rationality: A Response to the Postmodern Challenge* (Bloomington: Indiana University Press, 1992).

11. See *HCT*, 298, where Heidegger connects Dasein's understanding with various instances of either–or.

12. Utilitarian "benevolence" is not so much an existential disposition; it stems more from the standpoint of an "ideal observer" who can consider all interests impartially. See Williams's analysis in *Ethics and the Limits of Philosophy*, 81ff.

13. I leave aside a discussion of rule utilitarianism as an attempt to correct for some of these problems in so-called act utilitarianism. I can only say that it is not clear how one can measure the utility of a rule, or how rule utility does not eventually trace back to the utility of acts, or how rule utility does not lose the flexible responsiveness to circumstance that has always been an attractive feature of utilitarianism.

14. Could not a power advocate who accepts possible defeat consistently will the power principle? Could not disobedience of a political authority on behalf of moral conscience be seen to fail the universalization test? In the essay "What is Enlightenment?" Kant allows that an officer may dispute the legitimacy of a certain policy in the sphere of public discourse, but may not disobey the policy in the performance of public duties. This essay is included in *Kant's Political Writings*, ed. Hans Reise (Cambridge: Cambridge University Press, 1970).

15. The problem with Kant's universalization test and with John Rawls's related proposal to suspend our interests in the "original position" behind a "veil of ignorance," is that such schemes are existentially untenable. They are ingenious and instructive in many ways, but human situations do not exemplify these scenarios. We cannot fully suspend traditional influences, interests, and situatedness without becoming so vacuous as to perhaps not even be able to reason. The distance between these schemes and concrete existence impedes their capacity to affect human behavior. See Rawls, *A Theory of Justice* (Cambridge, Mass.: Harvard University Press, 1971).

16. W. D. Ross tried to remedy this problem in Kantian ethics by distinguishing between prima facie duties and actual duties, in *The Right and the Good* (Oxford: Oxford University Press, 1930). It is not clear in many cases, however, how one's actual duty is determined, and whether it can supersede baseline conflict. See Hampshire, *Morality and Conflict*, ch. 2, for an effective discussion of irresolvable conflicts of duties.

17. The work of Jürgen Habermas is an enormous contribution to moral philosophy and a significant improvement over standard Kantian models of rationality. In place of monological, subject-based reason, Habermas works out the dialogical intersubjectivity of rational practices that permeate the life-world. Communicative action and discourse, the unforced search for mutual understanding, consensus, and action-coordination, go all the way down in everyday life. Assumptions of objectivity, agent responsibility, and validity claims are built into communicative practice. Philosophy can reconstruct this tacit rationality and draw from it implications of universal principles and norms. Everyday validity presupposes warrants that surpass individual cases, which together with the impulse toward mutual understanding implies, for Habermas, a direction toward universal agreement, where all uncoerced discourse partners can come to a consensus. This does not presume what universal agreement entails from an a priori standpoint, because it must be an achievement of actual conversants, measured by standards of ideal speech conditions that are distortion-free, coercion-free, inclusive, and without time constraints or a pressing need to make decisions. See Habermas, *The Theory of Communicative Action*, two vols., trans. Thomas McCarthy (Cambridge, Mass.: MIT Press, 1984, 1987), and *Moral Consciousness and Communicative Action*, trans. Christian Lenhardt and Shierry Weber Nicholson (Cambridge, Mass.: MIT Press, 1990). Habermas presents a brilliant analysis of what I have termed existential rationality, which he claims presupposes a graduation to elements of modernist rationality. This last step I take to be an unwarranted leap. And ideal speech conditions raise the same questions of existential feasibility that were posed to Kantian and Rawlsian techniques. Ideality, even Habermas's dialogical version, can issue exclusionary effects by underwriting a charge of moral intransigence against one or more parties in a sustained disagreement, a dispute that in fact may be an intractable conflict that no amount of time or goodwill could resolve.

18. Later I draw this point from the thought of Aristotle.

19. Heidegger wants to stress that inwardness is not exhaustive of selfhood. The notion of the self as an inwardness differentiated from the outward environment and other selves

is a strong part of our tradition, but it is a historical development that took shape amid other dimensions of experience, and so it is not an eternal property. See Taylor's finely tuned analysis of this point in *Sources of the Self*, chs. 5–12. For an analysis of ancient thought that details the development of selfhood in relation to spheres of experience that Heidegger wants to retrieve, see my *Myth and Philosophy: A Contest of Truths* (Chicago: Open Court, 1990), especially chs. 2–6.

20. Heidegger writes: "The object we have taken as our theme is *artificially and dogmatically curtailed* if 'in the first instance' we restrict ourselves to a 'theoretical subject' in order that we may then round it out 'on the practical side' by tacking on an 'ethic'" (*BT*, 363–64).

21. I prefer to leave *Fürsorge* untranslated to capture the senses of caring for and caring about that can be missed in the standard translation "solicitude." In German, *liebesvolle Fürsorge* means loving care, *soziale Fürsorge* means social welfare or social service.

22. Nancy J. Holland develops this point in *The Madwoman's Reason: The Concept of the Appropriate in Ethical Thought* (University Park: Pennsylvania State University Press, 1998), 8–9, 103–10.

23. For a very important essay on everyday ethical comportment, see Hubert L. Dreyfus and Stuart E. Dreyfus, "What Is Morality? A Phenomenological Account of the Development of Ethical Expertise," in *Universalism vs. Communitarianism*, ed. David Rasmussen (Cambridge, Mass.: MIT Press, 1990), 237–64. Here a nuanced articulation of skill acquisition is coordinated with the development of moral maturity. Deliberation and choice emerge out of a prior sphere of "spontaneous coping," and moral development moves from more deliberate modes to more proficient modes of intuitive skill, and to a mix of both modes in complex situations.

24. Much of what follows is taken from Jonathan Bloom-Feshbach and Sally Bloom-Feshbach, eds., *The Psychology of Separation and Loss* (San Francisco: Jossey-Bass, 1987).

25. *The Psychology of Separation and Loss*, 2–3.

26. *The Psychology of Separation and Loss*, 8ff.

27. *The Psychology of Separation and Loss*, 97. The sharpening of experience involves a more urgent, sustained attention on the nature of desires and the things desired.

28. *The Psychology of Separation and Loss*, 22. Additionally, around the third year, mostly facilitated by language development, the child develops a sense of object constancy, that absent things can still exist, and in such a context, memory and anticipation help mollify anxiety and promote a toleration of separation (17).

29. *The Psychology of Separation and Loss*, 8ff.

30. See Frederick A. Olafson's insightful discussion in *Heidegger and the Ground of Ethics: A Study of* Mitsein (Cambridge: Cambridge University Press, 1998), 23–25.

31. See Jerome Kagan and Sharon Lamb, eds., *The Emergence of Morality in Young Children* (Chicago: University of Chicago Press, 1987).

32. Evidence for the ekstatic nature of imitation can be found in the phenomenon of "invisible imitation," where infants will operate imitatively with parts of the body such as the face that are not visible to the infant. Jean Piaget had suggested that such a capacity requires the development of a "body schema" around the age of eight to twelve months. But there is evidence of this mimetic capacity right after birth, for instance with tongue protrusion. This early capacity suggests an immediate outward immersion that need not

require some inner-formed sense directed outward. See Andrew Meltzoff and M. Keith Moore, "Imitation of Facial and Manual Gestures by Human Neonates," *Science* 198 (1977): 75–78, and "Newborn Infants Imitate Adult Facial Gestures," *Child Development* 54 (1983): 702–9.

33. Robert M. Emde, William F. Johnson, and M. Ann Easterbrooks, "The Do's and Don'ts of Early Moral Development," in *The Emergence of Morality in Young Children*, ch. 5.

34. See Judy Dunn, "The Beginnings of Moral Understanding," in *The Emergence of Morality in Young Children*, ch. 2.

35. Moral development is neither pure cultural transmission nor a child's own self-construction; it is a child's reconstruction and re-creation of cultural meanings. See Carolyn Pope Edwards, "Culture and the Construction of Moral Values," in *The Emergence of Morality in Young Children*, ch. 3. Even at an early stage, then, Heideggerian conceptions of interpretation and authenticity are evident to a certain degree.

36. For Hume, moral sentiments are natural to the human condition. Although these sentiments are not objective in the scientific sense, they do exhibit an intersubjective objectivity, rather than a mere preferential subjectivity. See Nicholas Capaldi, *Hume's Place in Moral Philosophy* (New York: Lang, 1989). With Hume's naturalism, it is clear that a radical is–ought divide should not be attributed to his philosophy. A better candidate is Kant, who wanted to protect the freedom of the moral will by separating it entirely from natural conditions.

37. See Arne J. Vetlesen, *Perception, Empathy, and Judgment: An Inquiry into the Preconditions of Moral Performance* (University Park: Pennsylvania State University Press, 1994). It should be said that Kant answers the question of motivation in ethics with the "moral feeling" of respect (*Achtung*), which is a feeling generated by reason, as distinct from the sensible feelings of nature. Respect is a kind of awe at the dignity of a rational agent's self-regulating transcendence of natural self-love (see the *Critique of Practical Reason*, ch. 3). From a historical standpoint, we can see Kant celebrating the import of rational autonomy, as opposed to external directives that had marked traditional social norms. Yet a Heideggerian emphasis on mood as constitutive of all modes of knowing is much better able to address moral motivation than is Kant's attempt to conjure up some special feeling out of a rational faculty that is otherwise divorced from affects.

38. See Vetlesen, *Perception, Empathy, and Judgment*, 159ff.

39. The later Heidegger's turn to poetry as a richer mode of disclosure than abstract concepts can be associated with the important role that literature can play in moral education. The narrative specificity of literature can touch people in ways that principles alone might not (think of the impact of Charles Dickens's novels in sensitizing people to the plight of the poor). The complex intricacy of great literature also attests to the ambiguities of ethical life. Two works that take up the role of literature in ethics are Richard Rorty, *Contingency, Irony, and Solidarity* (Cambridge: Cambridge University Press, 1989), and Martha Nussbaum, *Love's Knowledge: Essays in Philosophy and Literature* (Oxford: Oxford University Press, 1990).

40. Part of ethical upbringing involves instructing children in recognizing various circumstances *as* having ethical import, and also in discerning the appropriate kind of ethical import in this or that circumstance: for instance, showing that what was taken as a deliberate injury was actually an accident, or what was taken as laughing mockery was actually an expression of delight. On this and other relevant matters, see Nancy Sherman, *The Fabric of Character* (Oxford: Clarendon Press, 1989), ch. 5.

41. For an important study that works with the hermeneutics of Gadamer and Ricoeur to provide a space for ethics in between postmodern contingency and universal moral constraints, see Nicholas H. Smith, *Strong Hermeneutics: Contingency and Moral Identity* (New York: Routledge, 1997).

42. See Sisela Bok, "The Search for a Shared Ethics," *Common Knowledge*, vol. 1, no. 3 (Winter 1992): 12–25. Ironically, it may be the standard of indefeasibility that creates an overly distorted picture of conflict in ethics, in that we are prompted to consider any imaginable objection in order to shore up the validity of a proposed norm. We might do better to begin with our actual proclivities and to wait for sincere, forthright disputes. For instance, let us wait for actual radical egoists to advance (and live by) their positions, and let us gauge ethical prospects by way of the actual conduct of the engagement with such persons.

43. Two classic works are Carol Gilligan, *In a Different Voice: Psychological Theory and Women's Development* (Cambridge, Mass.: Harvard University Press, 1982), and Nel Noddings, *Caring: A Feminine Approach to Ethics and Education* (Berkeley: University of California Press, 1984).

44. Those who would interpret authenticity as separable from ethical norms must take note of a passage (*BT*, 435) where Heidegger associates Dasein's heritage with notions of the "good" and expressly states that such cultural orientations make authentic existence *possible*. Accordingly, nothing in Heidegger's thought rules out the idea that an authentic individual would have to be well socialized in a certain manner.

45. See Taylor, *Sources of the Self*, ch. 2.

46. See *BT*, sections 58–59.

47. A helpful analysis is Frank Schalow, "The Topography of Heidegger's Concept of Conscience," *American Catholic Philosophical Quarterly*, vol. 69, no. 2 (1995): 255–73.

48. See Werner Marx, *Is There a Measure on Earth? Foundations for a Nonmetaphysical Ethics*, trans. Thomas J. Nenon and Reginald Lilly (Chicago: University of Chicago Press, 1987), ch. 2.

49. One problem in the text involves Heidegger describing factical action and being good as "conscienceless" (334). I take this as referring to a sharp distinction between ontological being-toward-death and being absorbed in the world and with others. I prefer to think that this apparent segregation of modes of conscience can be overcome. For an analysis, see Lawrence Vogel, *The Fragile "We": Ethical Implications of Heidegger's Being and Time* (Evanston, Ill.: Northwestern University Press, 1994), 14–24.

50. For example, Heidegger disparages the everyday sense of guilt and bad conscience as a kind of balance-sheet reckoning, along the lines of a "court of justice" model attributable to Kant (*BT*, 338–39).

51. As Heidegger puts it in terms of ontological conscience, "the call comes *from* me and yet *from beyond me and over me*" (*BT*, 320). Ricoeur provides a phenomenology of ethical conscience in terms of the self speaking *as another*, drawn from a baseline sociality. Conscience is the source of being claimed in ethics, as a mode of being-enjoined. See his *Oneself as Another*, trans. Kathleen Blamey (Chicago: University of Chicago Press, 1992). Ricoeur takes Heidegger's ontological conscience to be divorced from ethical meanings and possibilities. I disagree.

52. As Vogel remarks, moral conscience need not be construed as telling one what to do in a situation; rather, it "simply orients one to a world beyond the immediate horizon of one's own needs, interests, and prejudices" (*The Fragile "We,"* 101).

53. I suppose it is possible that such an experience of guilt and conscience is not really world-disclosive, that it is simply a conditioned response or some kind of regulatory fiction, a cultural overlay upon an otherwise indifferent, self-regarding, or malicious self. All I can say is that instances in my experience of guilt and conscience suggest a direct sense of being claimed and called, of existing in and as such a claim, rather than some hidden script of forces that ultimately makes my apparent responsiveness actually specious. I trust that I am not alone in making sense of my experience in this way.

54. I thank Tom Neill for alerting me to this line of thinking. For an important work in the analytic tradition that opens up avenues of ethical truth in contrast to noncognitivist, internalist approaches, see David Wiggins, *Needs, Values, Truth*, 3rd edition (Oxford: Oxford University Press, 1998).

55. See Olafson's fine discussion of the relation between responsibility and trust in his *Heidegger and the Ground of Ethics*, 60–68.

56. Ethical responsibility construed as a response to the unevadable need of the Other is powerfully expressed in the work of Emmanuel Levinas. See his *Totality and Infinity*, trans. Alphonso Lingis (Pittsburgh: Duquesne University Press, 1969), and *Otherwise than Being or Beyond Essence*, trans. Alphonso Lingis (The Hague: Martinus Nijhoff, 1981). In part as a reaction to Heidegger, Levinas insists on the priority of ethics over ontology. In Western thought, being has been construed as a generality that subsumes differences, and so it amounts to a reduction of the Other to the rule of the same. Levinas is wrong, however, in taking Heidegger's ontology in this way. For Heidegger, otherness is part of being. In any case, the Levinasian Other is a primal resistance to the self, and it is encountered as a face. A face is different from other entities in the world; it looks back at me as a witness to my actions. Here is an original ethical force, because the face of the Other repels my attempts to control or destroy it, it counters my self-assertion and puts me under an infinite obligation. Levinas's work is not an ethics per se, as much as a phenomenology of a basic ethical dynamic, the force of obligation and responsibility issuing directly from the human face.

57. As Aristotle says, "thought by itself moves nothing" (*NE*, 1139a35).

58. Hannah Arendt calls this element of action "natality." See her *The Human Condition* (Chicago: University of Chicago Press, 1968).

59. Kant wrestled admirably with the problem of moral freedom, in terms of the difference between ethical action and causal relations, a problem brought on by the mechanistic conception of nature in modern science. If human actions are part of the natural causal nexus, then they are necessary outcomes of causal laws, and thus not freely chosen among alternative possibilities. But since we do not praise or blame people for things that could not turn out otherwise, scientific naturalism seems to cancel out moral responsibility, the very heart of ethics. Kant's solution was to limit scientific theoretical reason to phenomena, or things as they appear to the thinking subject, as opposed to noumena, or things in themselves. This maneuver gave Kant room to stipulate the possibility of noumenal freedom in practical reason, which can act contrary to the necessities of nature. But since moral freedom was still measured by the dictates of rationality, Kant underplayed the radical finitude intrinsic to moral freedom. He also had to resort to the bifurcation of a phenomenal and noumenal self in order to protect the locus of moral freedom, a bifurcation that can render moral agency in the natural world unintelligible. From a Heideggerian orientation, one can simply take Kant's distinction between theoretical and practical standpoints as phenomenologically evident, and thus make room for freedom without having to provide metaphysical scaffolding for these different modes of disclosure.

98   *Chapter Three*

60. See Taylor, *Sources of the Self*, 64ff.

61. The most important figure in value theory was Max Scheler, whom Heidegger much admired. Scheler's main work was *Formalism in Ethics and Non-Formal Ethics of Values*, trans. Manfred S. Frings and Roger L. Funk (Evanston, Ill.: Northwestern University Press, 1973). Scheler counterposed a material, phenomenological ethics to Kant's formal ethics. Scheler agreed with Kant that ethics should have an a priori, unconditional ground, as opposed to the contingent ends of consequentialism. But Scheler advanced a "material a priori" to challenge Kant's view that material desires and feelings were necessarily confined to a sphere of self-regard and contingency. Scheler believed that there are basic phenomena of moral experience that can exceed self-regard and provide an objective reference to ground ethics. The Heideggerian charge of subjectivism may not apply to Scheler, since he took phenomena such as kindness and love to be "given" in experience, not posited by the subject or the will. Yet for Scheler, morality remains grounded in a priori intuitions of supratemporal value "essences" that are independent of particular empirical goods. This is simply the flip side of a Kantian essentialism, which remains susceptible to a Heideggerian critique. For a very helpful analysis of Scheler and Kant that includes a discussion of Heidegger, see Philip Blosser, *Scheler's Critique of Kant's Ethics* (Athens: Ohio University Press, 1995).

62. Joseph Kockelmans makes this point in *On the Truth of Being* (Bloomington: Indiana University Press, 1984), 258, 261.

63. See Charles E. Scott's evocative reading in *The* Question *of Ethics: Nietzsche, Foucault, Heidegger* (Bloomington: Indiana University Press, 1990), 142–47.

64. Joanna Hodge, *Heidegger and Ethics* (New York: Routledge, 1995), is a rich account of this register in Heidegger's thinking, but it does not do much to address familiar concerns in moral philosophy. For Hodge, what is "ethical" in Heidegger's thought is its critique of metaphysical closure. Another important piece in a manner similar to Hodge is Silvia Benso, "On the Way to Ontological Ethics: Ethical Suggestions in Reading Heidegger," *Research in Phenomenology* 24 (1994): 159–88. Benso suggests some reciprocity between ontology and ethics, which is promising.

65. See *IM*, 133, where being is associated with differentiated rankings of value. Ernest Joós aims to articulate a "concept of values" that accords with Heidegger's thought, in *Dialogue with Heidegger on Values: Ethics for Times of Crisis* (New York: Lang, 1991). Here there are questionable interpretations of Heidegger because of an emphasis on Kantian categories, but there is an important effort to locate value as a world phenomenon. See also Robert Sokolowski, *Moral Action: A Phenomenological Study* (Bloomington: Indiana University Press, 1985), and Hans Reiner, *Duty and Inclination*, trans. Mark Santos (The Hague: Martinus Nijhoff, 1983). Both writers advance a phenomenologically nuanced account of values that can avoid much of Heidegger's critique. Reiner in particular lays out an environmental conception of moral action that can exceed the boundary of subjectivity.

Chapter Four

Heidegger and Aristotle

In many respects there is historical precedent for the kind of ethical analysis I am trying to draw out of Heidegger, namely the ethics of Aristotle. In this chapter I want to explore the philosophical links between Heidegger and Aristotle, offer a sketch of Aristotle's ethical thought, and discuss some Heideggerian modifications of Aristotle's approach that mark the path I am taking in this investigation. The value of considering the Aristotle connection is that it helps situate Heidegger's ontology and its ethical potential within a significant strand in the history of Western philosophy, thereby lending further credence to Heidegger's insistence that he was aiming to think in and through the tradition, rather than beyond it.

HEIDEGGER'S DEBT TO ARISTOTLE

Several of Heidegger's writings and lecture courses were concerned with the philosophy of Aristotle. Heidegger declared that his early work on Aristotle was "decisive" in the development of his phenomenology (*TB*, 78).[1] His estimation of the Greek philosopher was enormous, to the point of saying that no one has surpassed the greatness of Aristotle (*PS*, 8). Of particular importance for Heidegger was Aristotle's phenomenological method.

> Aristotle was the last of the great philosophers who had eyes to see and, what is still more decisive, the energy and tenacity to continue to force inquiry back to the phenomena and to the seen and to mistrust from the ground up all wild and windy speculations, no matter how close to the heart of common sense. (*BP*, 232)

As opposed to the transcendent tendencies in Platonism and the abstract deductions typical of earlier philosophers, Aristotle's method amounted to "saving appearances." Investigation should always begin with phenomena as presented to

99

us, through which the search for explanations and causes can properly proceed (*Parts of Animals*, 640a15ff). Phenomena are the "witnesses" and "paradigms" for philosophical inquiry (*Eudemian Ethics*, 1216b26ff). Contrary to speculative metaphysics and aetiological stories, Aristotle insists that the "why" and the "what" of things cannot be examined before the "that" (*to hoti*) of things (what Heidegger would call their concrete presencing); to reverse this order "is to inquire into nothing" (*Posterior Analytics*, 93a15–28). Aristotle takes his point of departure, not from theoretical constructions, but from what is immediately apparent in perceptible encounters.[2]

There are also clear indications in Aristotle of Heidegger's sense of the hermeneutic circle. Aristotle begins most of his investigations with a survey of historical precedents, with the aim of sorting out what in these sources is appropriate and inappropriate to phenomena. He initiates discussion in terms of familiar meanings and usages that he takes as given, and he then moves to think with and through these meanings toward clearer and deeper insights.[3] Aristotle also gives decisive importance to language in this technique by continually referring to what "we say" or what "is said."[4] Regarding Aristotle's reference to human beings as *zōon logon echon* (see *NE*, 1098a3–5), usually translated as "rational animal," Heidegger prefers a richer conception of *logos* and renders the definition as the animal "having" (*echon*) language, understood as speech and discourse (*AM*, 102ff). Rounding out the sense of a hermeneutic circle, Aristotle also maintains that philosophical inquiry should consult both the "many" and the "wise" (see *Topics*, 100b22ff), that is, both common beliefs and refined insights. The implication is that philosophical findings should be neither so unusual as to outstrip ordinary senses of things nor so familiar as to rest solely with customary meanings.

There are several ways in which Aristotle's thought represents a premodern precedent for Heidegger's alternative to the ontologies of modern philosophy and science. Aristotle was a thoroughgoing realist and naturalist, in the sense that human beings belong in the world and are at home in it. Heidegger also found in Aristotle's ontology a recognition of particularity, plurality, and movement, which was akin to his own phenomenological alternative to the metaphysics of constant presence that marked most of the Western tradition.

Consider Aristotle's concept of *ousia*, the primary sense of being as the unified reference for descriptions. Heidegger points to the pretechnical meaning of *ousia* as household belongings available for use, which he calls "possessions" or "havings" (*Habe*), in line with his sense of environmental *zuhanden* relations. As indicated in the examples of fabricated things illustrating the four causes, Aristotle understands beings initially as modes of productive use, not as bare "objects" (*AM*, 374–75). Heidegger associates this sense of *ousia* with the "having" of language, which Aristotle himself takes as a kind of "middle voice" in between self and world, which thus accords with Heidegger's holistic structure of being-in-the-world.[5] And *ousia*, for Aristotle—unlike the Platonic conception of being and the connotations of the Latin translation "substance"—is primarily a "this something" (*tode ti*), an immanent, concrete presence in experience (*Categories*, 3b10–12). Species and genera are *ousia* in a secondary sense, in that they reveal something about being, but not in a primary sense (*Categories*, 2b29–31). The primary sense of *ousia*, then, suggests the radicality of the "that" over the "what," which Heidegger takes to mean the sense of presencing in temporal experience (the Greek word for presence is *parousia*). *Ousia* is a unity in the sense of being a stable reference point for an account of things, but there are as many unities as there are beings in experience (*Metaphysics*, 1003b23ff), and the temporality of nature shows that *ousia* is in each case finite.

Aristotle's ontology does not set itself apart from motion and change, and thus it accommodates negation. Heidegger calls Aristotle's *Physics* a straightforward phenomenology of movement (*AI*, 387). In this work Aristotle investigates the explanations and ordering principles of nature (*phusis*), which is directly identified with movement and change (*Physics*, 200b12). Aristotle specifically correlates the notions of *phusis*, being, *ousia*, and movement (*Physics*, 185a12ff, 192b32–35, 201a8), thereby separating himself from philosophies that had counterposed being and change (*Physics*, 191a25ff). Things of nature have an intrinsic principle of movement, as distinct from things brought into being extrinsically by production (*Physics*, 192b10ff). *Phusis*, then, has to do with self-manifesting beings.[6] The task of analysis is to make sense out of change and movement, which Aristotle accomplishes by way of the concepts of matter and form, which are given a dynamic sense in the concepts of potentiality (*dunamis*) and actualization (*energeia*).

It is important to stress that both *dunamis* and *energeia* are active concepts for Aristotle. The two together represent a single model of process (*Physics*, 201a10ff). *Dunamis* as potentiality is not simply logical possibility, but an active capacity to develop, and *energeia* as actuality is not simply a finished state, but being at work (*ergon*) in the actualizing of potential. Form (*eidos*), then, cannot be understood simply as a static "shape," but rather as the active self-*organization* of a developing being (*Physics*, 194b27). Heidegger notices *energeia* and *dunamis* coordinated with *telos* in Aristotle's coinage of *entelecheia* (literally "having-an-end-in" one's being), so that the movements of *phusis* involve a being-toward, a self-emerging being-on-the-way-toward a not-yet that appropriately can-be—that is to say, a presencing of an absence (*ECP*, 217–28). Being, then, involves a self-surpassing "otherness" (*AM*, 85).[7] In thinking of *ousia* as a concrete occurrence in natural experience, Aristotle is able to give movement, change, time, and negation their appropriate sense of being (*AM*, 181).[8]

In Aristotle's text on the soul (*psuche*), we find a great deal that fits Heidegger's phenomenology of Dasein as an active, temporal movement animated by possibility. The soul is the form of the body's matter, but in the unified sense of being the actualization of potentials in a living being, an active capacity to function and develop (*On the Soul*, II.1). Aristotle specifically identifies the human soul with all the elements that Heidegger finds so significant in Aristotelian phenomenology: *phusis, dunamis, energeia, ousia,* and *logos* (*On the Soul,* 412a20ff), all of which suggests a dynamic capacity to be-in-the-world. Heidegger shares completely Aristotle's notion that the self is essentially an activity, not a static essence.[9]

Heidegger's alternative to subject–object bifurcations in modern philosophy also finds a precedent in Aristotle's reflections on the soul, which offer a bipolar conception of self and world. The soul is potentially the same as the things it thinks, without being identical to them (*On the Soul,* 429a15–17). Thinking is nothing until it thinks something in the world and what it thinks must *be* in thought (*On the Soul,* 429b3–431a1). The actively thinking soul *is* the things it thinks (*On the Soul,* 431b16–18). The mention of activity (*energeia*) can direct us to sections of *Physics* (III.1–3), where we are told that in activity, the agent and patient are the same, as a single process of actualization (illustrated by teaching and learning, building and a house being built). The agent is not something self-contained in an interior zone separate from the object of its activity. The potential of *both* is actualized in a single bipolar process. Here we have something very much akin to Heidegger's sense of being-in-the-world, as an ekstatic placement of the self *in* its environment. Such a bipolar construction also gives a dramatic presentation of Aristotle's realism that in certain respects is carried on by Heidegger, namely that the activities and disclosures of the human self are appropriated to the world and indeed can be called the world's own self-emergent activity.

As in Heidegger, the realism of Aristotle is not of a uniform kind. Aristotle offers a kind of pluralism that Heidegger takes to be significant. First there is the plurality of being. Aristotle tells us that being is spoken of in many ways (*Metaphysics,* 1003a34). Whatever unity there is in the notion of being will at best be analogical, since being cannot provide a universal genus (*Metaphysics,* 1042a23).[10]

Aristotle also gives a pluralistic account of truth in book VI of the *Nicomachean Ethics* that was of enormous importance in Heidegger's early development.[11] Aristotle mentions that there are two basic modes of the soul's "having *logos*" (*logon echon*): (1) that pertaining to beings whose origins cannot be otherwise (necessary being), and (2) that pertaining to beings whose origins admit of being otherwise (contingent being) and thus call for *bouleusis,* or deliberation and decision (*NE,* 1139aff). The virtue of each mode is its own proper function or work (*ergon*) in being appropriated to the different kinds of beings by way of a certain familiarity with them (*PS,* 19ff). This leads to a discussion of five virtues of thought: pertaining to the first mode of *logos* are *epistēmē* (scientific knowledge), *nous* (intuitive insight), and *sophia* (wisdom); pertaining to the second mode are *technē* (skill in making) and *phronēsis* (practical wisdom or acting well in human affairs). Aristotle then identifies these five virtues with five modes of truth, which are defined as the different functions and dispositions of the different virtues; indeed, the virtues are five ways in which the soul is *alētheuei,* or "in the truth" (*NE,* 1139b12–18). As Heidegger puts it, Aristotle is here associating truth with Dasein's very being, the soul as *ousia* (*PS*, 16).[12] What is key for Heidegger is that truth is not limited to statements of scientific exactitude; it also applies to inexact modes of discerning appropriate action in spheres such as ethics. And truth understood as unconcealment is certainly more appropriate for this multiple conception of truth than is the correspondence model. For Aristotle, there is truth (appropriate disclosure) in matters of making (*poiēsis*) and human living (*praxis*) that do not reduce to precise "agreement" with external objects or conceptual principles.

HEIDEGGER AND ARISTOTLE'S ETHICS

Heidegger gives some attention to Aristotle's ethics and the prospects of an ethics inspired by Aristotle. An early lecture course, *Phänomenologische Interpretationen zu Aristoteles* (*GA* 61), offers some fascinating material regarding the relationship between Heidegger and Aristotle's thought and the possibilities for ethics in Heidegger's early ontology.[13] In this text, Heidegger highlights the problems in absolutistic, transcendental moral systems, owing to their detachment from a more worldly, finite, lived morality (*GA* 61, 64). It is Aristotle's *Nicomachean Ethics*, particularly its critique of Platonic moral philosophy, that gives Heidegger a historical focus for a new beginning, both in ontology and in ethics. Heidegger suggests an ethics that will accord more with the human world, that will renounce the comfortable, undisturbed, lofty distances of moral theories that foreclose any realization of ethical possibilities in the actual experience of finite conditions (*GA* 61, 164–65).

Nevertheless, Heidegger's primary interest in Aristotle's ethics was not in its articulation of the moral sphere, but in the avenues it opens up for alternative conceptions of being and truth. In a discussion of book VI of the *Nicomachean Ethics*, Heidegger specifically brackets Aristotle's (ontical) ethical problematic in order to draw out its ontological implications—witness his characterization of Aristotle's intellectual virtues as modes of the "truthful safekeeping of being" (*AI*, 377).[14] This is in keeping with Heidegger's long-standing disinterest in ethics. What I am trying to accomplish is a kind of feedback loop regarding Heidegger and Aristotle. As Heidegger drew inspiration from Aristotle's ethics for his ontological analysis, I am taking Heidegger's ontology as inspiration for an ethics that in part revisits Aristotelian territory. Heidegger's intimate association with Aristotle permits an articulation of a Heideggerian approach to ethics by highlighting elements in Aristotle that Heidegger did not explore. In doing so, however, Heidegger's radically finite ontology calls for certain modifications of Aristotle's moral philosophy. In effect I am trying to open up an ethics with Heidegger's ontology that moves through, yet beyond, Aristotle's thought. To that end, let me present an outline of Aristotle's ethics.[15]

THE ORGANIZATION OF DESIRE

I have already shown that for Aristotle the being of the human soul is the active capacity to lead a life. And the capacity (*dunamis*) that moves human life is desire (*On the Soul*, 433b1), understood as a striving toward conditions in the world affecting the actualization of potential. Desire (*oreksis*) cuts across all three parts of the human soul: as appetite in the vegetative part, emotion in the sensitive part, and wish in the rational part (*On the Soul*, III.10). Even rational thought is necessarily moved by desire (*On the Soul*, 433a23–24). Desire involves the experience of an absence with respect to a desired condition (*orekton*), which then opens up the structure of striving toward a desired end (*telos*), as well as modes of deliberation regarding ways of actualizing such a potential end. Deliberation is needed because different desires can come in conflict (for instance, dieting to limit appetite for the sake of health concerns). Deliberation about desire has an essentially temporal structure, in considering the future in terms of present impulses in the light of past experiences (*On the Soul*, 433b5–10).[16]

Ethics for Aristotle begins with the recognition that "good" indicates a desired end (*NE*, 1094a1–5). And like being, goodness takes a plurality of forms (*NE*, 1096a24–25). Living well amounts to an organization of a plurality of desires in various practical milieus, in such a way as to allow the development of human potential. It is important to stress that the "rationality" of ethics in Aristotle should not be understood in terms of modern models of reason based in the subject–object dichotomy. The soul's bipolar relation to the world suggests that living well is environmentally responsive—the movements of the soul are likewise the opening up of the world—as opposed to the modern theoretical model of constructing moral principles and applying them to experience as rules for action. Desire indicates complex intersections of self and world that call for appropriate balancing in practice, rather than some kind of theoretical governance. Accordingly, ethical thinking for Aristotle has neither the exactitude nor the operative procedures of modern conceptions of reason. The word usually translated as "reason" in the text is *logos*. In Greek *logos* has a rich array of meanings, and there are occasions where Aristotle clearly takes *logos* to mean a kind of proportional ordering and attunement.[17] Since *phronēsis*, as I develop, is central to ethics and does not exhibit demonstrative certainty, it is better to see the "rationality" of ethics as an emergent ordering and balancing of desires in the midst of contingent practical environments.

EUDAIMONIA

The unifying term for the good life, for Aristotle, is *eudaimonia*. The usual translation of "happiness" does not sufficiently capture Aristotle's meaning, which is better rendered as human flourishing, living well, the active realization of human

potentials and attainment of various natural goods. Beginning with the phenomenology of desire, ethics is the consideration of various orderings and judgments
concerning better and worse choices—because some desires are necessary
(needs) and some are contingent (wants), because some desires come into conflict
with each other, and experience teaches a distinction between real and apparent
goods. *Eudaimonia* will require the exercise of virtue (*aretē*), which is better rendered as excellence, or a mode of high-level functioning. In other words, virtues
are the character traits, habits, and dispositions that disclose appropriate choices
and judgments regarding the ordering of desires, all for the sake of living well.

Aristotle's ethics is specifically counterposed to Platonic tendencies toward a
rationalistic, universalistic, perfectionist ethics.[18] Reflection on the good cannot
bracket tradition and received opinions, but must begin with cultural appearances,
which can then be submitted to analysis, clarification, and puzzle resolution (*NE*,
1095b3, 1145b3–7). Both common opinions and the insights of the wise must be
considered (*NE*, 1095a14ff). The good must also be a *human* good, reflecting the
finite condition of a desiring being experiencing lacks and limits, and so should
not be measured by divine perfection (*NE*, 1096b30–35, 1178a5–15). The good
is also pluralized, not uniform (*NE*, 1096a24–25), particular, not universal (*NE*,
1109b22–23), contingent, not necessary (*NE*, 1139b7–10), temporal, not eternal
(*NE*, 1096b4), immanent, not transcendent (*NE*, 1196b30–35), inexact, not precise (*NE*, 1094b20–25), and difficult to achieve, not easy (*NE*, 1106b30–35).
Finally, the good life and *eudaimonia* cannot be taken as conditions of the solitary individual, but must include the larger order of social and political environments (*NE*, 1094a27ff, 1097b8ff).

The good has a decidedly performative meaning for Aristotle, since it is identified with activity and *ergon*, which means function, task, or work (*NE*, 1097b24ff).
Eudaimonia is called the activity of the soul in accordance with virtue, or moral
excellence (*NE*, 1098a15–17). We should think of virtue here in the sense of "vir-
tuosity," as excellence of performance, as effective, successful action in social life.
Eudaimonia is also analyzed in terms of a specific temporal structure of activity,
as a process of coming into being and thus not as the constancy of a "possession"
(*NE*, 1169b29–32). *Eudaimonia* is also understood in terms of the comprehensiveness of the virtues and the course of a complete life (*NE*, 1098a18–21)—in
other words, as the overall temporal structure of a life fulfilling potential, and not
simply a focus on a particular event or experience. This is why the familiar association of "happiness" with "good feeling" is so misleading; *eudaimonia* is a comprehensive and ongoing *achievement*, not a "state of mind."

Eudaimonia is measured by the fulfillment and achievement of various goods that
are naturally beneficial for human beings: goods of the environment, the body, and
the soul (*NE*, 1098b13ff). Living well is a constellation of material goods, bodily
health, sensual satisfactions and enjoyments, social relationships and achievements,
productive activities, and intellectual understanding—in other words, a well-
rounded life of physical, sensory, social, productive, and cognitive development.

VIRTUE

Virtues are the capacities, dispositions, and habits that enable a person to orchestrate all the various possible goods, measured by the successful performance of a
well-rounded life. In this regard, Aristotle insists on the importance of good
upbringing prior to mature reflection on the good life. Aristotle seems quite pessimistic about the prospects for an ethical life without the cultivation of good
habits and dispositions from early on (*NE*, 1095b4ff, 1103b21–25). He connects
character (*ēthos*) with habit (*ethos*) and says that virtues arise mostly through
teaching and learning, and they require time and the accumulation of experience
to develop (*NE*, 1103a14ff). Aristotle maintains that the virtues are neither purely
natural nor purely artificial, but are natural capacities and potentials to live well
that must be cultivated by training, habit, and performance (*NE*, 1103a24ff). This
is why Aristotle points to the limits of rational argument in ethics (*NE*, 1179b1ff).
There is just so much you can say to a person inclined to vice, and people open
up to ethical matters in ways other than strict analysis of beliefs and their rational
justification (*NE*, X.9).

Virtues are defined as the capacity to discover a mean (*mesotēs*) between
extreme conditions of excess and defect, of too much and too little (*NE*,
1104a25ff). For instance, the virtue of moderation in pleasure seeking is a mean
between overindulgence and ascetic denial or insensitivity. Acting well according
to virtue, however, is a performance that does not operate on the basis of theoretical formulas or rules to guide action. Virtuous activity is inexact and can only
be executed by a competent person in the context of a particular *kairos*, a particular situation at a particular time (*NE*, 1104a5ff)—indeed, the *telos* of an action
is specifically identified with a *kairos* (*NE*, 1110a12–13).

This is why the practical virtue of *phronēsis* is so important in Aristotle's
ethics. Aristotle characterizes *phronēsis* as the ability to discover the mean (*NE*,
1107a1–2). Rather than some kind of rationalized subjective agency, *phronēsis* is
the disclosure of ethical truth (*NE*, 1140b5), in the sense of disclosing an appropriate path in pursuit of an aim in the midst of conflicting forces—what I would
call a *balancing act*. When the mean is associated with *orthos logos* (*NE*,
1138b20–25), usually translated as "correct reason," the phrase is connected with
aiming at a target and with a tightening and relaxing that suggests either a bow
string or tuning a lyre string; at another point (*NE*, 1109b24–27) Aristotle says
that finding the mean is facilitated by tending toward the excess and defect, again
suggesting a "tuning." Since *orthos* can mean the successful accomplishment of
an aim, *orthos logos* can mean successful action in a practical milieu, accomplished by an attunement of the soul with its milieu, something very different
from "correct reason." *Phronēsis*, then, is much more suggestive of Heidegger's
Dasein-world attunement than something like rational agency. *Phronēsis* could be
called a capacity for practical discernment, or an ethical finesse, a cultivated apti-
tude to uncover the appropriate balancing and ordering of practical possibilities.

Aristotle specifically says that *phronēsis* is not mere knowledge; it must include action (*NE*, 1152a8–9). Moreover, as a developed disposition and "having" (*hexis*), it is registered in a person's very being, and so it cannot be "forgotten," as can factual knowledge (*NE*, 1140b28–30).

Discovering the mean is relative to a particular person's situation (*NE*, 1106b1). This makes virtuous action difficult, because it is context-dependent. Formal compliance with a rule is easy; judging the proper balance and appropriate action in a certain situation, in a certain way, at a certain time, to a certain degree, for a certain purpose, is hard (*NE*, 1109a24ff). For example, generosity or charity could vary in its suitability or vary in degrees according to the circumstances, persons, resources, prospects, and so forth. What is appropriate can only be rendered at the time and in the situation of a particular agent, and it demands an *experience* of particulars, which is neither exact nor universal (*NE*, 1109b22ff). Consequently, Aristotle's ethics does not involve moral axioms or formulas that can transcend and govern the specificity of experience. To be sure, ethics can involve certain generalizations presented in an unqualified (*haplōs*) form (It is good to be generous), but ethical practice will always have to confront qualifications in experience (*NE*, 1134a25ff).

Aristotle appears to be advocating a kind of decisionism or intuitionism in ethics: The measure of virtuous action is the virtuous person (*NE*, 1113a25ff); the measure of the good is that which appears to the good person (*NE*, 1176a17ff). An ethical decision cannot be arbitrary, however, since it must respond to the environment at hand and must stem from good upbringing; but *as* a contextual decision it is saturated with temporal and cognitive limits, and its contingency is inevitable because at the time of the decision the outcome is unclear and the proper action is undefined (*NE*, 1112b8–10). To be educated in ethics is not to have decisive knowledge; anticipating Heidegger's insistence on different modes of truth, Aristotle says that the mark of an educated person is seeking only the degree of precision that the nature of an endeavor will allow (*NE*, 1094b23–25). Accordingly, the philosophical discipline of ethics cannot issue exact rules and measures, it can only be sketched in broad outlines (*NE*, 1104a2) with an eye toward its instantiation by the virtuous person in concrete circumstances.[19] Truth in ethics can only be judged in terms of performances in living, otherwise it is mere words (*NE*, 1179a18–23). It should be clear that such an outlook is perfectly in line with Heidegger's notion of formal indication.[20]

ETHICS AND FORTUNE

Virtue and vice, for Aristotle, are in our power and constitute the realm of voluntary action (*NE*, III.5).[21] In connecting virtue with *eudaimonia*, Aristotle clearly alters the older notion of *eudaimonia* as good fortune granted by a sacred power (*daimon*). Aristotle does recognize, however, elements of good fortune that contribute to *eudaimonia* (*NE*, 1099b1ff, 1153b17), and one can see an analogy to the older notion in Aristotle's insistence on the necessity of good upbringing. Aristotle also exhibits resonances of the Greek sense of the tragic when he recognizes the possibility of bad fortune limiting or even ruining *eudaimonia* (1100b23ff). In other words, the good is not necessarily inscribed in reality or the human condition. It is possible for a fully virtuous person to come to grief in life, without any transcendent rectification or compensation (as in Platonism or Christianity). So it is possible for a good person to not flourish, to not experience *eudaimonia* (*NE*, 1153b14–25). Aristotle seems to acknowledge finite limits to the good life and fundamental limits on the aspirations of the human self.[22] *Eudaimonia* is not guaranteed, and indeed a realization of the full and complete contours of *eudaimonia* seems quite difficult and relatively rare. Nevertheless, *eudaimonia* can still serve as a measure for life, and a good upbringing and the practice of virtue can certainly enhance the prospects of its attainment to whatever extent possible.

HEIDEGGERIAN MODIFICATIONS OF ARISTOTLE

Aristotle's notion of *phronēsis* shows itself to be an inexact ethical finesse that discloses appropriate courses of action with respect to desired ends, or that for the sake of which human beings act. The human good involves striving to actualize natural potentials through deliberative choices. Such an ethical field connects well with Heidegger's sense of prereflective understanding, which is associated with Dasein's potentiality-for-being and for-the-sake-of-which (*Umwillen*) animating Dasein's existence.[23] Ethics for Aristotle involves human potentials and the means and conditions needed to actualize these ends. A similar kind of ethical developmentalism can be read out of *Being and Time*, although in that text there is a radicalization of Aristotle's formulations. Kierkegaardian influences in *Being and Time* show an even more dynamic, open, and contingent atmosphere than Aristotle would allow. For Heidegger, Dasein's potentiality is never filled up in any way or compensated by the comfort taken in a metaphysics of divine actuality. Dasein *is* potentiality, so full actuality is ruled out in principle. And despite the acceptance of tradition in Heidegger's analysis, the notion of authenticity opens up issues relating to the tension between individuation and conformity, which goes far beyond the gesture toward particularity in Aristotle, and which presents a more contemporary range of ethical topics regarding how we should engage social norms and controls.

Heidegger stresses elements of negativity and absence that are given only a muted voice in Aristotle. Despite Aristotle's attention to potentiality, movement, and desire-as-lack, despite his recognition of limits and the contingency of ethical truth, Aristotle still displays a (Platonic) preference for more stable modes of knowledge and the self-sufficient perfection of a divine realm. Aristotle ranks *phronēsis* lower than *sophia, nous,* and *epistēmē*, which provide necessary knowledge (*NE*, 1141a20ff). Human ethical life is constituted by limits, lacks, and needs, which is why Aristotle denies that the gods exhibit moral virtue, since they are completely self-sufficient, and thus they need or lack nothing (*NE*, 1178b10–16). The life and activity of the gods is identified with intellectual contemplation (*theoria*), which is wholly self-referential and needs nothing outside itself (*NE*, 1178b20ff). Accordingly, Aristotle names contemplation the pinnacle of human *eudaimonia*, since it is what is most godlike in humans—most self-sufficient and least burdened by desire, external needs, and relations with others (*NE*, X.7). Although Aristotle, being a good phenomenologist, sees the human, natural world as constituted by temporality and limits, he nevertheless reaches for the compensation of a metaphysics of constant presence in the divine sphere.[24]

For all Aristotle's recognition of limits in the sphere of ethics, perhaps it is the metaphysical comfort of his theology that accounts for the rather secure, undisturbed tone that resonates in his ethical works, the sense of a clearly defined, organized harmony that marks *eudaimonia*, and the relative ease and confidence with which the virtuous person seems to move through life. A Heideggerian take on *eudaimonia*, or living well, might involve more openness to negativity, disruption, and unsettlement, thereby subverting Aristotelian comforts. For Heidegger, the experience of potentiality highlights the futurial openness that marks the temporal structure of ethical decisions, and that therefore includes a more acute awareness of *not* being grounded or secured in any strict sense. A Heideggerian perspective on ethical decisions would not be restricted to various "positive" states, conditions, or dispositions. But I have also shown in Heidegger how negative dimensions play an essential role in disclosing the meaning of existential conditions. For this reason, a Heideggerian approach would have to be suspicious of the seeming security of the Aristotelian good life.

Although Dasein is always situated in a social world and shaped by tradition, the dynamic of authenticity shows that the individual self cannot be securely grounded in a community, custom, or habitual practice. The disclosing of authentic care follows from the *Unheimlichkeit* of an anxious separation from familiar supports. Heidegger identified *phronēsis* with his notion of conscience (*PS*, 39). Conscience, in Heidegger's ontological sense, calls Dasein to the nullity of its being-toward-death, and accordingly conscience "speaks" in the manner of silence (*BT*, 318). Such silence gives voice to Dasein's loss of actual supports, but it also prepares Dasein's discovery of its own possibilities. Heidegger therefore offers a radical finitization of Aristotelian *phronēsis* and potentiality, and so the ethical *kairos*, or temporal context of decision, now takes on a certain tremble. On the plus side, however, the enhanced openness of Heideggerian *phronēsis* is less tethered to its cultural milieu, and so it permits more innovation and a sharper sense of *self*-actualization of potential than is likely in the more socially composed agency of Aristotelian *phronēsis*. In the next chapter, I have more to say about this opened sense of *phronēsis* and its ethical implications.

In a way we can understand Heidegger's ontology as a radicalization of Aristotelian teleology that inscribes creative openness into temporal development.

Heidegger can affirm an Aristotelian *telos* as a being-toward, but also unsettle its confinement to the actualization of definable forms in nature and its ethical paradigm of *eudaimonia* as the full actualization of potentials in an organized harmony. For Heidegger, the ultimate *telos* of Dasein is death, which resonates to bring more edge and unease to the seeming composure of Aristotelian virtue and its unvexed naturalism.

The dynamic of authenticity is able to accommodate Nietzsche's insight that creative individuals experience and instigate a conflict with normal organizations of life; they cannot be described as seeking "happiness" in the sense of contentment or a balanced harmony of all human capacities. Nietzsche alerts us to the ambivalent coexistence of culture and creativity—in that culture is furthered by innovations that must exceed and disrupt existing cultural forms. Aristotle's world seems too conservative in lacking this creative energy. Nevertheless, Heidegger's sense of authenticity can turn to the decidedly active and performative character of Aristotelian *eudaimonia* and simply open it up to include creative departures from the norm.[25] In other words, human flourishing and living well can include certain excesses and tensions that are no less appropriate to human nature than are the more normal patterns of the social world. The advantage of the Heideggerian–Aristotelian take on this matter is that although creativity by definition cannot be managed or pressed into social normalcy, it should not be seen as utterly anarchic or separable from cultural structures either.

RETHINKING NATURALISM

It is possible to employ Heidegger's radically finite ontology to revise and unsettle Aristotle's ethical naturalism. Usually a thing's "nature" or what is "natural" is taken to mean a universal kind or a fixed essence. That is why talk of "human nature" or what is natural to human beings is a red flag in many circles of contemporary thought, because it suggests a kind of essentialism that is oppressive of otherness or difference. But this study has aimed to show that in Heidegger's thought, what is natural or intrinsic to being includes otherness, absence, movement, change, tension, and variation. In this way Heidegger departs from Aristotle by way of Hegel's insights into the historical character of being. For Heidegger, what is "natural" is always historical (*WT*, 39). The influence of Nietzsche, however, takes Heidegger beyond Hegel's progressive, systematic conception of history. The natural can be connected with Heidegger's peculiar reading of "essence" (*Wesen*), as a coming to presence that is constituted by openness rather than fixed conditions or outcomes.

It should be said that there are some interesting suggestions of such an approach to nature in Aristotle's own thought. In the *Nicomachean Ethics* (1134b18–35) he discusses the distinction between nature (*phusis*), understood as the invariant and universally valid, and convention (*nomos*), understood as the variable and relative. But he suggests that there is a sense of *phusis* that is change-able, that *phusis* may be unchangeable for the gods, but in our world nature can admit change. With his example of developing ambidexterity to overcome the natural dominance of one hand, we see that this admission of change allows more than simply the process of development in natural forms toward a completed state; it includes the possibility of altering natural conditions. In the *Politics* (1332a4ff) Aristotle states that human beings are made good by nature (*phusis*), habit (*ethos*), and reason (*logos*). All three conditions must optimally be in har-mony, but such harmony is often achieved by reason going *against* nature and habit. This remarkable passage offers some relief from Aristotle's supposed con-servatism, suggests a conception of harmony that unfolds by way of conflicting tensions (anticipating Hegel), and provides another angle on the variability of what is natural. This constellation of forces also anticipates, I think, the conflu-ence of thrownness, *das Man*, and authenticity in Heidegger's thought. With Heidegger, though, one can say in a more pronounced way that "human nature" can exhibit change, adaptation, alteration, and divergence.

With both Aristotle and Heidegger, one can at least suggest a conception of the natural that can challenge radical conventionalism and skepticism—as well as the theoretical habit of bracketing established conditions—without having to depend on some invariant order, causal necessity, or fixed essence.[26] In both thinkers can be found what I would call a "presumptive naturalism" with respect to their phe-nomenology of what is given in everyday, ordinary practices. In ethics one can talk of a presumption in favor of norms and values that have taken hold in human practice over the course of time. This would not mean that such norms and val-ues are justified as such, because we can admit the (equally natural) possibility of openness and interrogation. But the burden would be on the interrogator to show *internally* how and why a certain norm should be challenged, modified, or replaced—without the presumption of a theoretical framework that mandates a priori grounds for criticism. An ethical naturalism would be a "presumption of immanence" because it dismisses transcendent sources, wholly alternative worlds, and radical divisions between reason and nature (as in Kant), and so it proceeds on the assumption that nature would not likely operate by way of whole-sale errors (see *NE,* 1098b27–30). Both human practices and their possible alter-ations would be understood as emerging out of and within the immediate lived environment.

Our analysis might also help articulate the complexities surrounding ques-tions of the natural versus the cultural, and nature versus nurture. The relation between the natural and the cultural is often taken to mean the difference between what is given in nature and what is (merely) conventional, or intro-duced by human artifice. The manifest variety of human cultural forms encourages this division because the natural is usually taken to mean an invari-ant order (clinched by the modern objectification of nature). But we have already noticed how such a division can be disrupted. We can begin a reconstruction of this question by distinguishing between the *natural*, the *arbitrary*, and the *cultural*. The natural is what is intrinsically self-manifesting; the arbitrary is what is merely conventional, or externally superimposed; and the cultural can be located in between these polarities rather than on one side or the other. Since we have seen that the natural need not be identified with the fixed and invariant, then variations in human culture need not mean that cultural forms are arbitrary. Accordingly, we would be prompted to investigate complex intersections of nature and culture in human life.

With respect to ethics and social norms, we might begin by identifying as natural certain bearings that seem intrinsic to the human condition and that are relevant to ethical norms: for instance, the impulses to avoid pain, and to care for children. On the other side we could identify as arbitrary practices that seem utterly discretional: for instance, whether to use eating utensils, or what kind of utensils to use. Certain differing cultural norms need not be called arbitrary but rather variations on natural conditions: for instance, different modes of caring for children, and differences in the range of common human values such as compassion. So the natural and the cultural can escape the distinction between the invariant and the variant and be understood as the intrinsic and its modifications.[27] Intersections of the natural and the cultural make for complicated overlaps. Cultural variation as such can be considered natural if mutability and adaptability are recognized as intrinsic to the human condition and advantageous for human development. In fact, it may be that because of this overlapping openness, very little in human life winds up being arbitrary in the strict sense.[28]

The nature–nurture division also does not hold up under scrutiny. The consensus among most investigators into this question is that a child's nature is neither strictly biologically determined nor wholly malleable by the environment. The "second nature" of developed habits and skills represents a confluence of nature and culture that cannot be reduced to either brute facts or arbitrary superimpositions.[29] The intersection of nature and nurture is not even clearly delineable into two discrete cooperating factors. Even the womb is a contributing environment for the biological development of the fetus, and an infant's behavior will influence how caregivers in the social environment will respond to the child (and vice versa).[30] We have mentioned how language requires both an intrinsic capacity and a prompting environment for it to develop in a child. Then language itself becomes a crucial environment influencing human development (simply saying something cruel or kind can have as much impact on a child as a physical event). With Heidegger this linguistic environment is intrinsically open, since language is able to give presence to the absences of past and future, and accordingly extend immeasurably the possibilities of, and influences on, human experience, thought, and action. In sum, from a Heideggerian perspective, what is natural to the human condition can be understood as anything but fixed and invariable.

NOTES

1. For two important essays on the Heidegger–Aristotle connection, see Franco Volpi, *"Being and Time*: A 'Translation' of the *Nicomachean Ethics?"* and Walter Brogan, "The Place of Aristotle in the Development of Heidegger's Phenomenology," in *Reading Heidegger from the Start: Essays in His Earliest Thought*, ed. Theodore Kisiel and John van Buren (Albany: SUNY Press, 1994).

2. See the analysis of Aristotle and mathematics in *PS* (section 15), which mirrors Heidegger's later interrogation of modern science.

3. See *AM*, 40–46.

4. For example, *NE*, I.1 and 4.

5. Aristotle analyzes "having" (*echein*) as something "in between" the haver and the thing had (*Metaphysics*, V.20), and even as something that can "have" the haver, as when a fever "possesses" a man (V.23). In this way, *zōon logon echon* can express Heidegger's contention that language just as much possesses Dasein as Dasein possesses language. See Theodore Kisiel's analysis in *The Genesis of Heidegger's* Being and Time (Berkeley: University of California Press, 1993), 281–301.

6. *Phusis* is derived from *phuō* meaning to grow or emerge. Heidegger concludes that Aristotle does not consider *ousia* or being as static or unchanging, but as fully consonant with temporal emergence and development (*ECP*, 186–208).

7. Heidegger's analysis certainly helps us make sense out of Aristotle's unusual claim that privation (*sterēsis*) is in a way an *eidos* (*Physics*, 193b19–20), and that negative states have a kind of being (*Metaphysics*, 1004a10ff).

8. Heidegger admits that his own work is stressing implications that Aristotle himself did not fully work out and that Aristotle did not articulate a radically temporal ontology. Nevertheless, the seeds are there in Aristotle's analysis of *dunamis* and *energeia* (*AM*, 189ff).

9. Aristotle offers an unmistakably unified correlation of potentiality, actuality, making, doing, and being in an interesting passage from the *Nicomachean Ethics* (1167b31–1168a10), which describes a producer as loving his product because it is his being, understood as the actualization of potential. Aristotle's argument runs as follows. Being (*einai*) is what is desired and loved by all; our being is given in activity and actualization, since we *are* a living and doing; a work (*ergon*) is the maker actualized, and so it is the being of the maker; so the maker loves his work because he loves his own being. All of this is described as part of nature (*phusikon*), in the sense that the process of actualizing a potential is the very revelation of a thing's being.

10. Key examples are accidental being, being true and false, the being of the categories, and the being of *dunamis* and *energeia* (*Metaphysics*, 1026a33–b2). See Heidegger's analysis in *AM*, 9–33. Aristotle also suggests multiple senses of being in terms of different as-operators that disclose things variously from different vantage points (see *Metaphysics*, 1042b155ff). This compares with Heidegger's interpretive as-structures.

11. See *PS*, sections 4–26.

12. Aristotle, like Heidegger, specifically connects the notions of being and truth: "to the extent to which a thing has being, to that extent it has truth" (*Metaphysics*, 993b30–31).

13. See John van Buren, "The Young Heidegger, Aristotle, Ethics," in *Ethics and Danger: Essays on Heidegger and Continental Thought*, ed. Arleen Dallery and Charles E. Scott (Albany: SUNY Press, 1992), 169–85. See also Robert Bernasconi, "Heidegger's

Destruction of *Phronēsis*" *Southern Journal of Philosophy*, vol. 28 supplement (1990): 127–47, which includes a survey of the literature on this topic.

14. See also Heidegger's extended discussion of Aristotle in *PS*, sections 4–26.

15. I will not be engaging various issues and problems surrounding the interpretation of Aristotle's ethics. Some significant scholarly studies include Amélie Oksenberg Rorty, ed., *Essays on Aristotle's Ethics* (Berkeley: University of California Press, 1980); John P. Anton and Anthony Preus, eds., *Aristotle's Ethics* (Albany: SUNY Press, 1991); Sarah Broadie, *Ethics with Aristotle* (New York: Oxford University Press, 1991); and Nancy Sherman, ed., *Aristotle's Ethics: Critical Essays* (Lanham, Md.: Rowman & Littlefield, 1999).

16. See Heidegger's analysis of striving as a being-toward (*AM*, 128) and of deliberation as the temporal confluence of a "not yet" and an "already" (*AI*, 381). It should be noted that *oreksis* can be associated with Heidegger's sense of being-toward, since it is derived from the verb *oregō*, meaning to stretch out or reach out.

17. See *Physics*, 194b27, where form is called the *logos* of a being, as in the case of octave ratios, and *On the Soul*, 407b34, where *logos* is connected with attunement (*harmonia*). For details on the complex and varied meanings of *logos* in Greek, see W. K. C. Guthrie, *A History of Greek Philosophy*, vol. I (Cambridge: Cambridge University Press, 1962), 420–24. In addition to standard philosophical meanings of reason, law, principle, and argument, *logos* expressed many "nonlogical" senses such as anything spoken, a story, an account, news or tidings, conversation, mention or notice, esteem, thought, truth, measure, relation, and proportion. As Guthrie indicates, for the Greeks it was possible for many of these meanings to resonate together.

18. For a rich and extensive study of the differences between Aristotle and Plato on the good life, see Martha Nussbaum, *The Fragility of Goodness* (Cambridge: Cambridge University Press, 1986).

19. Thus Aristotle would find fault with the Rawlsian ideal of a "moral geometry." See John Rawls, *A Theory of Justice* (Cambridge, Mass.: Harvard University Press, 1971), 121. Rawls's aim for a "reflective equilibrium" between moral theory and our given intuitions bears some connection with an Aristotelian approach (see 48–51). Nevertheless, differences in what is meant by rationality remain an obstacle for any coordinating efforts here.

20. Van Buren develops this connection in "The Ethics of *Formale Anzeige* in Heidegger," *American Catholic Philosophical Quarterly*, vol. 69, no. 2 (1995): 157–70.

21. Aristotle does not offer a doctrine of metaphysical freedom along the lines of some modern projects, but simply a phenomenology of actions that are self-activated rather than compelled (*NE*, 1135a24ff).

22. For a rich discussion of the intrinsic limits of ethical life in Aristotle, see Nussbaum, *The Fragility of Goodness*, ch. 11.

23. Hans-Georg Gadamer, who was greatly influenced by Heidegger's early Aristotle lectures, takes up the relation between *phronēsis* and *Verstehen*, especially in *Truth and Method*, trans. G. Barden and J. Cumming (New York: Seabury, 1975). See also *The Idea of the Good in Platonic–Aristotelian Philosophy*, trans. P. Christopher Smith (New Haven, Conn.: Yale University Press, 1986). For an articulate application of Gadamerian hermeneutics to ethics, see P. Christopher Smith, *Hermeneutics and Human Finitude: Toward a Theory of Ethical Understanding* (New York: Fordham University Press, 1991). Smith does important work in bringing finitude to bear on moral philosophy, although from my perspective there is an overemphasis on community and tradition.

24. The eternal presence of immaterial form in the divine mind gives Aristotle an ultimate metaphysical reference point to resolve the negativity of the natural world. Although in each natural phenomenon potentiality precedes actuality, perfect form in the divine mind represents the paradigmatic basis for the strivings and movements of natural developing forms. It is at this level that "actuality is prior to potentiality" (*Metaphysics*, 1072a9). Without such a divine reference point, we would be forced to give ultimate priority to potentiality, in which case we would be left with the unacceptable notion that things arise out of "nonbeing" (*Metaphysics*, 1072a19ff). Heidegger's phenomenology can be understood as a reversal of Aristotle's classic metaphysical proposition; for Heidegger, potentiality is prior to actuality.

25. In an early work, Heidegger associates Aristotelian *eudaimonia* with "the authenticity of human Dasein" (*PS*, 118).

26. For some, ethical naturalism entails reducing values to facts, moral properties to nonmoral properties. With Heidegger we can sidestep this model, avoid the fact–value binary, and simply argue that moral phenomena have a kind of "being" and are intrinsic to human life, rather than being merely conventional or subjective. Ethical naturalism too often has assumed that the natural can only be understood according to the modern conception of disenchanted nature, which of course makes the association with values problematic from the start. On this point, see John McDowell, "Two Sorts of Naturalism," in *Virtues and Reasons: Philippa Foot and Moral Theory*, ed. Rosilind Hursthouse, Gavin Lawrence, and Warren Quinn (Oxford: Clarendon Press, 1995), ch. 6. See also Bernard Williams's discussion of the naturalistic fallacy and its shortcomings in *Ethics and the Limits of Philosophy* (Cambridge, Mass.: Harvard University Press, 1985), ch. 7.

27. See Stuart Hampshire, *Morality and Conflict* (Cambridge, Mass.: Harvard University Press, 1983), 142–43. In chapter 7, Hampshire overplays the distinction between nature and social conventions, which I think lies behind his overstatement of the extent of conflict in moral life.

28. See Phillippe Descola and Gísli Pálsson, eds., *Nature and Society: Anthropological Perspectives* (New York: Routledge, 1996), a collection of papers arguing against the strict distinction between nature and culture. For a discussion of the unfeasibility of the natural–human binary, see Steven Vogel, "Nature as Origin and Difference: On Environmental Philosophy and Continental Thought," *Philosophy Today*, vol. 42 supplement (1998): 169–81. Evolution theory certainly suggests the natural advantages of open adaptability over rigid routines for biological organisms. I leave aside a treatment of recent discussions of ethics from an evolutionary perspective, although I think a Heideggerian orientation can be profitably brought to bear on such discussions. Doing this matter justice, however, would take an entire chapter of its own, which length constraints will not permit. For a provocative study that aims to coordinate evolution with Aristotelian ethics, see Larry Arnhart, *Darwinian Natural Right: The Biological Ethics of Human Nature* (Albany: SUNY Press, 1998).

29. For important discussions of second nature in response to various conundrums of modern philosophy, see John McDowell, *Mind and World* (Cambridge, Mass.: Harvard University Press, 1994). McDowell's work has some affinities with Heideggerian thought, especially his notion of meaning-laden concepts taken as an openness to the world.

30. See Elliot Turiel, Melanie Killen, and Charles C. Helwig, "Morality: Its Structure, Function, and Vagaries," in *The Emergence of Morality in Young Children*, ed. Jerome Kagan and Sharon Lamb (Chicago: University of Chicago Press, 1987), ch. 4.

Chapter Five

Virtue

For much of the twentieth century, moral philosophy was primarily engaged in debates between deontological and consequentialist theories. Then what has come to be called virtue ethics came on the scene, in part as a revival of an Aristotelian orientation.[1] Virtue ethics is not restricted to human actions, the consequences of actions, or rules and principles to guide actions; it focuses on character traits and dispositions at the heart of human actions, capacities that are needed to lead a good life and to act appropriately in ethical situations. Virtue ethics gives voice to the way in which we assess persons and not just actions. When we admire a benevolent person, for instance, we extol more than simply benevolent acts. Someone who performs a helping act, but simply with an eye toward reciprocation or reward, would not be considered a benevolent person. When we think of a benevolent person, we think of certain dispositions, such as a genuine interest in the well-being of others. Virtues, then, involve existential capacities, motivations, aims, and bearings that mark *how* one lives ethically. Virtues point to the very being of the self in Heideggerian terms—that is, not simply what one does, but who one is and how one exists in the world.

A vivid portrayal of the question of virtue can be found in book II of Plato's *Republic*, where a story is told of a man who finds a magic ring that renders him invisible, which symbolizes absolute impunity. The man proceeds to violate various norms of behavior in pursuit of his own interests. The point of the story is to advance a version of psychological egoism, namely that human beings follow ethical norms only because of external forces such as punishment, that they have no internal motivation or interest in, say, refraining from abusing others. A main concern of Socrates in the course of the dialogue is arguing for the possibility of virtue, of an internalized sense of the good that would prompt right action even in the absence of external constraints. In other words, virtue allows for a self-motivated ethical life as opposed to merely following rules or avoiding penalties.

Virtue, then, in the terms of my discussion, can be construed as ethical authenticity, in the sense of coming to one's own interest in, capacity for, and commitment to ethical practice.

Virtue in this sense would not be sufficient for ethics, however. Environmental and institutional constraints will likely always be a part of social life. But the question of virtue is at least opened up by considering the relationship between the ethical and political spheres. Political and legal institutions reflect in one way or another the norms and values of a society, but with the addition of tangible and coercive penalties in response to transgressions. Such institutions could be said to embody the limits of virtue, of a self-motivated ethical life. Public regulations represent an external force governing the self, but the issue of virtue is still a central concern in addressing how human beings exist ethically in a lived sense. Virtue ethics comes closest to the kind of treatment I am pursuing in this investigation. Virtue construed as authentic being-ethical-in-the-world can provide a richer treatment of selfhood than can be found in modern conceptions of moral agency that aim to move from external governance to *rational* self-governance, which certainly provides self-directedness but at the cost of bypassing the complex range of existential forces that shape being-in-the-world.

The sense of virtue I am drawing from Aristotle and Heidegger should not be taken simply as an agent-centered ethics as opposed to an act-centered ethics, nor should it be confined to a discrete self as distinct from environmental factors and institutional forces. Virtue not only introduces affective, dispositional, and performative elements to disrupt the modern emphasis on subject-centered reason, it also disrupts the modern ideal of autonomy, strictly construed. Virtue as ethical authenticity would not be separable from Dasein's upbringing, cultural inheritance, sociality, thrown situatedness, and especially its ekstatic, environmental responsiveness. That is why it is a mistake to counterpose virtue and institutional forces. Not only do educational institutions play a crucial role in the cultivation of virtues, but sometimes coercive legal constraints are needed not only to enforce certain norms, but also to trigger or open space for shifts of social moods and attitudes that would otherwise be suppressed or lie dormant. A good example of this is the long-term effects of civil rights legislation in the United States. In short, virtue should not be overinternalized or individuated, since it intersects with environmental settings.[2]

ARISTOTLE AND VIRTUE

I have shown that Aristotelian virtues are moral excellences that allow for the fruition of human potentialities and the appropriate organization of desires in pursuit of human goods. Each virtue is characterized as the capacity to discover a mean state between two extremes of excess and deficiency. I have suggested the notion of a balancing act to better express what Aristotle construes as a mean. In the next section I explore the complexities and difficulties attaching to the idea of a mean, which can imply a stable and decipherable locus that even Aristotle's texts call into question. For now I can say that Aristotelian virtue involves the dynamic disclosure and performance of appropriate ethical bearings in the midst of conflicting tensions.

For Aristotle, each virtue involves (1) a certain situation or context of action, (2) a certain affect, attitude, and capacity for action with respect to that situation, (3) vices of excess and defect with respect to the affect, attitude, or capacity, and (4) the virtue of the appropriate mean between the two vices. For example, in dangerous situations, regarding the attitude of fear, the virtue of courage is the mean between cowardice (too much fear) and foolhardiness (too little fear). In the situation of helping others, regarding the desire to help, the virtue of generosity is the mean between extravagance and miserliness. In the situation of self-appraisal, regarding the attitude of self-affirmation, the virtue of pride is the mean between boastful vanity and false modesty or self-debasement. Regarding insults, injuries, and the emotion of anger, the virtue of proper indignation is the mean between ill-tempered irascibility and apathy or submissiveness.

In Aristotle, a virtue becomes a mode of the soul's being, a *hexis*, or "having" (*NE*, 1106a13), a capacity to make appropriate choices in various ethical contexts. A *hexis* does not arise in the soul automatically; it requires prior training, cultivation, and repetition until it becomes habit, or second nature (see *NE*, 1152a31–34). Just as one becomes skilled in playing a musical instrument by training and practice, one becomes courageous and understands courage by performing courageous actions (*NE*, II.1). An ethical habit, for Aristotle, is not some mechanical operation or instinctive drive, but an acquired capacity to act well that eventually can become relatively unforced and natural, without strain. As an appropriated manner of being, we could call habit a mode of dwelling, or in-habiting an ethical environment.[3]

Aristotle seems to be saying that a truly virtuous person will do the right thing without much analysis or difficulty. A summary of Aristotle's ideal conception of virtue can be gleaned from his discussion of *akrasia*, or weakness of will (*NE*, VII.1–10). Aristotle distinguishes persons as being virtuous, morally strong, morally weak, and vicious. A virtuous person does good effortlessly, habitually, even with pleasure (*NE*, 1099a6ff). A morally strong person knows what is good but struggles to do it. A morally weak person knows what is good but fails to do it. A vicious person acts badly without regret. We would tend to call the morally strong person virtuous in many respects, but Aristotle would not. Aristotle's ethical ideal, though difficult to achieve, seems to be a self-composed person who moves through life with relative ease, whose desires have become properly organized, and who possesses all the virtues as a unified whole (*NE*, 1145a1–2).[4]

UNCONCEALMENT AND VIRTUE

I want to suggest an alternative reading of Aristotelian virtue drawn from Heidegger's ontological construal of *phronēsis*, in such a way as to bring more openness and finitude to the apparent comfort of Aristotle's doctrine of the mean. In his lecture course *Parmenides*, Heidegger offers an ontological rendering of *phronēsis* in terms of unconcealment. He provides a fascinating discussion of the concluding myth in the *Republic* (*P*, 118–21), presumably in light of the double-movement of being-toward-death and care. Heidegger interprets the souls drinking from the river *Ameles* (carefreeness, indifference) as follows: The river represents concealment, and souls must drink a *proper measure* of its water before returning to earth, the realm of unconcealment. Those who drink too much of the water cannot return to earth because they lack the proper "insight" (in Plato's text, *phronēsis*) that balances concealment and unconcealment. A few pages later (*P*, 123), Heidegger argues that complete concealment, measureless oblivion, is contrary to human essence, which should be seen rather as a "measure" of concealment and unconcealment—that is, the two forces are always correlated. Pure concealment is the oblivion of nothingness. Pure unconcealment is the metaphysics of constant presence generated from a fallen immersion in beings. This suggests that humans dwell, or should dwell, in an ontological balancing of concealment and unconcealment, a balancing, in the language of *Being and Time*, of being-toward-death and care. And Heidegger specifically associates such balancing with *phronēsis*.

I can link this discussion to the ontical–ethical meaning of Aristotelian *phronēsis* as the discovery of a mean between extreme ontic conditions—which *as* extreme conceal each other and the proper virtue in between. In other words, each vice conceals by unconcealing too much, and virtue would be the measured balance of these extremes that discloses what is concealed by each vice. This suggests that virtue is a kind of blending of the force of opposing conditions that discloses an otherwise concealed truth. This sense of blending is suggested in the *Eudemian Ethics*, where Aristotle writes that "the extremes are opposed to one another and to the mean," and "the mean is each one of the opposites in relation to the other" (1220b31–33).[5] Courage, then, could be construed as a balance between the force of cowardice and foolhardiness (between too much care and too little care). What is provocative here is that too much of a good thing (caution or risk) is no longer good. Too much unconcealment, unbalanced by otherness, creates an absence, a concealment of its appropriate apportionment in ethical action. It is as though courage arises within a continuum of force in two directions and is disclosed as a balancing of both directions of force. An excess of caution and an excess of risk conceal what *both* contribute to the appropriate condition of courage. Ethical situations can be seen as a play of concealment and unconcealment in the tension of human possibilities. *Phronēsis* can be understood as the balancing of this tension at moments of decision, as the capacity for responsive and appropriate action.

With the radical finitude of Heidegger's ontology, we can push further the implications of Aristotle's openness to contingency in his departure from the perfectionism of Platonic ethics. We might do better in rendering ethical experience by substituting an oscillating *balancing act* for the notion of a mean, because a mean suggests some "middle point" between two poles that even distorts the sense of virtuous action displayed in Aristotle's texts. The ethical mean, for Aristotle, is not like a numerical or spatial mean, which would be uniform for all cases (*NE*, 1106a27ff). As I have indicated, virtuous action varies according to the context, the specific individual, and the temporal situation (*kairos*). Sometimes the mean will be closer to one of the extremes than to the other (*Eudemian Ethics*, 1222a22ff): for instance, some situations might demand more or less generosity. Sometimes degrees of deficiency or excess can be praiseworthy (*NE*, 1109b16ff), as in the case of certain strong passions that might be useful in leadership. A general account of the mean is difficult to articulate, since it is relative to particular cases and perceptions (*NE*, 1126b3–4).

Even if we consider specific discoveries of the mean by particular individuals, what would tell them that they had found some "middle point" (suggested in *NE*, 1109a26)? If there is no general formula for finding the mean, why formalize the matter at all by suggesting some measure borrowed from mathematics? Instead we can call *phronēsis* a balancing act in the midst of counterforces, and in the manner of an oscillating attunement. This would be consistent with Aristotle's remarks about finding the mean by tending toward the extremes (*NE*, 1109b2ff). The measure of virtuous action would not be some generalizable or even particularizable locus of precision, but more a mode of disclosure (recall the association of *phronēsis* with truth) that unfolds as an experiment in learning how to live well, an experiment that proceeds by experiencing conflicting forces and possibilities, and discovering balances that foster successful living. As Aristotle says, individuals have different natural tendencies and aims, and they come to learn what works well by tending in conflicting directions and gauging—by consequent pleasures and pains—the appropriate path (*NE*, 1109b2–7).

In light of Heidegger's ungrounded dynamic of unconcealment and disclosure by way of negation, the Aristotelian sense of the mean does not so much define or locate a proper action, as much as set the negative boundaries for what is out of line (the vices), and open space for individual appropriation and disclosure somewhere between these boundaries. Virtue as a call for a balancing act within these boundaries can be called an ethical version of Heidegger's notion of formal indication, that is, a general outline that can only be actualized in concrete cases and in different ways. In certain respects, many moral theories can be understood as an emphasis on the formal element at the expense of the indicative element, as an attempt to decisively govern concrete cases by the force of general principles.

Heidegger's phenomenology of finite being-in-the-world can help illuminate what prompts these theoretical tendencies. As Aristotle says, the specificity of virtuous action entails that it is difficult to achieve (*NE*, 1106b16–35). There are a number of ways to understand the difficulty of virtue. It is easy to simply follow any and every impulse that arises. From a deliberative standpoint, it is likewise easy to act according to a general rule (Follow every impulse, Never lie, Always support your friends). The formal–indicative character of virtue, however, is difficult in that it demands attentive finesse with regard to the variances, complexities, and contingencies of concrete circumstances, a finesse that is formally unstable in being case-specific.

This suggests another kind of difficulty that Heidegger emphasizes. The specificity of virtuous action entails that there is no external or formulaic support for ethical action, which is thus ungrounded in the sense of being unconcealed in a finite process of immediate disclosure. The formal character of virtue (Find the appropriate balance between extremes) does not "ground" the indicative character of virtuous action (What *is* the appropriate balance in this situation?); rather, it "points" to the task of its discovery. This existential difficulty can generate anxiety in the face of an ungrounded task, which can prompt an interest in, or need for, a refuge in various stable forms of support (religious commands, traditional customs, social patterns, laws, rational principles). Here Heidegger's analysis of the finite burden of authenticity in relation to the familiar comforts of inauthentic existence can be given an ontical, ethical meaning in the light of Aristotelian virtue. And indeed, Heidegger connects resoluteness (authentic, care-ful action in the midst of being-toward-death) with *aretē* (*P*, 74).[6]

In view of the radical finitude of a Heideggerian *phronēsis*, Aristotelian virtue can be modified as a more open and less stable phenomenon. And given Dasein's situatedness, a contextual analysis of virtue can be advanced that is not restricted to qualities of the self, but rather open to different kinds of performance and involvement. In other words, virtue as a balancing act can be seen as a shifting measure depending on context and circumstance, which can present different and even conflicting types of bipolar extremes that call for balancing. Virtue, then, could be expanded beyond Aristotle's somewhat singular and harmonized model to include more complexity and tension, both within and between selves.[7] So the formal indication of "living well" need not be structured identically across the spectrum of human lives, and need not require an overarching harmonious order within any particular human life. This is not to invite chaos but rather a sense of limits regarding any and all structures.[8]

A contextual analysis can show different and conflicting senses of virtue that cannot always be harmonized or paralleled. As has long been recognized, the virtues of a soldier in many respects diverge from civilian virtues. There are overlaps between the two spheres, but soldiers have to find balancing acts regarding risk, aggression, and violence that in other contexts would be considered vices. Aside from the obvious traumas of warfare, this ethical schism has been the source of some of the deepest and most lasting psychological troubles. Positions of political and organizational leadership also entail certain capacities and qualities that can be quite different from those appropriate for other associations (such as with relatives, friends, or co-workers). The roles of management, decision making, and responsibility for outcomes will elicit performances and call on virtues that can appear problematic from other standpoints; yet these differing virtues are generally appropriate for the different contexts. People in leadership positions must inhabit these divergences and experience their tensions.

Heidegger's phenomenological pluralism can help account for ineluctable ethical conflict and ambiguity. Recall the multiple as-structures in the case of a tree discussed in the first chapter. The disclosure of a tree as a thing of beauty and as an obstacle in a road site can issue conflicting standpoints regarding the same phenomenon. In the same way, a human posture *as* a parent and *as* an employee and *as* a citizen can come into conflict in an ethical setting. Consider the case of a whistle-blower with a family to support. With Heidegger one can say that each hermeneutical "as" has its legitimate status, and that a resulting conflict is not always a deficiency that needs resolving by sorting out the true from the untrue postures, the important from the unimportant postures. This tensional pluralism fits well with our experience of many moral situations *as* conflicts, rather than as nothing more than challenging and complex problems waiting to be solved by the application of some formula. Sometimes moral conflicts are unresolvable and we must simply dwell in ambivalence.

One issue that greatly concerned Heidegger was the conflict between creativity and normalcy. Inspired by Nietzsche, Heidegger wanted to contest the common patterns of everydayness and *das Man* on behalf of the innovative work of artists and thinkers. As I have said, Heidegger would not segregate creativity from normalcy, since the former arises from, and is made possible by, the latter.[9] With authenticity, Heidegger makes room for creative divergences from established patterns. Yet, as Nietzsche has expertly shown, creative activity and creative types exhibit different characteristics from the norm: Creative people are more comfortable with, even excited by, risk, disorder, and openness; they tend to have more productive energy and stronger passions; they experience discontent with established conditions and procedures; and they take pleasure in challenging the commonplace.

The obvious problem is that creativity seems to be at odds with the Aristotelian mean, yet culture can be and has been advanced by creative types and their divergences. This problem need not call for a segregation of creativity from ethics on the assumption that ethics is the sphere of normalcy and regulated behavior. On the contrary, my analysis permits a shifting measure of virtue that can accommodate an "ethics" of creativity. We need not be confined to a generalized conception of a mean that sees any excess or intense condition as a vice. Certain aspects and contexts of creativity suggest that sometimes a reach toward a more extreme state is *better* than a more moderated balance. Here I simply radicalize Aristotle's sensitivity to context, difference, contingency, and his remarks about tending toward extremes to find the mean. A more open sense of *phronēsis* can both make room for creative experience and articulate its appropriate virtues, its own balancing acts. Creative activity is not sheer chaos; it operates as a mix of disrupting existing forms, experiencing the open horizons of new possibilities, and shaping new forms. All of this can involve its own sense of appropriate balancing (too much disruption and openness can be disintegrating and unproductive). The context of creativity, however, is quite different from other contexts, and from the standpoint of normal settings it can prompt anxiety, fear, and resistance. Here are two spheres that in many respects would seem to be incommensurable. How could we normalize creativity or recommend divergence as a general norm? And yet both spheres are necessary for culture, and the tensions between them (and the experiencing of these tensions) would seem to be an ineradicable feature of life. Indeed, where would ethics be without certain elements of creative divergence in its history?

This Heideggerian take on Aristotelian virtue suggests an ungrounded, heterogeneous, unregulable finesse that dwells with the task of disclosing appropriate balances in the midst of tensional forces. Its ungrounded character would not stand as support for sheer license, however, because of the stipulation of prior socialization and the need for responsiveness to the different ethical environments. Yet in light of Heideggerian notions of possibility and being-in-question, virtue must include an openness to the complexities, ambiguities, contingencies, and incommensurabilities in ethical life that normal patterns of socialization and some moral theories tend to conceal.

One could even draw from Heidegger a basic virtue of "negative capability," which can be construed as an openness to finitude, a capacity to dwell with negative conditions and limits in one's existence.[10] Heidegger's thought helps us see that such a virtue is much more than simply a tolerance of finitude. It is a disposition that prompts sensitivity to the complexities of life and restraint of the tendencies toward simplification, universalization, and homogeneity. And given the correlation between limit conditions and meaning, negative capability is a virtue that permits a fuller, richer, more acute sense of the meaning of ethical possibilities in their tensional character.[11] Finally, negative capability can have the ameliorating effect of spawning attitudes that are less dogmatic, polarized, and sanctimonious, and less susceptible to despair or resentment.

In sum, virtue can be called a phronetic, experimental capacity to discover in various contexts appropriate balancing acts in a tensional environment. Such a phronetic element can also apply to ethical *thinking* as well, and thus to moral philosophy. Rather than search for an overarching, uniform theory to govern action, we can find in historical contributions to ethics various polarities that call for balancing acts in addressing social possibilities: egoism and altruism, individuality and community, responsibility and fortune, virtue and regulation.

VIRTUE AND DESIRE

Two main virtues in Aristotle's analysis are moderation (*sōphrosunē*) and courage (*andreia*), respectively having to do with pleasure and pain. In the light of my analysis, I want to explore a modified and expanded treatment of these ethical capacities to illustrate how a Heideggerian approach to virtue can be fleshed out. The virtue of moderation involves bodily pleasures and desires, and is marked by a balance between overindulgence and insensitivity or abstinence. For Aristotle, desire permeates all parts of the soul, and pleasure as well can be experienced in all forms of virtue. I would like to draw from this a general discussion of the ethical significance of desire, supplemented by a notion of authentic desire that can be drawn from Heideggerian phenomenology.

In Aristotle, desire is the *dunamis* that moves human life, and so it indicates what Heidegger calls Dasein's being as potentiality. Desire exhibits a temporal toward-which structure, a striving that is animated by an experienced lack or absence in relation to a desired end. Desire, in Heideggerian terms, is the existential presence of an absence that draws Dasein's concern for something in the world. With Aristotle and Heidegger, what is provocative about the phenomenology of desire is that it need not be reduced to crude biological drives or forces counterposed to more cognitive states, and it need not be confined to the self or subject. For both thinkers, human desires, as interests, are saturated with understanding and so could not be reducible to so-called irrational drives that need to be "conjoined" with cognitive structures in order to be properly directed or shaped. And the bipolarity of desire as a mode of being-in-the-world suggests that desire can be implicated in world-disclosure. As I suggested earlier, desire is not simply a condition of the self, but also the world's "beckoning" to be opened up. This strange-sounding notion is given more plausibility when considering the ekstatic in/there/with structure of Dasein. The experience of desire is often prompted by ekstatic fascinations, absorptions, and interests, and thus is much more ambiguous than a simple stimulus–response structure or an inside-out phenomenon grounded in something like the will.[12] In one work, Heidegger associates desire (*oreksis*) with a double-movement that suggests the kind of middle voice in between subjectivity and objectivity, activity and passivity, that has always marked his reflections on being (*BP*, 136).[13]

What can this contribute to ethics? First of all, the long-standing correlation of goods and desires can be given ontological weight and emancipated from overly subjective constructions. Second, the temporal structure of desire and its intrinsically open character as possibility capture the ungrounded elements of ethical life that cannot be reduced to conditions of actuality. Finally, desire coupled with the trajectory of fallenness in Heidegger's analysis can speak to perennial ethical concerns about desire as an existential problem, that is, an excessive absorption in, or attachment to, life interests or things in the world. It is important, however, to distinguish a Heideggerian approach to desire in this vein from certain traditional strategies of scripting the problem of desire as a lure to surpass the world or insulate the self from the sensuous conditions of earthly life. With Heidegger, the solution to the problem of desire would not be an overcoming of desire, but a phronetic balancing act that can be illuminated by the bipolarity of desire as world-disclosive care.

I have noted the double-movement of care and being-toward-death in Heidegger's thought, the intrinsic correlation of meaning and unmeaning. Heidegger's finite ontology affirms the significance of *unheimlich* experiences. Yet the phronetic balancing of unconcealment and concealment avoids extremes in either direction. A life without estrangements and losses would be a life without meaning and growth. Yet too much estrangement can lead to disintegration, trauma, incapacitation, or perhaps excessive attachments as a refuge from finitude. As I indicated in an earlier chapter, the plausibility of the proposed balancing movement is borne out by developmental psychology.[14] In early life, experiences of loss and responses to separation are an index to a child's development and adjustments in later life. Too much care and too little care are both detrimental. Overprotectiveness stifles growth and resiliency. Parental neglect, withdrawal, or abuse can produce excessive separation experiences that make coping with loss even harder, which explains the irony that it is often harder for children to leave an abusive home.[15] Early experiences of acute insecurity or deprivation make toleration of loss more difficult, and can also spawn excessive self-regard and hyperattachments to compensate for looming stress and anxiety.[16]

The phenomenon of desire gives some existential specificity to Heidegger's care structure and the dynamic of inauthentic fallenness. First of all, desire is obviously a mode of care, an interest in the world and human possibilities.[17] Second, desire as an open striving resonates with Heidegger's alternative to ontologies of actuality. Third, the force of desire can be implicated in the fallen absorption in beings and actualities, which conceals or suppresses the primacy of finite possibility. In short, desire is a dynamic mode of disclosure that can involve both the openness of potentiality and the closure of actuality. A phronetic balancing of these forces could suggest something like "authentic desire."[18]

The bipolar structure of desire, which can be characterized as an ekstatic interest-*in*-something, fits, I think, the Heideggerian notion of appropriation, the belonging together of being and human existence. Could we say that, leaning on the human side, desire is experienced as an absence that prompts a towards-which, while on the being side, desire intimates a beckoning-withdrawal that discloses the world as open possibility and the captivating allure of hidden prospects? We should recall that authentic care out of being-toward-death breaks the hold of familiar actualities to reveal their finitude, which now *as* possibilities illuminated by negation can be more richly disclosed by the sharpened attention of Dasein. Finite care does not look past the world but is an acute responsiveness to concrete situations (*BT*, 346–48), as opposed to the superficial evasions and concealments of fallen everydayness. We can redescribe authentic care in this sense as responsive desire, a middle-voiced bearing that is neither the refuge of clinging need nor a disengagement from the world.

Inauthentic fallenness may be an inevitable consequence of desire-as-lack, where the force of anxiety looming in absence experiences can spawn an excessive attachment to actuality in order to "fill up" the lack and keep it at bay. Authentic engagement with the world is made possible by an openness to the negativity of desire-as-withdrawal, to its inevitable excess of possibility. Authentic desire, then, could follow from being educated in the finitude of being, where one can overcome the "addiction" to presence and actuality that prompts a flitting about in search of perpetual fixes of surface stimulation, acquisition, and consumption.[19] Such addiction is not only an alienation from the meaning of being in general, but also from a deeper sense and appreciation of specific phenomena in the world. Authentic desire without fixation would be more attuned to *what* one is interested in than simply to its capacity to fill up or ward off a lack.[20] Can we say that the beckoning-withdrawal on the being side of desire is a kind of perpetual invitation to search further than surface stimulation or exigency, to *dwell* with things in their intricate richness and openness, which is concealed by a compulsion to satisfy urges, meet practical needs, and take comfort in fixed results?

Heidegger suggests something along these lines in an early lecture course (*HCT*, 295–97), where he distinguishes between urge (*Drang*), inclination (*Hang*), and authentic care (*echte Sorge*). All three are modes of care, but authentic care is distinguished first from the compulsiveness of urge, which is a blind confinement to need satisfaction that conceals the "full structure of care," and second from the involved attachment of inclination, which improves upon urge in being drawn by the "what" and not just the need, but which conceals the open finitude of genuine care because of excessive absorption. Heidegger insists that both urge and inclination (need and attachment) are inevitable in human experience, yet they can be expanded and fulfilled by authentic care.

This might serve as a model for authentic desire, which can be called a responsive openness, something different from either attachment to, or detachment from, the world. The element of *openness* stems from the negativity of desire. Human beings tend to take refuge from finitude in either existential or theoretical ways. An existential refuge can be found in a fallen attachment to life interests, things, or need satisfactions, or in an ascetic, religious, or pessimistic withdrawal from life. A theoretical refuge can be found in objectivism and thought constructions that screen out the contingencies of lived experience (and that thus share some of the tendencies of existential withdrawal). The element of *responsiveness* in authentic desire fulfills Heidegger's unique approach to finitude. The negativity of being does not cancel out meaning; it enhances meaning by banking on the "charge" that limit conditions bring to illuminating things. And from a structural standpoint, note how the three refuges cited above (attachment, withdrawal, and theorization) are all compressed within the needs and concerns of the self or reflective subject—and thus are *different* from a more responsive openness to things as they show themselves (what Heidegger calls letting-be). Authentic desire, then, would be neither a fallen attachment to the world nor a withdrawn detachment from the world. Each extreme can be diagnosed as a flight from both finitude and appropriate disclosure. Authentic desire is an existential bearing that is interested, involved, responsive to its world, and attuned to limits.

The phenomenon of desire helps illuminate how and why humans become enmeshed in inauthentic fallenness, and it also opens up the possibility of authentic responsiveness. Dasein's in/there/with structure shows how both fallen absorption and responsive openness are possible. Desire is existentially problematic when its force prompts an excessive confinement to human interests, spawning all manner of self-centered or subject-centered outlooks. Authentic desire exhibits an appropriate balancing of human striving and an openness to the world.

This analysis of desire is certainly applicable to ethics in a number of ways. It speaks to the strong attachments and self-regarding interests that make certain ethical appeals hard to fulfill. Most of what counts as immoral living should not be characterized as a fundamental departure from some pristine condition, or a refusal of some transcendent good, or an outcome of a radically divided self, but rather as a consequence of excessive care, stemming from a need to ward off finite limits, and with the effect of blocking off appropriate ranges of responsive involvement with others in the world. In other words, both unethical and ethical bearings are capacities that are intrinsic to the structure of care.[21]

As I show in the next chapter, this discussion of desire speaks to the possibility of affective dispositions that are less compressed and self-regarding, and more openly responsive to others. Consider again the example of benevolence and how it might be implicated with authentic desire. It would seem that the most laudable kind of benevolence would involve a felt concern for, and responsiveness to, the needs and interests of someone else, and a capacity to act on that concern. Benevolent people exhibit bipolar, engaged disclosure in being interested in someone other than themselves and being open beyond an attachment to their own interests. Such a balanced bearing would be different from selfish disregard, of course, but also from acts of assistance based mainly in self-interest or in abstract theoretical principles. The bipolar structure of desire drawn from Heidegger's constellation of being-in-the-world makes possible an ethical bearing that is grounded neither in the self, nor in affects subjectively construed, nor in abstract constructions of theoretical reason, nor in mechanical compliance with custom or tradition; it stems, rather, from an engaged openness and responsive world-disclosure.

The notion of authentic desire, charged by finitude and responsive to the richness and depth of things, can issue an ethical attentiveness that is more disclosive than the simplicities and superficialities that commonly seduce us in moral matters. Too often, ethical choices and attitudes follow the quick satisfactions of surface accounts and routine assessments, which can offer an attractive substitute for the difficulties of a deeper consideration and understanding.

COURAGE

Aristotle defines courage in relation to pain (*NE*, III.6–9). A courageous person is someone who is steadfast in pursuit of a good in the midst of pain or the risk of pain. A coward is someone who cannot or will not act for the good because of pain or the fear of pain. Aristotle seems to say that a courageous person does not experience fear (*NE*, 1104b7–8, 1115a10–20), but other passages suggest that the courageous person lacks overwhelming fear (*NE*, 1115b11ff). The latter sounds more plausible, yet the former may reflect Aristotle's ideal condition of silencing conflict. In any case, it seems to me that courage should be distinguished from fearlessness. In line with Aristotle's performative sense of virtue, we should understand courage more as an activity than a state of mind. A courageous person is someone who acts despite fear, even strong fear. It seems odd to say, for example, that a good soldier should not fear death, or that someone who gives a speech despite strong stage fright is not genuinely courageous (here we can assign the virtue of courage to someone Aristotle would describe as simply morally strong). Indeed, I would tend to gauge a person's courage as proportionate to the degree of fear accompanying the act: I could call a fearless person courageous, but I would call a person who acts despite fear *more* courageous.

Heidegger connects courage with essential anxiety and the capacity to withstand the negativity at the heart of being (*PM*, 234). Accordingly, we can examine courage in terms of Dasein's temporal finitude and the capacity to experience the presence of absences, of lacks, losses, and threats, or their perceived possibility. Contrary to Aristotle's condition of ideal courage, the force of pains and losses can still have a presence in courage; such force need not be overcome for there to be "genuine" courage, indeed it may be constituent for the sustained existential meaning of courage (as was suggested in an earlier discussion of virtue). Although Aristotle's discussion emphasizes the obvious example of courage in battle, we can add all sorts of pains, losses, and risks, and thereby greatly expand the meaning of courage and cowardice in the sphere of ethics. I would even suggest that courage is the most important of the virtues, and our analysis of finitude can help articulate why this might be so. Courage could be called a basic negative capability that cuts across all aspects of ethical life.

Heideggerian ontology involves a reconciliation with finitude, with the limit conditions of existence. The dynamic of fallenness includes an absorption in beings or conditions of actuality as a refuge from radical finitude. Authenticity, then, involves a release from this fixation and a capacity to dwell finitely, to accept more readily the movements of presence and absence. It seems that such a capacity is precisely what courage means in ethical life. Much of human possessive or abusive behavior that is morally problematical can be understood as stemming from a *fear* of finitude, of the pain of lacks and losses. A good deal of greed, hatred, and violence can be traced to a self-absorbed fallenness that serves as a refuge from, or response to, loss or the threat of loss. Losses can be material, psychological, social, ideological, situational, and so on; and in the face of any such negations, human beings will go to great lengths to protect or achieve desired conditions at the expense of other people. Ethical reflection on such matters would have to include the general dynamic of courage and cowardice, in terms of the challenge of facing finite limits.

Even moderation can be connected with courage, in that people who indulge their appetites at the expense of others or themselves are cowardly in the sense of not being able to withstand the "pain" of an unfilled desire, experienced as a lack. Or perhaps indulgence is compensation for other types of pains or anxieties. The excesses of addictive behaviors, for example, involve more than simply the objects of desire; they include flight responses. Overcoming addictions, then, would include the courage to confront the source of the flight.

The dynamic of courage and cowardice can also help articulate how and why we often fail to live up to an ethic we affirm in principle and want to enact (moral weakness). In many respects, acting according to ethical norms involves risks, sacrifices, and uncertainties, which makes such enactment difficult and challenging. Honesty, for example, is not something risk-free or cost-free. The honest person is courageous in the sense of accepting such conditions, while the liar is in this respect a coward.[22] So it could be concluded that liars are not really affirming deceit as a good, as much as they are fearing the consequences of telling the truth. It can be said that a key task in ethics is not a radical interrogation of values—who would propose the abandonment of truth telling?—but a recognition of how much courage it takes to lead a moral life.

This account of the virtue of courage highlights and augments a central conviction of my study: that Heidegger's general conception of authenticity can underwrite a conception of ethical authenticity, understood as the capacity for responsive dwelling in the finitude of ethical situations and decisions.

VIRTUE AND MORAL PRINCIPLES

Virtue ethics comes closest to capturing the spirit of Heidegger's thought, but it need not be exclusive in rendering the contributions to moral philosophy I am trying to develop in this study. We should remember that Heidegger does not dismiss objectivity, reflection, and abstraction, and so it is possible to make room for moral principles and abstract regulations, and yet not reduce ethics to these formulations or to theoretical megaprinciples. The next chapter takes up this question in more general terms, but presently I can offer some preliminary remarks on the relation between virtue and moral principles.

Aristotle notes that not everything in ethics involves the phronetic balancing act of virtue. For instance, adultery, theft, and murder do not admit a mean (*NE*, 1107a9ff). As Aristotle says, their very names entail wrongful action ("murder" is wrongful killing). Certain vices are implicated in such actions, of course, but here we can employ an abstract construction that connotes more than simply characteristics of the self or an individual appropriation of ethical guidelines.

Aristotle also indicates a genetic relation between virtues and the abstract formulation of rules or laws (*nomos*). Rules and laws enjoin virtuous actions and forbid vicious actions (*NE*, 1129b20–25, 1130b20–25). Laws, rules, and penalties are needed because of people's limited capacity for virtue (*NE*, 1179b5ff), owing to bad upbringing or moral weakness. Yet the authentic resolve of virtue remains the measure of moral worth. In addition, Aristotle suggests a certain phronetic flexibility in the application of laws and rules when he discusses *sungnōmē*, which can be translated as consideration or pardon (*NE*, 1143a19–24), and which is connected with *epiekkeia*, or decency (*NE*, 1137a35). The sense here is to warn against a rigid adherence to the letter of the law, which thus allows for flexibility, attention to mitigating circumstances, qualified judgments, and even pardon and forgiveness.

Abstract principles can also be accommodated in Aristotle's claim that we do not deliberate about ends, only about the means to ends (*NE*, 1112b13ff). For instance, a doctor does not deliberate about whether to cure patients, only about how best to do this. So there is room for articulation of certain principles that are contextually appropriate and obligatory, along the lines of my earlier discussion of thrownness and presumptive obligations. Thus one can say with confidence that doctors should do their best to cure their patients. Not everything in ethics is a matter of virtuous dispositions.

It is clear that moral principles can often be correlated with virtues. Abstract formulations such as "Be truthful" or "Care for others" can be considered place-holders for the virtues of honesty and benevolence—very much like what Heidegger calls formal indication, a conceptual construction that points to concrete performance. The advantage of tracing certain principles to virtues in this sense is twofold: (1) the complexities and contingencies of ethical action in concrete circumstances are not canceled out by the formal structure, but rather anticipated in the gesture toward the phronetics of virtue (When, and to what extent, is truth telling appropriate?); and (2) the enactment of the formal principle entails existential dispositions and capacities that give the principle its animation (benevolence implies caring about others, sacrifice, and generosity; honesty implies an interest in truth, a disinclination to conceal oneself, and the courage to be forthcoming despite possible costs).[23]

Construing a moral principle as a formal indication with an eye toward virtuous enactment is different from conceiving a principle as the necessary determination of moral right, or as the rational governance of a decision procedure. The formal–indicative character of "Lying is wrong" or "Be truthful" can be articulated by various qualifications to the principle that can arise in circumstances of performance. "Be truthful" need not mean "Always tell the truth." If Aunt Sally asks how her outfit looks, it might be cruel to tell her it looks awful. One might revise: "Be truthful unless it causes pain." But sometimes I cause pain by telling students what I think of their work. Revise: "Be truthful unless it causes unnecessary pain." But then questions arise: What is unnecessary pain? What are people's different capacities in handling necessary pains? What circumstances call for revisions of what counts as necessary or for modifications of people's capacities? In some circumstances we can notice a proliferation of "ifs" and "unlesses" until we arrive at what Aristotle calls a *kairos*, a specific temporal situation that calls for phronetic choice by a responsive agent who cannot rely on precise guidance from a formal rule.

Say I know that a good friend's wife has cheated on him and he asks me if she has. Knowing him, I think the revelation would shatter him and could end the marriage. I know that his wife regrets what she did and loves her husband. I know that certain difficulties stemming from my friend's disposition toward his wife probably prompted her to stray. The larger complex "truth" here and its possible ramifications can subject the principle "Be truthful" to so many qualifications that it becomes little more than a guidepost in the difficult terrain of ethical action (among other guideposts, given the tensional mix of ethical claims in this situation). I am here burdened with the task of creating an ethical outcome (of disclosing ethical truth) in a contingent atmosphere of uncertain possibilities. Yet a disposition of environmental responsiveness, which indeed has uncovered the complexity of the situation, at the same time ensures that my decision cannot be considered arbitrary or groundless in the strict sense. If I tell the truth or conceal the truth, the hope is that the decision can be appropriate, and therefore ethical. It is possible, then, to measure the quality of phronetic discernment according to the extent of responsiveness and attentiveness to the circumstances at hand. Snap judgments, decisions taken from a narrow perspective, or perfunctory applications of a rule can be deemed deficient in certain respects.[24]

SOCIALITY

As a transition to the next chapter, I briefly note the sociality of virtue in Aristotle's thought. For Aristotle, the human being is a *zōon koinōnikon*, an associational animal that lives a shared life (*Eudemian Ethics*, 1242a25). *Phronēsis* is not an isolated faculty of the soul, but a social endeavor (*NE*, 1112b10–11). The virtue of justice is necessarily related to the good of others (*NE*, 1130a4–5). Friendship (*philia*) is an essential part of the good life (*NE*, 1155a5ff), and is characterized as a mutual loving and reciprocal goodwill (*NE*, 1155b27ff). Despite Aristotle's extensive discussion of friendship (*NE*, VIII–IX), and despite the centrality of emotion in virtue, Aristotle's ethics seems to underplay certain social emotions, at least when compared to the Judeo–Christian tradition, which stresses fellow-feeling, compassion, and benevolence to a greater extent than does Greco–Roman ethics. In this vein, I turn next to a consideration of empathy.

NOTES

1. A key work in this development is Alasdair MacIntyre, *After Virtue* (South Bend, Ind.: University of Notre Dame Press, 1981). Significant earlier works are G. E. M.

Anscombe, "Modern Moral Philosophy," *Philosophy* 33 (1958): 1–19, and Iris Murdoch, *The Sovereignty of Good* (New York: Schocken, 1970). A good representative collection is *Virtue Ethics*, ed. Roger Crisp and Michael Slote (Oxford: Oxford University Press, 1997).

2. In the sphere of education, there have been movements recently in advancing "character education," wherein public schools consciously incorporate into the curriculum the fostering of certain character traits such as honesty, tolerance, patience, and so on. Such movements have met with objections or worries about "teaching values" in public schools. It is true that modern life is much more complex and open than the supposed homogeneity of times past, and that education in values runs a risk of undue constriction and conformity. Blanket objections to character education, however, are shortsighted. Any school embodies a project of cultivating certain existential outcomes. Few educational institutions are seen as simply the depositing of information and cognitive skills. Learning includes social development and the cultivation of habits and dispositions that presumably will make students better persons. Even teaching critical thinking cannot be restricted to learning logical rules and patterns; it includes social skills and dispositions such as curiosity, open-mindedness, attentiveness, even courage. The point is that character education is simply an explication of tacit values that seem intrinsic to the project of education. Specific attention to such traits *as* existential bearings, as part of students' lives and not simply as tokens for rules and norms, can go a long way toward influencing ethical development. When I discuss cheating in my classes, I have found it far more effective when the discussion passes beyond the regulation as such to existential questions such as: Why do students cheat? What does it say about their priorities? What does cheating say about a person? Would anyone be proud of being a cheater?

3. Mention should be made of the importance of John Dewey's work in such matters and its affinities with an Aristotelian–Heideggerian orientation. Dewey presents a dynamic naturalism, in which human experience is embodied, transactional, social, value-laden, and open. He provides significant insights into the prereflective sphere of knowing-how in terms of habit formation. A habit, for Dewey, is not a mechanical routine but a formed disposition and readiness to act in the world. Habits can also be altered in transactional adjustments between the self and its environment. See Dewey, *Human Nature and Conduct*, vol. 14 of *John Dewey: The Middle Works, 1899–1924*, ed. Jo Ann Boydston (Carbondale: Southern Illinois University Press, 1988). See also Larry Hickman, ed., *Reading Dewey: Interpretations for a Postmodern Generation* (Bloomington: Indiana University Press, 1998).

4. In some respects Aristotle's ideal is more demanding than Kant's rational regulation of the passions—since, for Aristotle, not only should vices be silenced, but one should enjoy the practice of virtue. See Julia Annas, "Aristotle on Virtue and Happiness," in *Aristotle's Ethics: Critical Essays*, ed. Nancy Sherman (Lanham, Md.: Rowman & Littlefield, 1999), 38–39.

5. Aristotle *Eudemian Ethics*, trans. Michael Woods (Oxford: Clarendon Press, 1992), 16.

6. In an early course on Aristotle, Heidegger specifically cites the passage in the *Nicomachean Ethics* on the difficulty of finding the mean as a reference for the difficulty of philosophy's formal–indicative character, as contrasted with the ease of a fallen immersion in customary conceptions of being and life (*GA* 61, 108–10). In general terms, Heidegger associates inauthentic *das Man* with the tendency to evade the burdens of choice (*BT*, 443).

7. Aristotle's neatly organized picture of happiness as the fulfillment of "human nature" was actually aristocratic and exclusionary. It generally reflected the life and ideals of Athenian gentlemen. Barbarians, slaves, and women were not thought to be capable of full virtue. Even productive labor was taken to be beneath the man of virtue. Certainly Aristotle's conception of virtue has much to contribute to human ethics in general, but rather than correct for his myopia by simply extending his ethical ideal to all humans, I suggest that such a full extension will inevitably destabilize and complicate his ethics. After all, it can be said that the comfortable structure of Aristotle's moral vision was sustained, both intellectually and culturally, by exploiting, suppressing, or demeaning other human beings and modes of life. An affirmation of these modes will not only subvert aristocratic privileges, it will also open up difficulties in life that aristocrats have been shielded from (like working for a living).

8. Stuart Hampshire argues against the notion of an organized harmony of the virtues, claiming that conflicted capacities can still be seen as natural to the human condition. See *Morality and Conflict* (Cambridge, Mass.: Harvard University Press, 1983), 143–48. The many conflicts of modern life can be understood as appropriate responses to the developing complexities of the environing-world, rather than as a deterioration of some harmonious order presumed to be intrinsic to "human nature."

9. Even Nietzsche saw the importance of both innovation and regular structure for culture generally and even for creative types. See my discussion in *A Nietzschean Defense of Democracy: An Experiment in Postmodern Politics* (Chicago: Open Court, 1995), 141–44. One way to understand this is to consider Aristotle's analysis of habit. If habit is understood as a kind of mechanical repetition, then it seems to conflict with creativity. Yet if habit is understood as an acquired skill that becomes second nature, its association with creativity is made clear. Creative uses of language in the literary arts, for example, bank on the background habits of linguistic competency. This is why forgoing or curtailing a certain discipline in early schooling, in everything from social norms to language skills (presumably for the sake of children's creativity and individuality), can be a significant mistake.

10. This is a term coined by the poet John Keats in "Letter to George and Thomas Keats," December 1817. Dwelling in the world, for Heidegger, includes what he calls "*das Heimischwerden in Unheimischsein*," becoming at home in being not at home (*GA* 53, 150–51).

11. In this regard, is it possible that Aristotle's ideal of perfect virtue, where one no longer experiences the pull of conflicting tensions, can amount to a flattened or diluted sense of the meaning of a virtuous condition?

12. For Heidegger, the will presupposes Dasein's transcendence and care (*BT*, 227, 238).

13. For an insightful analysis of this question, see Ben Vedder, "Heidegger on Desire," *Continental Philosophy Review*, vol. 31, no. 4 (1998): 353–68.

14. See Jonathan Bloom-Feshbach and Sally Bloom-Feshbach, eds., *The Psychology of Separation and Loss* (San Francisco: Jossey-Bass, 1987), 42ff.

15. *The Psychology of Separation and Loss*, 44.

16. Maurice Merleau-Ponty makes the important point that children who experience acute emotional conflict and stress are more likely to develop rigid, polarized thinking for psychic protection. Children in more stable emotional environments are more likely to fathom intellectual complexity and ambiguity. See "The Child's Relations with Others," in

The Primacy of Perception and Other Essays, ed. James E. Edie (Evanston, Ill.: Northwestern University Press, 1964), 105.

17. Heidegger translates the Greek term for desire in Aristotle's first line of the *Metaphysics* as the German word *Sorge*, or care (*BT*, 215).

18. This is Vedder's construction in "Heidegger and Desire," 361ff. Some of my remarks that follow are found in Vedder's article, and they originated in a commentary of mine on an earlier conference version of this article.

19. In this regard, see *BT*, 240–41. See also Heidegger's discussion of *Neugier*, or curiosity (*BT*, section 36). Most of our modern economy, including cultural and intellectual production, is driven by the constant allure of novelty for its own sake, a criterion of fashion that both wards off boredom and eclipses (or relieves us of) the demands of more authentic creativity and sustained attention to important works.

20. This provides a deeper sense of what might be ethically wrong with addictions, beyond questions of overindulgence or loss of self-control. The addict becomes compressed with a narrow sphere of self-regard, narrower than even the self's possibilities in the world, to a point where the only thing that matters or registers affective import is immediate need satisfaction. In other words, addiction fractures the ekstatic in/there/with structure of human experience.

21. This point relates to Heidegger's claim that both good and evil unfold out of being (*LH*, 260–61), and that the capacity-to-be-evil belongs essentially to Dasein's capacity-to-be, a remark found in his *Zollikoner Seminare* (Frankfurt am Main: Vittorio Klostermann, 1987), 208–9.

22. Aristotle suggests the feasibility of such an analysis when he says that avoiding burdens is cowardly (*NE*, 1116a15).

23. For an intriguing study that aims for a correlation of virtue and principle in ethics, see Nancy Sherman, *Making a Necessity of Virtue: Aristotle and Kant on Virtue* (Cambridge: Cambridge University Press, 1997). Sherman works to coordinate Kant and Aristotle by drawing on each thinker and how they intersect. The charge of formalism against Kant ignores the important role of material ends in his later thought. See especially Kant, *The Doctrine of Virtue*, trans. Mary J. Gregor (Philadelphia: University of Pennsylvania Press, 1964). For a discussion, see Ping-Cheung Lo, "A Critical Reevaluation of the Alleged 'Empty Formalism' of Kant's Ethics," *Ethics,* vol. 91, no. 2 (January 1981): 181–201. Hans-Georg Gadamer argues that Kantian principles are not rational arbiters of action, but the constitution of the moral sphere as a province of duties that need bolstering against sensuous inclinations and naive malleability. The chief force of such constitution is to shape an ideal that develops character, or the capacity to not be ruled by inclinations. See Gadamer, *Kleine Schriften*, vol. 1 (Tübingen: Mohr, 1967), 179–91. Nancy J. Holland offers a looser interpretation of Kantian duties as formal schemas for appropriate action that must be fitted to circumstances, in *The Madwoman's Reason: The Concept of the Appropriate in Ethical Thought* (University Park: Pennsylvania State University Press, 1998), 44–57. It is possible to interpret Kantian ethics in such a way that agents may need virtuous discernment and may even need to yield on a duty in certain circumstances. Reason could still stand as the constitution of moral right and as an ideal measure, while adjusting to the exigencies of a finite existence (note how the noumenon–phenomenon distinction can function here). But such ideal constitution can still be questioned on philosophical grounds. Moreover, one of the virtues of a consequentialist approach is that it can

preclude a "purist" standing for the right at any cost and claiming the higher moral ground over the "corruption" of compromise.

24. Calvin O. Schrag explores an "ethic of fitting response" in *The Self after Postmodernity* (New Haven, Conn.: Yale University Press, 1997). Holland's *The Madwoman's Reason* is a cogent reflection on the role of appropriateness in ethics, particularly in terms of a contextual, historical discernment that can be critical without strict foundations. Jürgen Habermas acknowledges the contingency of the life-world in moral performance, and also the role of emotion, interests, and value pluralism in ethics. He also has taken up questions of motivation, context, and application in the life-world, beyond questions of norm validity. See his *Justification and Application: Remarks on Discourse Ethics*, trans. Ciaran Cronin (Cambridge, Mass.: MIT Press, 1993). Yet Habermas still resists neo-Aristotelian movements because of worries about conservatism and relativism. Universal validity remains the overarching measure and the consummation of communicative rationality.

Chapter Six

The Role of Empathy in Ethics

Empathy has played an important role in moral philosophy, given that some thinkers (David Hume, Arthur Schopenhauer, and Jean-Jacques Rousseau, for instance) have maintained that sympathy or compassion is essential to ethics, as a kind of shared affect that is prior to rationality, principles, or rules. Empathy signifies a central concern in ethics: a sensitivity to the weal and woe of others, a caring about and for others that can both prompt beneficence and stave off harm and abuse. Modern moral philosophy, however, in its subject-centered orientation, has generated a variety of problems surrounding empathy and its implications. With the presumption that the self is an isolated individual consciousness, there has arisen a general skepticism about empathy and its concomitant altruistic expressions: Empathic concern is a puzzle along the lines of the problem of other minds; empathic altruism is either a fiction (psychological egoism) or morally dispensable (ethical egoism). With the presumption that feelings and emotions are merely internal psychic states, there has arisen the concern that an affective ethics would collapse into egoism; in response to this concern, the subject has been bifurcated into rational reflection and emotional self-interest, and ethical norms have been formulated in constructions of disinterested reason (utilitarianism and deontology).

   The aim of this chapter is to address these questions in light of Heidegger's thought. I will rehearse the ekstatic nature of Dasein's finite being-in-the-world, the primacy of *Befindlichkeit* and mood, and Heidegger's occasional remarks on empathy (*Einfühlung*). In the course of this analysis I want to establish the following: (1) empathy is a natural capacity in human experience, and it should not be understood as a "subjective" phenomenon; (2) the role of empathy in ethics shows the limits of reason and the structural defects in utilitarian and deontological theories; (3) findings in social psychology can reinforce Heidegger's phenomenology, and the latter can help surmount flawed assumptions in the former; and (4) empathy cannot be sufficient for an ethics and should be coordinated with reason and principles in moral life. Though empathy is not sufficient, I hope to show that it is necessary from the standpoint of moral development and enactment. By way of Heidegger I aim to establish that empathy is a primal existential condition that makes ethical life possible.

THE EKSTATIC NATURE OF BEING-IN-THE-WORLD

I have discussed how Heidegger undermines the subject–object bifurcation and the notion of an isolated, unencumbered self by showing how human Dasein is being-in-the-world; is ekstatically *there* in its circumstances; and is involved and immersed in its concernful dealings and social relations, prior to reflective distance that instigates various divisions between mind and world, self and others. I have summarized Dasein's primal comportment toward the world as an ekstatic in/there/with structure. What is important for my analysis is that this ekstatic structure indicates a being-in-the-there, and not a "projection" from an inner state of consciousness.[1] Consciousness is not the origin of the presence of beings; we are *already* ekstatically standing-in being before we distinguish consciousness and things. As Heidegger says in the context of language, Dasein is not first "inside" and then expressed "outside." Being-in-the-world is *already* outside (*BT*, 205). We have seen this ekstatic structure expressed in *zuhanden* relations, where one is immersed in a practice, animated by concern for one's project and guided by a tacit circumspection of the situational milieu. We have also seen how breakdowns in the situation reveal its tacit meaning and allow for delineations of "objective" (*vorhanden*) properties and "subjective" intentions. Such delineations, however, are derived from a more original practical sphere that is neither strictly objective (being concernful use) nor subjective (being ekstatic).

We have seen that Dasein's being also involves being-with other Daseins and that being-toward-others is ontologically different from relations with things in the world. Other Daseins are not person-things but likewise finite, needful, concernful being-in-the-world. Dasein's Mitsein involvement is characterized as *Fürsorge*, which is essential to Mitsein: Dasein "exists for the sake of Others" (*BT*, 160). This does not mean that Dasein always does care about others, but it does suggest something originary because Heidegger calls indifference a "deficient" mode of *Fürsorge*, distinguished from "positive" modes (*BT*, 158). Positive modes are marked by two extremes: a standing in for people's care (which can be paternalistic domination) and a releasing of people to and for their authentic care (*BT*, 158). It is important to note that Heidegger recognizes mixed forms in between these two positive extremes, but he interjects that articulating these forms would lead him away from his purposes (*BT*, 159).[2]

I have indicated that *Fürsorge* is essentially different from *vorhanden* and *zuhanden* relations, but that an analogy can be drawn between ethical Mitsein and certain features of the *zuhanden–vorhanden* dynamic. I want to ask if empathy can be considered an ekstatic mode of *Mitsein* that is implicated in *Fürsorge* and that can clarify the derivative nature of indifference as a deficient mode of *Fürsorge* in a way analogous to the derivative nature of the *vorhanden* out of ekstatic, practical involvement. I stress the limits of the analogy, however, because as Heidegger says, indifference is still a mode of *Fürsorge*, and so is nothing *vorhanden* (*BT*, 158). Still, Heidegger does draw an analogy between *Fürsorge* and the circumspection of *Zuhandenheit* (*BT*, 159). I want to see if empathic concern can show itself as ekstatically *there* in Dasein's social world. I am encouraged in this by the fact that Heidegger initiates a discussion of empathy (*Einfühlung*) right at the end of his treatment of Mitsein and *Fürsorge*.

BEFINDLICHKEIT

I have shown that Heidegger associates being-in-the-world with the notion of dwelling. I have summarized Dasein's existence as an ekstatic dwelling with a coordinated in/there/with structure. I have also discussed *Befindlichkeit* and mood as affective attunement, which is not an interior or subjective condition because it is an ekstatic disclosure of how the world matters, providing the medium for all thinking and acting (*FCM*, 68). I also noted how mood is intrinsic to Dasein's sociality (*FCM*, 67).

Why is the question of mood important for moral philosophy? It helps identify an ekstatic, disclosive, existential mode of dwelling, and its in/there/with structure allows us to talk of being-ethical-in-the-world in a way comparable to Heidegger's ontological analysis. Mood, as I have indicated, can open up questions of motivation that have been the province of moral psychology and also speak to the limits of cognition in explaining or affecting moral action. A Heideggerian orientation, however, avoids the trap of subjectivism or egoism that usually haunts a promotion of affects and that prompts the rationalized alternative of an "impartial" subject, whose reflective disinterest can appear problematical in the existential milieu of moral situations. We can also bypass the way in which rationalistic theories talk of actions as grounded in "beliefs," which can be phenomenologically suspect. We can take moods and affects as disclosive of "moral import," prior to the isolation of beliefs and various appeals to rational inferences and implications.[3] We can then better understand why a reference to reasons, principles, or rules often does not *matter* to people, and why moral change often arises from a shift in affective ambiance— whether from an attempt to tap into moods or from a gradual evolution of a social atmosphere. In any case, Heidegger helps us see that mood shifts are not something that can be controlled or directed, but they can be "awakened" (*FCM*, 59ff). I repeat that mood cannot be sufficient for ethics, but it may be necessary, or "essential" in Heidegger's verb-sense of *Wesen*, as a coming to presence of moral import. Rules and principles may still be important for ethics, but the question is whether moral *philosophy* can reduce ethics to rule formation or rule following.

EMPATHY

I want to focus on empathy as a moral mood, as an originary, disclosive ethical attunement, and on how Heidegger's ekstatic in/there/with structure can be located in the phenomenon of empathy. I begin with characterizations of empathy drawn largely from the field of social psychology, but such notions eventually are refined with the help of Heidegger.[4]

Empathy has been defined as a feeling-with-another, as a vicarious sharing of an affect, which is most clearly shown when one is not directly undergoing the Other's feeling or circumstance. Empathic affect is disclosive of something outside oneself and so is to be distinguished from more immanent, self-regarding affects. Empathy is not a "matching" with someone else's feelings, but rather "an affective response more appropriate to another's situation than to one's own."[5] An empathic relation is not a "union" of self and Other (contra Rousseau and Schopenhauer); it requires a distinction between self and Other in order to be experienced *as* related to the feeling of an Other and *as* one's own experience of this relation. Empathic relations can also have an intersubjective reciprocity. For example, empathic exchanges in a love relation help show the bipolar, reciprocal element well. Such emotional transactions amount to a co-constitution of selves; each person is *altered* by the relationship, which is different, then, from a mere "sharing" of feeling. The intersecting feelings in a love relation are *productive* of self-awareness, rather than simply an exchange between selves. I would suggest that all empathic relations have a certain degree of reciprocity in their dynamic. An empathic response is just as much a force *from* the Other *to* oneself as it is a movement from oneself to the Other.[6]

The emergence of empathy seems to be contextual and situational, stemming from an understanding of another's specific life circumstances. Empathy is by no means constant, and it is not universally or uniformly exhibited (there being variations both between and within individuals). Finally, empathy should not be seen as affective only, because it has cognitive dimensions as well (empathic understanding), and it connects with processes such as memory, symbolic association, imagination, and role taking. Mature empathy, then, should be understood as multidimensional, as a blend of affective, cognitive, and participatory elements.[7] Nevertheless, the affective element seems to be developmentally primal and appears to make the other elements possible.[8] We will concentrate on the affective dimension, although the remarks here show that empathy can be richly disclosive and can function in different ways in ethical considerations.[9]

Empathy and compassion are often used interchangeably, but empathy should be seen as the wider term and as that which makes compassion possible. Compassion is an empathic awareness of another's suffering, prompting an interest in alleviating that suffering (or at least dwelling with another's woe).[10] Empathy can include the sharing of positive feelings (one can share the joy of someone's freedom or success), and so it has a wider application than compassion. But since suffering and injury are clearly prominent in moral concerns, it is no surprise that compassion is highlighted as a crucial form of empathy.[11] Empathy and compassion seem to be positively associated with prosocial behavior, although the association is certainly not a necessary one. Developmentally and otherwise, empathy seems to correlate with altruistic action, the formation and use of moral principles, and the operation of moral judgment.[12] One might conclude, then, that empathy is an existential precondition for a moral life.[13]

Historically speaking, the term "empathy" originated as an English translation of the German term *Einfühlung*, which had been used in German aesthetics to explain how one experiences an aesthetic object. Empathy was taken up in early-twentieth-century experimental psychology to explain how one experiences the affects of others. In any case, *Einfühlung* had generally been understood as a process of "feeling oneself into" another object or person, as a projection from "inside" oneself out "into" the Other. This viewpoint made sense in terms of the prevailing notion of selves as individually constituted and self-contained, so that awareness of another's affect would have to involve the projecting of one's own experiential states into the Other, which would then double back as a perceived experience *of* the Other's condition.

I would like to spotlight the *"ein"* in *Einfühlung* in order to link up with Heidegger's conception of being-in, which would be different from a projective "into" that Heidegger himself saw as problematical.[14] In other words, I want to interpret empathy in terms of Heidegger's ekstatic in/there/with structure, so that empathy is an attunement *disclosing* the weal and woe of others, *there* in the world, *with* us, and *in* us in that it matters. Heideggerian ekstatics can contribute to moral philosophy by helping us overcome self–Other bifurcations that have created classic problems associated with empathy. For example: (1) empathy as a surprising anomaly (How can we experience the misfortune of someone else if we are not directly undergoing it?); (2) empathy as a mysterious process that needs an explanation (If understood as a projection, how does such a "transfer" from inside oneself into the Other occur?); (3) skepticism about empathy (How can one truly apprehend the experience of another that is directly inaccessible to one's own consciousness?); and (4) cynicism about empathy (Given the priority of individual consciousness and self-awareness, should we not say that empathy is really only the projection of one's own interests and a surreptitious strategy for enhancing those interests?). If empathy is understood as ekstatic attunement, however, much in this catalog of problems can be dissolved.

HEIDEGGER ON *EINFÜHLUNG*

At the end of section 26 of *Being and Time*, after the discussion of *Fürsorge*, Heidegger offers some remarks about *Einfühlung* (he had also treated this topic in *HCT*). He begins by saying that disclosure of the Other arises primarily out of being-with the Other (*BT*, 161). He then mentions the theoretical problem of the psychical life of others (*fremden Seelenlebens*) and the proposal of *Einfühlung* as the original way in which being toward others is made possible. But he finds the term *Einfühlung* regrettable (*BT*, 162) and critiques the theory as phenomenologically inadequate, because of its sense of empathy as a "bridge" between a solitary subject that feels itself into the Other who is initially closed off.[15] With such self–Other divisions, disclosure of the Other will always remain a puzzle. In *HCT* (243) Heidegger rejects the "problem" of empathy (How can one apprehend the experience of others by "feeling oneself into" them?) as a pseudoproblem, one that is as absurd as the problem of the reality of the external world.[16] In general terms, the projective model of empathy is rejected because Dasein's world is always already a co-world as being-with-and-toward-others, which is called an "autonomous, irreducible relationship of being" (*BT*, 162); indeed, Dasein is *essentially* an *einander Verstehen*, an understanding of one another (*HCT*, 242) because each self is embedded in a nexus of shared meaning structures that precede delineations into discrete selves. Empathy does not produce being-with because it is made possible by being-with (*BT*, 162). For this reason empathy is not a primordial existential phenomenon (*BT*, 163).

It is important to clarify Heidegger's critique here. It is not the phenomenon of shared feeling that is rejected, but rather the theoretical model that presumes isolated selves that somehow must venture out to each other. In fact, the implication is that disclosure of the Other is an original element of Dasein's being. Heidegger does not pursue an examination of *Einfühlung* along the lines of his phenomenological analysis of being-in-the-world, but he opens a door that I am trying to enter (particularly by reading "*ein*" ekstatically rather then projectively). He admits that *Miteinandersein* and *Einfühlung* still need "phenomenal clarification," that the "ontological existential originality" of *Miteinandersein* is not obvious or self-evident, that it still needs to be pursued as an *ontological* problem (*HCT*, 243). He even mentions the possibility of a "special hermeneutic of empathy," which will have to show how genuine understanding of the Other gets suppressed, obstructed, and misled—for example, in the direction of an inconsiderate reckoning with others "without seriously 'counting on them' or even wanting to 'have anything to do' with them." A "proper" understanding of the Other will have to presuppose this hermeneutic (*BT*, 163).

There are some remarks in *Fundamental Concepts of Metaphysics* that are helpful for my analysis. Although, again, Heidegger rejects the theoretical construction of *Einfühlung* and its polarized problematic (*FCM*, 203), he claims that there *is* a phenomenon in which people can "share one and the same comportment *with one another*," an "immediate experience" of a *Mitgang*, a going-along-with (*FCM*, 205). Although there are questions concerning the extent of this capacity, such a phenomenon shows that human beings can have an essential "transpositional" relation with others (*FCM*, 205). Heidegger then tries to experiment with a language that can avoid the theoretical traps of *Einfühlung*. His venture in fact resonates with the kind of interpretation I am attempting to bring to the phenomenon of empathy. Consider his remarks about "self-transposition" (*Sichversetzen*) as a "going along with":

> In general the question at issue concerns the possibility of man's transposing himself into another being that he himself is not. In this connection self-transposition does not mean the factical transference of the existing human being into the interior of another being. Nor does it mean the factical substitution of oneself for another being so as to take its place. On the contrary, the other being is precisely supposed to remain *what* it is and *how* it is. Transposing oneself into this being means going along with what it is and how it is. Such going-along-with means directly learning how it is with this being, discovering what it is like to be this being *with* which we are going along *in this way*. (*FCM*, 202)

Heidegger complains that usually such self-transposition is described as merely cognitive and hypothetical, as opposed to an existential inhabiting of the Other's sphere. Such descriptions miss the direct experience of *my* being with the Other.

> This moment does not consist in our simply forgetting ourselves as it were and trying our utmost to act as if we were the other being. On the contrary, it consists precisely in we ourselves being precisely ourselves, and only in this way first bringing about the possibility of ourselves being able to go along with the other being while remaining *other* with respect to it. There can be no going-along-with if the one who wishes and is meant to go along with the other relinquishes himself in advance. "Transposing oneself into . . ." means neither an actual transference nor a mere thought-experiment that supposes such transference has been achieved. (*FCM*, 202–3)

I want to work with these suggestions to explore a richer phenomenology of empathy. I have already sketched the possibility of empathy as an ekstatic being-in-there-with-the-Other, of empathic concern as a fundamental element of Dasein's social world, of indifference as a derivative and deficient mode of being-with (analogous to the *zuhanden–vorhanden* dynamic). Consider a face-to-face encounter with someone undergoing pain or misfortune. I assume that there can be moments of spontaneous, direct, affective response wherein we are immersed in/there/with the other person: We might wince, or tears might well up, or sadness might come, and so on—all in direct response to what is seen/sensed/felt in and from the person's words, tones, gestures, facial expressions, and body language. Analogous to the phenomenology of tool use that undermines the model of cognitive steps—of forming beliefs, drawing inferences, transferring to manual maneuvers, and out to the tool—empathic concern shows moments when we are simply affectively in/there/with the person, without a sense of conjuring up feelings or beliefs "inside" and then transferring them to the other person, or processing perceptual data as "misfortune" and then triggering an affect and then casting it out to the Other—all of this in an inferential procedure of external reception, internal processing, and projective transmission. No, the shared affect simply *happens*.[17]

Empathy, then, is a direct disclosure of a co-presencing that is more than merely subjunctive or hypothetical (how I would feel if I were in another's situation). And empathic disclosure need have nothing to do with the question of "accurate" perceptions of others, something which again is generated by projective presuppositions and reflective divisions of self and Other. In the midst of an empathic experience, we do not take it as an exercise in accurate perception (only an epistemologist would see it that way). There simply emerges an affective co-presencing of another's fate. If I felt sadness in the presence of another person's misfortune, and someone were to ask: "Do you think you genuinely felt as he did?" or "Do you think you rightly perceived what was in his consciousness?" — I would blink in bewilderment. Cognitive categories of sameness and difference are not thematized in empathic moments, although such moments do exhibit a vague and ambiguous intersection of togetherness and apartness.

Of course we might sooner or later become reflective or even self-conscious about an empathic experience and split it up into zones of "self" and "Other" in various modes and for various reasons.[18] But I think we can recognize genuinely ekstatic moments when we are not reflective or self-conscious (or strategizing or faking or merely edifying), but simply *there*. Speaking for myself, these moments are not very frequent, but when they happen I take them as authentic and satisfying as a clearly worthy, enhanced, and exemplary mode of human interaction and response; in other words, as fully *appropriate*. I would like to think that such moments are possible for others regarding me as well. The point is that we have here an intimation of a fitting engagement, a deep sense of involvement that feels right. As Heidegger puts it, "do we not experience a new sense of elation in our Dasein each time we accomplish such going-along-with in some essential relation with human beings?" (*FCM*, 206).

In Heideggerian terms, one can talk of the appropriation of self and Other, of their "belonging together." As was mentioned earlier, empathy can exhibit intersubjective reciprocity, that is, not just a one-to-one "withness" but a productive co-presencing, where both sides *alter* each other. This is why the projective "from-into" model fails; not only is my empathic concern directly disclosive, something happens *to* me as well; it says something about me as much as my relation to an Other. I feel a kind of exalted openness, that I *am* with someone, that is, *not* taken "out of myself" to some other region; rather, it is an enlargement of my self.

Conversely, I take deviations from these moments to be deficient in a sense, and noticeable *as* deviations. I am more likely in moments of indifference to ask myself why I do not care, whereas in moments of empathic concern I am not likely to ask myself why I care. I suggest then that we take empathic moments to be primal, and that indifference (or worse) is noticed as "negative." Here is an analogy to Heidegger's analysis of *Zuhandenheit*, where a breakdown in tool function is noticed as a disruption, which accordingly illuminates the meaning of the more primal mode of involvement. If we notice disengagement as a deviation (recall Heidegger's description of indifference as a deficient mode of *Fürsorge*), we might have phenomenological evidence for the primacy of empathic concern. Empathy could then serve as an existential exemplar, as a kind of measure for a significant range of ethical matters.[19]

EMPATHY AND SOCIAL PSYCHOLOGY

I will here highlight some findings in social psychology, especially in the area of child development, which I believe can reinforce Heideggerian phenomenology and suggest developmental roots of an ekstatic in/there/with structure. Moreover, Heideggerian phenomenology can help us interpret these findings in a philosophically deepened way and challenge certain subjectivistic assumptions and prejudices that prevail in the social sciences.[20] In any case this discussion can effectively address questions such as: How is it that we come to care about others? How does caring get blocked? How might caring be nourished?

Face-to-face play between parent and infant (at two to three months) entails the sharing of emotion and develops an affective attunement that may be the precursor to later empathic responses.[21] At ten to twelve months, babies begin to sense the emotional meaning of facial expressions; this begins their social development, which soon exhibits a capacity to respond vicariously to emotional expressions and behaviors.[22] Some cases: A nine-month-old becomes overwhelmed at the distress of other infants; a fourteen-month-old sees another infant crying and she begins to cry and looks to her mother; a fifteen-month-old is arguing with another child, who begins to cry, and the first child leaves to fetch a teddy bear to bring to the crying child.[23]

Empathic experience seems to emerge in stages and in a way that makes an assumption of mere "conditioning" problematical.[24] In the first year, prior to self–Other differentiation, infants experience empathic distress, in which the distress of the Other is one's own. For instance, an infant will cry at the sound of another infant's crying. Such responsiveness would seem to be a developmental base that makes later empathic forms possible. In the second year, with self–Other differentiation, children can respond empathetically to the distress of others that they recognize is not their own. At two to three years, children learn more clearly that the feelings of others belong to these others, and this actually enhances responsiveness to their cues. With the learning of language, empathy can relate to more complex emotions and can be aroused by the mere recounting of an absent person's misfortune. Children in later years can begin to empathically generalize about groups or grasp larger life situations and their meanings. In maturity, a broadened understanding of life and its complexities can modify empathy in various ways.[25]

It appears that an empathic response may be biologically coded, yet a child's environment can influence whether it flourishes or withers. In addition to prosocial dispositions, empathy seems to be implicated in a wide range of social behaviors and attitudes: for example, self-awareness, communication skills, and social understanding.[26] Such findings would lend support to Heidegger's claim that the affective dimension of *Befindlichkeit* has priority in Dasein's being-in-the-world.[27]

What is particularly interesting in child development is the role of motor mimicry, which is essential to an extensive range of learning experiences, and which can be considered a primal form of empathy.[28] Motor mimicry is a mode of transpositional embodiment, in which we spontaneously wince at other people's pain, smile at their delight, recoil at their peril, ape their movements, and so forth. Such behavior has been generally perceived as a puzzle by psychologists.[29] Why is it done, especially when we ourselves are not undergoing the movements? It seems, though, that the role of motor mimicry in early childhood provides answers, and a Heideggerian ekstatics greatly contributes to an understanding of such behaviors. Mimetic response, especially in a child's early face-to-face engagements, would seem to be a fundamentally ekstatic phenomenon. In spontaneous mimicry we can presume, as I have suggested earlier, that the "outside" comes first in a way and is productive of the child's "internal" states. Indeed, psychologists speculate that an infant comes to learn about the self primarily through the emotional responses of others, a process that can then be looped back to allow vicarious learning about the experiences of others.[30] It is important to note here that empathy should not be understood as unidirectional from either side of self and Other; it is developmentally bipolar, *inter*personal rather than *intra*personal. It is not simply an "out to" or an "into" or even a mere "with," but a reciprocal co-presencing that prefigures a significant range of intersubjective processes. Empathic responses that a young child receives from others are both a factor in the self-formation *of* the child, and a prompting and reinforcement of the child's empathic responses *to* others throughout its development. The point is that the self from early on has *relational* needs in addition to mere biological needs based in "drives" of pleasure and pain.[31]

In general terms, research suggests that a projective model of empathy presuming a self-centered trajectory "into" an Other is reductionistically flawed.[32] The phenomenon of empathy in early child development would seem to bear out Heideggerian claims about the ekstatic nature of experience and about the derivative nature of various divisions between self and Other, the internal and the external. The subsequent Heideggerian philosophical move would be that ekstatic structure remains operative in mature experience as well.[33] Although reflective distance and various partitions of experience are necessary elements of human experience, Heidegger is at pains to point out how a reduction to such elements distorts our thinking and how philosophy must acknowledge and attempt to articulate an originary, prereflective, ekstatic dimension in Dasein's being. The point of this chapter is that ethics in particular can benefit from such a philosophical revision.

To conclude this section, research findings also speak to familiar questions of nature and nurture. The development of empathic concern seems to be a confluence of innate predispositions and environmental influences.[34] The latter highlights the importance of upbringing and education in matters of ethics. Mimetic processes are crucial for the development of numerous capacities, particularly language, but also a moral sense. Heidegger's ekstatic configuration of being-in-the-world helps show how and why this happens, and it cues insights into how something like empathy can be nurtured, reinforced, or as Heidegger says, facilitated in particular cases (*FCM*, 205).[35] But in addition to the importance of environment, research suggests that empathy is in some sense natural, not in the sense of being invariant and universal, but in the sense of being indigenous, that is to say, *not* artificial or culturally constructed. Empathy then would be part of human nature in the sense of not being mere social conditioning (or even a surreptitious strategy for advancing self-interest).

In other words, it is natural for human beings to care about others and feel for others. It should be reiterated that being-in-the-world shows nature and nurture not as opposites along the lines of binaries such as intrinsic and extrinsic, invariant and variable, but rather as intersecting co-constituents of human development. Calling empathy natural is simply to say that it shows itself spontaneously in human experience, that it is in some sense intrinsic to human comportment, though dependent on environmental influences for its flourishing (analogous to the natural propensity for language that is nevertheless not automatic or self-generating). We could call empathy a natural human capacity or potential, in the same way that Aristotle called virtue a natural potential fulfilled by habit.[36] So although empathy is not artificial or conditioned, its development is neither automatic nor necessary; it needs nurturing. Accordingly, empathy *can* be absent, concealed, or lost. This gives some relief from citations of exceptions or extreme cases (for example, the occurrence of radical selfishness in circumstances of acute deprivation) presumed to invalidate the naturalness of empathy, as though invariance or permanence were necessary conditions for the natural. The concept of potentiality provides a more balanced account.[37]

One significant consequence for ethics in all of this can be found in recent experiments that seem to validate empathic and altruistic behavior as a genuine part of human experience, contrary to egoistic suppositions that such behavior is either infeasible or ultimately based in self-interest.[38] If empathy is primal in human experience in some way, then to whatever extent empathic relations are indicative of an ethical sense (caring-about and caring-for), in this respect human beings do not "become" ethical as life proceeds, they are *already* ethical to a certain extent. It is commonplace that disaster situations typically elicit spontaneous concern, responsiveness, and assistance, often at surprising and heartening levels of decency. Here is another sense in which disruptions and breakdowns are dis-

closive, in this case disclosive of a natural ethical bearing that can lay concealed
in more normal circumstances.

EMPATHY AS ETHICAL ATTUNEMENT

I have shown in Heidegger the connection between the attunement of mood and
ekstatic dwelling. The word "dwelling" gives Heidegger an alternative to traditional subject–object ontologies because it captures in one stroke both human and
extrahuman features (existential meaningfulness and an environing habitat). In
Letter on Humanism, as I have pointed out, Heidegger considers the Greek word
ēthos in its sense of abode or dwelling place, and suggests that his ontological
investigations might be called an "original ethics." But we need not restrict ourselves to Heidegger's lofty ontological ethics; we can extend the notion of
dwelling to familiar ethical concerns, particularly with regard to empathy. I am
suggesting that empathy can be understood as a primal mode of dwelling or
attunement with the social world, as a capacity for ekstatic being in/there/with
others with respect to existential weal and woe.

If ethics in its evaluative aspect always has to engage certain preferences regarding better and worse ways of living, empathy can be understood as a preconcep-
tual, preregulatory, but nonetheless exemplary measure for the possibility of genuine ethical regard, particularly in terms of valuing benevolence over
malevolence. As ekstatic attunement, such a measure arises neither from sheer
self-regard nor from a reflective construction of principles that bypass existential
comportment—in other words, empathy exhibits *self*-involvement-with-*others*.
Here we can rehearse Heidegger's notion of *Jemeinigkeit* and further deflect mis-
conceptions of this complex term. The affective immediacy of empathy shows a
being-toward-others-that-is-mine, *my* being-toward-others. Empathy presupposes
a differentiation of self and Other, rather than sheer union. But as *my* felt concern
for others, mineness displays an existential mattering, in that the fate of others
matters to me. And I would surely prefer that others also be absorbed in their mineness regarding my fate—in other words, that their concern for me be heartfelt
rather than an instrumental calculation, or a mere mechanical obedience to rules,
or an impersonation of social expectations. So mineness in this context is anything
but egoistic self-regard.[39] As Heidegger says, Dasein's for-the-sake-of-itself "does
not assert ontically that the factual purpose of the factical Dasein is to care exclusively and primarily for itself and to use others as instruments (*Werkzeug*) toward
this end" (*BP*, 296). Indeed Dasein's selfhood as a *world* phenomenon is "the
ontological presupposition for the selflessness in which every Dasein comports
itself toward the Other in the existent I-thou relationships" (*BP*, 298).

Empathy, of course, exhibits various degrees of feeling, concern, and disclosure, which suggest a spectrum of measuring, including so-called cognitive
modes of empathic understanding and affective–cognitive blends such as a sensi-

tivity to people's needs, attitudes, and experiences. We should not hold to a strict separation between affective and cognitive empathy. As Heidegger says, every form of understanding and knowing has its mood or attunement. Even a strict conception of moral principle would seem to require that one have an *interest* in the principle, that one care about its importance and about living up to it. Ethics as lived demands that moral beliefs be *animated* in the sense of being charged with existential import. The various degrees of empathy can be taken as a primal source of such import.

In fact, developmental studies suggest that affective empathy passes through different stages and continues to be implicated in supposedly more abstract moral considerations. In infants empathic distress prepares the possibility of prosocial sympathetic distress, and empathy makes possible empathic anger at perpetrators of another's hurt, something exhibited in children as young as eighteen months old.[40] The emergence of guilt feelings at being the cause of another's hurt can be understood as a blend of empathetic distress, sympathetic distress, and self-directed empathic anger. Finally, empathic injustice arises when a child feels aversion to someone suffering undeserved misfortune or mistreatment, and this can be seen as a bridge between empathic concern and a more generalized sense of moral principle. Empathy and guilt function as motives for moral action and for affirming certain principles ("Care for the needy") that then can function as steps in moral judgments in various social or political milieus. From a developmental standpoint, empathic affects emerge prior to cognizance of moral principles, and the affects seem to predispose people toward, and help activate, moral principles. Empathy allows a moral principle to be a "hot cognition." Indeed, moral principles can become charged enough to the point where simply noting them can elicit empathic responses in moral situations.[41]

Here in the sphere of ethics we encounter the familiar distinction between the modern and postmodern conceptions of selfhood, between the unencumbered, disinterested, rational self and the situated, involved self. For all the supposed advantages of rational universality in cognitive ethical theories, what remain problematical for such theories are fundamental questions about moral constitution and moral motivation: How does one come to see a situation *as* a moral situation? Why should one *be* moral or come to see morality as an important part of one's life? Empathy can apply to such questions in being a primal mode of ethical *interest*, an involvement in the existential weal and woe of others. Such involvement can be understood in terms of Heidegger's early concept of care and his later notion of "nearness," which is meant to contrast with the "distance" of objectified modes of being perfected in modern technology. Cognitive moral theories consider rational disinterest to be a great advantage in guaranteeing universality and in preventing ethics from collapsing into the chaos of emotional forces. But we have seen that a turn to affect may in fact be a turn to the very origins of an ethical sense. Moreover, promoting disinterest should give pause because some of the most heinous human behaviors can be traced not to hatred, but to a radical emotional detachment, a distancing from the fate of others that objectifies them to the point of permitting brutal treatment in the name of duty, order, or efficiency.[42]

Empathy is not simply a feeling; it is a mode of *disclosure* that generates ethical import. In its atmosphere of affective nearness and its being-toward structure there arises the existential "draw" of the Other that can be called the prereflective condition for the possibility of, and openness to, important ethical forces such as responsibility, obligation, conscience, and guilt. In this regard we should recall Heidegger's hint that the ontological structures of conscience and guilt, though not indicative of a moral meaning, nevertheless can provide an existential basis for morality (*BT*, 332). The concept of thrownness can also provide a background for ethical senses of responsibility and obligation in a way quite different from modern criteria grounded in an individual's rational reflections and decisions. As I have discussed, one's obligations to one's children would seem to be better rendered as the claim of being *thrown* into parenthood than as the self-grounding construction of a rational inference.[43]

The ekstatic structure of empathy also helps defend against the gambits of moral skepticism, nihilism, and relativism, which in one way or another are governed by subjectivistic assumptions and the fact–value binary. A Heideggerian analysis allows ethical regard to show itself as a *world* phenomenon.

EMPATHY AND AUTHENTICITY

The preceding discussion helps undermine the belief that Heidegger's conception of authenticity indicates radical individuation and a divorce from the social world. I have shown how Dasein's authenticity indicates an openness to finitude, and how inauthenticity reflects the different ways in which Dasein covers up this finitude in its immersion in beings or familiar modes of understanding. Dasein's being-toward-death can shake off a dependence on the distortions, superficialities, and dispersions of everyday understanding. Now Dasein has the possibility of coming to its own understanding of its existence, appropriate to itself, no longer dominated by the commonplace.

Despite this clear sense of individuation, interpreting authenticity as a sheer break with the social world is a mistake. Dasein is always situated. Being-toward-death does individuate, since one's own death is nonrelational (*BT*, 294), but such individuation should be understood as a temporary *interruption* of world involvement that prepares a disclosive revisioning of the world, rather than a radical break with it (*BT*, 308). Dasein's transcendence surpasses all beings, and it surpasses *itself as well* (*MFL*, 190). That is why in choosing itself authentically, Dasein actually chooses not isolation but being with other Daseins and other beings in the world (*MFL*, 190). Dasein's transcendence is a capacity for "binding commitment," where Dasein "first can and even must hold itself to beings" (*MFL*, 196–97).

Several texts clearly suggest some ethical implications in the context of authenticity. Heidegger states emphatically that Dasein's for-the-sake-of-itself is nothing like a radical egoism; that would be "madness" and "outrageous nonsense." Rather, it is the condition for the possibility for Dasein "to be able to be with others, for them, and through them" (*MFL*, 186). The individuation of being-toward-death is still connected with Mitsein; it opens up the potentiality for being of *others* too (*BT*, 309). There remains a basic relationship between authenticity, resolution, and being-with-others (*BP*, 287–88). A later work (*GA* 39, 72–73) suggests an ethical sense of nearness and connectedness that recapitulates the disclosive double movement of death and care. The existential "nearness of death" can be the basis of an "original community" (*ürsprungliche Gemeinschaft*); its negativity can be the source of an unqualified belonging together (*unbedingten Zueinandergehörens*). In short, our common finitude can draw us toward each other. Finally, there is a remarkable passage at the very end of *Vom Wesen des Grundes* that organizes and coordinates the reciprocal movements of death, care, authenticity, and Mitsein:

> And so man, as existing transcendence abounding in and surpassing toward possibilities, is a being (*Wesen*) of distance. Only through primordial distance, which he forms toward all beings in his transcendence, does there arise in him a true nearness to things. And only the capacity to hear in the distance develops for Dasein as self the awakening to the response (*Antwort*) of Mitdasein; for only in Mitdasein can Dasein sacrifice its egotism (*Ichheit*) in order to win itself as an authentic self.[44]

In view of this strong social component in authenticity, I would like to suggest the possibility of an analogous ethical authenticity with respect to the phenomenon of empathy. The movement of being-toward-death to authentic care is a general ontological configuration that Heidegger provides as an interpretive path for the thinking of being. We have noticed certain ethical registers in authenticity and are free to explore possible parallels in the specific sphere of ethics.

Empathy (especially in developmental terms) seems to imply a primal ekstatic "nearness" along the lines of Heidegger's ontological analysis. And empathy in the form of compassion seems analogous to the double movement of authenticity, in the sense of being an openness to the finitude of suffering that discloses its meaningfulness and possible responses to it. Recalling two basic aspects of inauthenticity—(1) an immersion in presence as a refuge from radical finitude, and (2) a superficial leveling that conceals the depth of individuated appropriation—empathy could be understood as ethically authentic, as a dwelling-in-the-midst-of-finitude that discloses the meaning, depth, and appropriate particularity of a given existential situation. Moreover, in view of the first aspect of inauthenticity cited above, could we call indifference inauthentic, as a refuge from the negativity of suffering to protect the self from the burden of perceiving the pains of life? Given what I have said about the virtue of courage in connection with accepting pain and loss, could we say that empathy and compassion are forms of courage, and that indifference is a subtle form of cowardice, a psychological strategy to ward off the pain of direct attention to human misfortune? And regarding the second aspect of inauthenticity, could we call an ethics restricted to moral rules and principles inauthentic in a way, as a "flattening" of the ethical sphere into generalizations that conceal existential comportment and its specificity? Ethical authenticity, sharpened by finitude and situated by empathy, can provide a deepened register for familiar questions of moral motivation. Authenticity can open up a clearer, more immediate interest in ethics as an essential, urgent endeavor dedicated to human potentiality and what it takes to live well—a more vivid interest than the vague, indirect, or weak attitudes that are common in more everyday dispositions.[45]

THE LIMITS OF EMPATHY

It is important to reiterate that empathy and its implications cannot be sufficient for an ethics. I have tried to establish that it is a crucial element in ethics, that it can be exemplary, and that it may be a primal or originary ethical phenomenon, especially in a developmental sense. Nevertheless empathy must be seen as a limited ethical phenomenon, and Heidegger's ontology can help articulate this limit.

For Heidegger, every form of being is limited and balanced by otherness, and thus is always ambiguous regarding its nature. The same must be said for ethical concerns, and I have taken some guidance from Aristotle in this regard with respect to *phronēsis* as a balancing act between extreme possibilities. I also noted Heidegger's ontological conception of *phronēsis* as a balance between concealment and unconcealment. Heidegger's ontological phronetics of presence and absence can be shown to operate in ethical thinking and practice, as a balancing act that is indigenous to ethical finitude. For example, phronetics can negotiate a balance between self-regard and Other-regarding empathic concern. The debate between egoism and altruism can be diagnosed as a struggle between "purist" theories modeled on constant presence that cannot abide otherness or ambiguity. Ethical life can involve not only the coexistence of self-interest and altruism, it can also involve an ambiguous blend of self-regarding and Other-regarding attitudes and behaviors. If I experience pleasure in helping others or some vexation in a sacrifice I might make, such bearings would be problematical only for polarized conceptions of ethical regard.

One could also perform a phronetic analysis of the virtue of empathic concern as a balancing act between the following extremes: (1) indifference or objectification, a general alienation from the fate of others; and (2) empathic overload, which can lead to extreme personal distress (which can prompt indifference), an overprotection and overtaking of the Other, or a revulsion against suffering.[46] Such extremes can correspond to Heidegger's distinction between the deficient mode of *Fürsorge* and its problematic positive mode of standing in for another's care. We can also locate within this dynamic the importance of Heidegger's other positive mode of *Fürsorge*, which releases people to their authentic care. We should remember as well that there are modes of *Fürsorge* in between the positive extremes of overtaking and release.

Finally, there should be a balance between the extremes of empathy for no one and empathy for everyone. The former is sociopathic while the latter is unrealistic, if not impossible. A certain empathic partiality is probably inevitable because of the following factors: the contextuality of empathic experiences, the seemingly natural partiality toward intimates as contrasted with strangers, and the risks of emotional overload. But if empathy can remain exemplary, this can open up the importance and role of moral principles (such as "Feed the hungry") as "proxies" for the limits of direct empathic concern.[47] In addition, a tendency toward the abstract character of principles can actually help manage the intensity of empathic affects that can be psychologically overpowering.[48]

The importance of empathy, then, does not supplant the role of principles in ethics, nor is empathy immune to certain problems that lead us to see the significance of "distancing" in social life. It is well known that people who work in highly charged environments, such as emergency rooms, have to develop certain strategies of distancing to ward off emotional overload. It could be said that the extent of suffering and misfortune in life is an "impossible truth," in that its full disclosure is intolerable. Certain modes of concealment would be needed, then, to permit a balanced, tolerable bearing regarding both one's own suffering and one's awareness of suffering in the world. Hypersensitivity to suffering could be called too much truth, which can even go as far as prompting a denial of life (this was Nietzsche's diagnosis of religions and pessimistic philosophies such as Schopenhauer's that recommend detachment and anticipation of the end of life).

It is important to remember that Heidegger's ekstatic configuration of being-in-the-world does not discount or disparage objectification or reflective distance, but simply the *reduction* of ontology to these modes of disclosure. I am not recommending the elevation of ekstatic empathy to some kind of ethical ground or moral absolute.[49] A universal empathy seems implausible. Nevertheless, empathic circles can be widened, because often it is simply absence or distance that creates indifference.[50] Strategies of exposure can often instigate an empathic nearness that spawns an otherwise dormant ethical motivation. Consider how people's indifference toward the poor can be affected by literature, documentaries, or direct encounters. Recent famines received little response until television pictures triggered a worldwide stream of aid. Reflexive questions (What if that were you or your family?) can also prompt an extension of empathy.[51]

Regarding such possible enlargements of concern, one of the virtues of Heidegger's conception of correlative presence and absence with respect to the self is that we are never fully present to each other or even to ourselves, and this undermines closure of all kinds, especially in oneself. It makes possible a cultivation of openness that can have ethical implications: a disposition of expansiveness, an openness to "more," to novelty and otherness, which can be productive of relatedness without collapsing into conditions of "unity" that contain their own kinds of closure. It is important to keep in mind that empathy, in both affective and cognitive senses, does not operate as a "merging" of the self with the Other. There is always an awareness of difference (of *my* experience of someone *else's* situation). Accordingly, empathy can extend beyond immediate self-Other relations to include social or cultural lives different from my own. Although empathy depends on certain common human experiences (such as pain and loss), its original affective trajectory is an *openness* to the Other, *as* other. Empathic understanding can be seen as emerging out of this affective openness, and hence as a cultivated capacity to understand and even appreciate forms of life different from one's own. Empathy, then, is an ekstatic opening of the self that allows, even generates, a coexistence with difference. An existential capacity for expansive openness can be called a primary good in human life, because it works against closure of all kinds, especially closure within myself and a closed sense of the Other.

In sum, my contention is that empathy is developmentally originary, that empathic affect, rather than reason, uncovers ethical import and predisposes humans toward a range of moral conceptions, and that the ekstatic structure of empathy helps surmount certain problems that have bedeviled traditional moral philosophy, especially the notion that a turn to emotion in ethics invites a restriction to self-regarding dispositions.

EMPATHY AND PRINCIPLES

Earlier it was suggested that an ethical reduction to moral principles might be considered inauthentic, as distinct from the authenticity of empathic regard. Here I want to elaborate on this point and flesh out its complex implications. Although the authenticity of empathy is meant to suggest a kind of exemplary ethical measure, this does not rule out moral principles, even if they are associated with inauthenticity. Heidegger's authentic–inauthentic distinction is not itself a "moral" construction implying that one should reject the inauthentic. The distinction displays, rather, a multidimensional, layered dynamic, that is, movements between radical finitude and meaning, between wonder and familiarity, between originary depth and the commonplace, between individuation and the customary. Authenticity is a "modification" of the inauthentic (*BT*, 312), not its opposite. Even the climactic *Augenblick*, or "moment of vision," in authentic being-toward-death is just that, *momentary*; the *return* to inauthenticity is a positive part of Dasein's structure (*FCM*, 295–96). So the role of abstract moral principles is not to be ruled out in ethics. What is in question is the ontogenesis of moral principles and how they operate in ethical life. Abstract principles can have a certain moral force without having to purchase the opposition between reason and affect, impartiality and partiality, which has marked many modern moral theories. The issue here is whether or not principle formation in ethics is a strictly rational enterprise as conceived in the modern tradition, which accordingly would be governed by the stipulated rational requirements of universal consistency and indefeasibility. My proposal is that there are other ways to construe the formation and enactment of moral principles.[52]

In the previous chapter, I note that abstract principles could be coordinated with the performative sense of virtue along the lines of Heidegger's notion of formal indication. Here I want to extend this discussion in the context of empathy and try to organize the complex relation between abstraction and concrete performance. It needs to be said that not every moral principle has to do primarily with empathic concern for others. Truth telling, for example, need not be seen as a proxy for empathy in any direct sense. I do want to argue, however, that empathy in the broadest sense of an ambient attunement (*Befindlichkeit*), an ethical interest, *is* implicated in some way and to some degree in all ethical matters.

To begin this discussion, it would help to draw on a basic distinction introduced in chapter 3. Ethical concerns can be organized around two principal goods—freedom and care—two main areas of ethical interest that are exhibited throughout human life. Even in early childhood it is evident in the existential environment that it is good to be free, to be cared for, and to care for others. Such goods, however, also run up against situational constraints, limits, and correlative tensions. It is rare, if ever, that any of these goods can admit an abstract universality. Whatever generalizations can be constructed in ethics will likely require qualifications in practice. That is why the balancing act of virtue is an enduring factor in orchestrating the movements of an ethical life.

Both freedom and care in my analysis are, ontogenetically, existential conditions of being-in-the-world, and so they should not be seen as grounded in subject-centered reason. Most moral theories that have championed impartial reasoning based in abstract principles have done so because affect and interest have been construed as the self-centered origin of moral conflict and most forms of human abuse and injustice. An impartial commitment to a principle is seen as the best hope for a moral consensus and effective moral governance. In questioning such an approach, I am following Heidegger in delimiting rationality and expanding affect into an ekstatic openness that is not restricted to self-regard. I am not arguing that impartiality should play no role in ethics, nor am I denying that affect and interest can be ethically problematical. I am simply questioning basic assumptions about where problems and solutions in ethics originate and how ethics should properly execute its concerns.[53]

Both care and freedom can be coordinated with a sense of moral principle. A moral principle need not be construed as a rational universal that compels the mind's assent and that logically governs decision procedures applied to particular cases. Rather, a moral principle can be taken as a formal indication, a conceptual abstraction drawn from, and referring to, a concrete existential environment, especially in the wake of disruptions of social expectations and familiarities that prompt a reflective gaze, which opens the space for generalizations. Moreover, the ethical force of principles is also drawn from the existential environment, particularly in terms of relevant inhabitive signs of truth. With respect to care, concern for and about others is originally an existential bearing that can be converted into abstractions ("Help the needy") for various purposes: as proxies for empathic concern, as exhortations to action, as instructional references, as a kind of inductive shorthand that gears ethical bearings without having to start from scratch.[54]

The ethical import of freedom is, of course, originally disclosed for each of us in terms of our existential interests. The notion of reciprocal freedom, however, is much more amenable to the impartial force of an abstract principle, because honoring freedom for others entails noninterference and constraints against treating people solely on the basis of our own interests and inclinations. That is why the Kantian principle of justice as respect for persons is such an effective ethical formulation. Allowing people their freedom in general terms has become a pervasive intuition in our culture. The reach of freedom, however, can always be a question when we ask about what kind of freedom, in what context, for what purpose, and in relation to whom. And overdetermining individual freedom can distort, conceal, or suppress certain Other-regarding dispositions that are equally important in ethics. Finally, even a commitment to a principle of freedom is not itself utterly impartial, since it seems to require an *interest* in people's freedom (which Kant tried to capture in describing respect as a kind of feeling), an interest that can be traced to empathic regard (if we recall that empathy can involve something like taking pleasure in other people's successes) and that can serve as an Other-regarding interest that might outweigh certain self-regarding interests.[55] In sum, both freedom and care can be understood as existential bearings that can be modulated into an abstract sphere of principles.

Moral principles can also be seen as operating in the presumptive obligations discussed in chapter 3. If my interest leads me to become a teacher, then I am "thrown" into certain responsibilities and obligations intrinsic to the profession and correlated with the trust granted me by my students. I am obligated to treat students fairly, to assess them solely on the basis of the quality of their work, and to give my best effort in preparing my classes. Such requirements are not simply a matter of personal preference, or based solely in affective regard, or even simply a result of some rational inference. These are obligations that govern my behavior because they stem from my *being* a teacher, from my inhabiting this environment, and from a narrative sense of what it means to be a good teacher. There are impartial principles, then, that guide human behavior simply by virtue of taking up or encountering certain situations. Such obligations can be qualified, limited, or released in extreme situations or when trumped by other obligations. Obligations will not be amenable to sheer universality because they are context-specific, and indeed they might run into conflict with other context-specific obligations or expectations (consider how friendship or loyalty might clash with having to make a professional judgment).

A sense of impartial universality is much more appropriate in institutional structures, especially legal institutions (for example, equality before the law). Here is where deontological theories have their strongest case and application. Legal provisions can be seen as intrinsically geared toward such levels of reasoning in a way that ethical comportment alone is not. Ethical discernment would be indicated more at the level of lawmaking, which is less formally restricted. Even constitutional provisions that govern lawmaking emerge from a more open existential environment, when considered from the standpoint of historical inception. It should be added that even with the elements of impartial universality in legal institutions, prudential discretion is always a factor in legal practice.

The point here is that some sense of moral principle is possible as a constraint on certain modes of self-interest—without, however, constructing a baseline opposition between moral right on the one hand and self-interest and emotion on the other hand. Kant is famous for having stipulated such an opposition. For Kant, human desires and their subsequent material practical principles are all based in self-love.[56] That is why moral right requires the abstract, formal universality of the categorical imperative in order to save ethics from the force of self-regarding emotions. My discussion of empathy suggests that affect can be genuinely Other-regarding, and so it can be plausibly stated that only *certain* affects have prompted theorists to disparage the role of emotion in ethics. And one can easily grant that some emotions and passions cause a lot of damage in life without, however, committing to a wholesale dismissal of affect.

With Heidegger, it is possible to subvert the common division between emotion and reason. Heidegger insists that affect can be world-disclosing and that knowledge is always charged with existential interests. It is better to take emotion and knowledge as points on a continuum, within which both can be specified and yet co-implicated with each other to varying degrees. For example, self-regarding and Other-regarding attitudes can be seen as blended in the common recognition of reciprocity as a workable and desirable measure of human relations, which then can function as a mode of cognition guiding social practices. Here a form of moral reasoning can ensue that is generated from interest-laden dispositions. It should be noted that the complex bidirectional character of human affects can help disrupt the notion that reciprocal reasoning is nothing more than the mutually instrumental calculations of ego-based agents. Returning favors, for example, can involve a mix of self-interest, indebtedness, gratitude, and transactional pleasure.

An emotion–cognition continuum can also help illuminate certain passions that are obviously harmful and problematical from an ethical standpoint. Consider the example of hatred, particularly something like racial hatred. Hatred is far from simply an emotion or feeling; it is a very complex affect with a range of cognitive elements.[57] Hatred is different from anger because there is a deeper narrative involved than simply a reaction to a perceived injury. Hatred can prompt cruelty, or the deliberate infliction of suffering mainly for the satisfaction of the perpetrator. Hatred, then, seems to be the opposite of empathic concern because it is an intense emotion with a tendency toward injuring or eliminating an Other. The cognitive element of hatred is shown in the constructions of the Other that seemingly explain or justify the emotion. Racial hatred is not a matter of a direct encounter with a particular person; it is indiscriminately directed toward a racial group, indeed members of the group cannot be perceived as individuals but as embodiments of stereotypical constructions that have a fixed, abstract quality. The source of such hatred can be multifaceted and complex: a frustration over one's own inadequacies, a fear of difference, a general anxiety about the finitude of life that can prompt projection onto some tangible Other as the source of one's woe, an elevation of oneself through the castigation of an Other, or even a fear of weakness (which can explain why social hatreds are often directed at groups that are relatively weak or vulnerable). The point is that hatred and cruelty are constituted by complex associations and constructions, which shows the degree to which language and cognition are implicated in human emotions, in a manner not evident in other animals.

The ambiguity of the emotion–cognition continuum and the possibility of Other-regarding affects suggest that emotions are ethically problematical not because they are simply emotions, construed as natural forces of self-interest as opposed to the nature-transcending capacity of regulatory reason. We can say, rather, that *some* emotions or levels of emotions are ethically problematical, owing to a complex constellation of existential factors, in the face of which theoretical principles are relatively impotent. Solutions to such problems would have to reflect the complexity of their causes. As I have said, questions of moral constitution, motivation, and transformation cannot be answered solely on rational grounds, but would have to engage the existential, environmental, and affective elements suggested in this study. Given the possible sources of racial hatred mentioned above (an extreme example that can still bear on less severe but comparable levels of racial attitudes, and that can be analogically extended to other social attitudes), a principle of human equality or solidarity may have a certain ethical force, but it will be insufficient to affect ethical attention, much less ethical change. It is evident that a host of psychological, emotional, and cognitive factors are involved, and addressing them approaches the deepest issues of how one engages the world and others—particularly concerning Heideggerian insights about how the tension of finitude can prompt evasion, concealment, distortion, and refuge in fixed constructions. A principle can tell us that racial hatred and consequent behaviors are morally wrong in the abstract, but the environment out of which and in which such matters develop involves much more than the regulation of emotion by reason. Indeed, at a certain level, it is the complex phenomenon of world-disclosive affect (*Befindlichkeit*) that is at the heart of most ethical problems and solutions.[58]

Moral theory's dependence on subject-centered reason mirrors the modern disengagement of the self from the world by way of an abstract ordering of the existential environment. Consider the example of torture. Utilitarian and Kantian theories would judge torture to be morally wrong based on an impartial rational analysis. Utilitarianism would judge on the basis of calculating the balance of harm and benefit (and accordingly it might sanction torture in some instances). Kantianism would judge on the basis of a maxim's universal consistency. In neither case would the judgment be in direct response to the suffering of the victim or the character of the perpetrator. Kant would certainly praise compassion for the victim, but the *moral* assessment of torture would stem from an agent's conforming or not conforming to a rational law, not from the concrete conditions and effects of actions.[59] Even the "feeling" of respect, for Kant, is more for persons as rational agents capable of grasping the moral law, not as particular persons — this person here and now in this situation.

The virtue of empathy is different in generating concrete responses to concrete circumstances with an intrinsic ethical sense. Impartial moral theories are certainly right in pointing to the possible absence or diminishment of certain admirable affects, and especially to harmful consequences of certain other affects. Impartial reasoning is presumably offered as a safeguard against such possibilities. My objections concern the tendency toward a wholesale segregation of moral reasoning and affective regard, especially concerning questions of moral constitution, motivation, and transformation. In particular, if we recall the developmental continuum of affective empathy and more cognitive modes of empathy, we can notice important correlations between affective and cognitive forces in ethics. For example, I suggest that affective empathy first discloses a sense of "alikeness" that evolves, with the help of language, into more generalized, less immediate moral notions that are less affectively specific and that hence have a wider range. Immediate experiences of help and harm can be widened — by way of language's capacity for distancing and temporal extension — into a more abstract, cognitive understanding of the moral significance of help and harm. Such understanding can subsequently be generalized, fostered through imagination, and extended to absent Others.[60]

It is feasible, then, to propose a compensation for the limits of affective empathy in the direction of conceptual generality, and hence a widened horizon of commonality that is presumably the province of many moral principles. Such compensation, however, is ontogenetically dependent on affective empathy, which can be seen as still registering its traces in more abstract modulations. Accordingly, we should question the notion that moral concepts and principles are strictly cognitive phenomena. Rather, such constructions unfold in an affect–cognition continuum shaped by language. Recall that empathy is not simply a feeling or impulse, but an experience laden with an interpretive as-structure. Empathy is not simply about feelings, but a response to a person's existential *condition* and a prompt to engage that condition.[61] Various linguistic formulations simply extend this tacit content into further horizons.

An existential model of ethical understanding as a blend of cognitive generality and affective particularity is a richer conception than mere cognitive or

noncognitive models alone, and it clearly can address questions of moral constitution, motivation, and performance more effectively than strictly cognitive theories. In this light, moral principles and other basic ethical notions can be
defended, not in terms of strict rational standards of consistency or universality,
but in terms of the looser, situated conditions of inhabitive truth, in terms of
appropriateness, reliability, workability, and agreement. These conditions may
not provide an inviolable defense or a universal order, but they can surely provide
a certain intellectual force.[62]

An existential orientation can also address problems of feasibility facing rationalistic theories that extend conceptual generality into a sphere of universality and
rational necessity, which can press ethics into a rigid formalism or demonstrative
technique that can overreach or overburden an ethical environment. Consider the
notion that we ought to help the needy. First of all, "help" and "need" are complex
terms, and their import certainly originates in specific affect-laden circumstances
(indicated in usages such as "I need help"). Abstract concepts of help and need can
sustain and widen this moral import. But if the moral character of this notion is
converted into a universal principle of right, either on the grounds of rational consistency or the indiscriminate obligation to maximize well-being, then a commitment to helping anyone or everyone in need would seem to be rationally, and
hence morally, required. If I have more than I need and I do not agree to extend
my surplus to the needy, then I would seem to be guilty of a moral failing.[63] As I
have said, widening one's circle of concern is certainly important in ethics, but an
abstract syllogistic technique that would argue, for example, that only a global
redistribution of wealth would satisfy the moral claim at issue would be at least
unrealistic and at worst counterproductive (given the failings of certain sweeping
experiments in this direction).

We could talk of a certain presumptive obligation to alleviate suffering, especially since many face-to-face circumstances usually elicit spontaneous motivations to help. The question concerns how far one can or should extend this obligation. The importance of impartiality is that it stems from a (not impartial)
interest in extending the moral horizon as wide as possible (and thus not primarily from a dedication to rational consistency). Most human ethical motivations
and practices originate in the sphere of partiality toward intimates. Face-to-face
contact with strangers or specific appeals to specific contexts of need can elicit
comparable responsiveness. The more distant or wider the horizon, however, the
more difficult it is to tap into moral motivation. We can affirm the general notion
of widening the circle of ethical regard without insisting that only universal consistency can fulfill a moral obligation.[64]

Moral principles and abstract formulations can be called formal indications
that shape a sense of ethical bearings in a finite existential environment that is
marked by limits and contextual specificity, and that is distorted or even damaged
when governed solely by rational universals. Moral principles are more a con-

ceptual supplement than a rational reconstruction of ethical experience or a governing force in some decision procedure. I am not likely to alleviate suffering simply because a decision to do so was entailed by a moral principle in a chain of reasoning. And moral life need not require a self-conscious reflexivity that mandates a rational articulation of one's decision procedure.[65]

In sum, moral principles can provide ethical bearings, but in a manner derived from other ethical bearings that originally take shape in a complex affective, situational, practical, social environment. Language allows the articulation, specification, and transmission of much in this environment. A moral principle can be called a specified generalization stemming from such a linguistic articulation ("People should not be cruel"). The problem is, recalling the role of language in inauthenticity, that the sustainability of language beyond immediate uses and experiences permits the isolation of a linguistic formulation from its original milieu, which can produce and foster two kinds of distortion. First, the abstract quality of an isolated linguistic proposition allows an overlooking of the complex affective/situational/performative setting from which the proposition arose. Second, the separability of a proposition from other propositions permits an analytical segregation from the tensions and conflicts with other ethical bearings and their modulations into differing principles. A principle-based ethics, then, is predisposed to miss the ambiguities, ambivalences, and dissonances in ethical life.

In general terms it is possible to talk of an "ought" or a "must" in ethics that has an existential claim, without having to entail a necessity that would rule out divergence on pain of irrationality or moral failure. A rationalistic sense of obligation that trumps all comers is not appropriate to most lived senses of obligation.[66] Presumptive obligations unfold in particular contexts, without the assumption of universality beyond the context, and often without a sense of rules applied to cases.[67] How would my friends take it if I told them my loyalty to them issued from following a friendship rule? Even generalizable obligations such as "Be loyal to your friends" remain context-specific and can often run into conflict with other obligations.[68] A conflict of compelling obligations is not uncommon in ethical life, and it is more the stuff of tragedy than adjudication.[69]

NOTES

1. When Heidegger offers a critical discussion of "projection" he refers to *Projektion*; his own notion of *Entwurf* is far from an inside-out structure, in fact it is associated with the "throw" of *Geworfenheit* (*GA* 9, 377).

2. It is frustrating that Heidegger seems to find the time to discuss examples of tool use in some detail, but human relations seem to be a distraction.

3. Arne J. Vetlesen argues that emotion supplies the "constitution" of a moral object, as an affective discovery of the import of the weal and woe of others. See *Perception, Empathy, and Judgment: An Inquiry into the Preconditions of Moral Performance* (University Park:

162   Chapter Six

Pennsylvania State University Press, 1994), ch. 4. See also Justin Oakley, *Morality and the Emotions* (New York: Routledge, 1992), and Michael Stocker, *Valuing Emotions* (Cambridge: Cambridge University Press, 1996).

4. See Mark H. Davis, *Empathy: A Social Psychological Approach* (Boulder, Colo.: Westview, 1996), and Nancy Eisenberg and Janet Strayer, eds., *Empathy and Its Development* (Cambridge: Cambridge University Press, 1987). See also Hans Herbert Kögler and Karsten R. Stueber, eds., *Empathy and Agency: The Problem of Understanding in the Human Sciences* (Boulder, Colo.: Westview, 2000).

5. Martin Hoffman, "Affect and Moral Development," in *New Directions for Child Development*, ed. D. Cicchetti and P. Hesse (San Francisco: Jossey-Bass, 1982), 95.

6. It should be pointed out in this regard that Heidegger does not discuss to any significant extent the *inter*subjective elements of Mitsein, something treated extensively by Gadamer and Habermas. Heidegger does, however, call *Fürsorge* a "co-disclosure" (*BT*, 344).

7. See Davis, *Empathy,* throughout.

8. Eisenberg and Strayer, *Empathy and Its Development*, 63 and ch. 10.

9. The primacy of affective empathy can be seen as ethically significant because a cruel or sadistic person can be said to possess a kind of cognitive empathy. See Bernard Williams, *Ethics and the Limits of Philosophy* (Cambridge, Mass.: Harvard University Press, 1985), 91.

10. Empathy must be distinguished from "personal distress," which is an *aversive* experience of another's suffering that prompts various modes of flight to alleviate one's own distress (Eisenberg and Strayer, *Empathy and Its Development*, 7).

11. For a helpful discussion of the differences between empathy, sympathy, and altruism, see Douglas Chismar, "Empathy and Sympathy: The Important Difference," *Journal of Value Inquiry* 22 (1988): 257–66.

12. Davis, *Empathy*, ch. 7; Eisenberg and Strayer, *Empathy and Its Development*, ch. 4.

13. Vetlesen maintains that empathy is the human access to, and disclosure of, the moral domain, the import of the weal and woe of others (*Perception, Empathy, and Judgment*, 204–18).

14. I am not arguing that such a projective and reflective model of empathy has no sense or application, only that it is not primal.

15. Heidegger may have had Edmund Husserl specifically in mind here, since Husserl understood *Einfühlung* as the self feeling itself into the Other, with the self as the original reference point. See Rudolph A. Makkreel, "How Is Empathy Related to Understanding," in *Issues in Husserl's* Ideas II, ed. Thomas Nenon and Lester Embree (Boston: Kluwer Academic, 1996), 199–212. See also the study by one of Husserl's students, Edith Stein, *Zum Problem der Einfühlung* (Halle: Buchdruckerei des Waisenhauses, 1917). Wilhelm Dilthey offered a more nuanced conception of empathy as a kind of transposition based in shared cultural structures rather than as transferences between individual selves. See Rudolph A. Makkreel, "From Simulation to Structural Transposition: A Diltheyan Critique of Empathy and Defense of *Verstehen*," in Kögler and Stueber, *Empathy and Agency*, 181–93.

16. See Heidegger's forceful critique of the skeptical problem of the external world in *BT*, section 43.

17. Hume considered sympathy to be a natural capacity to share the pleasures and pains of others, which can serve as the wellspring for Other-regarding elements in ethics. See his *A Treatise on Human Nature* (Oxford: Clarendon Press, 1978), particularly books II and III. Hume provides vivid phenomenological accounts that suggest something like a Heideggerian ekstatics, but he also remains caught up in the modern framework of subjectivity by sometimes explaining sympathy in terms of projection and inferences (575–76).

18. Heidegger indicates that it is no accident that a polarization of self and Other has been conceived (*FCM*, 203), because part of being-with is an experience of being "apart" or merely "alongside," which can prompt a notion of a gap that needs bridging (*FCM*, 206).

19. On this point in general terms, see Werner Marx, *Is There a Measure on Earth? Foundations For a Nonmetaphysical Ethics*, trans. Thomas J. Nenon and Reginald Lilly (Chicago: University of Chicago Press, 1987).

20. Heidegger suggests positive prospects for ethnology and psychological research, but a phenomenologically adequate conception of "world" is needed before appropriate scientific findings can be considered (*BT*, 76–77).

21. Eisenberg and Strayer, *Empathy and Its Development*, 127.

22. Eisenberg and Strayer, *Empathy and Its Development*, 129.

23. Eisenberg and Strayer, *Empathy and Its Development*, 119.

24. Eisenberg and Strayer, *Empathy and Its Development*, 51.

25. Eisenberg and Strayer, *Empathy and Its Development*, 52.

26. Eisenberg and Strayer, *Empathy and Its Development*, 148–49.

27. The primacy of something like empathy is not something to be "proven," but something phenomenologically *shown* in the experience and behavior of children, and in parental responses to such exhibitions. What parent would not enjoy, prefer, and encourage a child's empathic responses in social relations, compared to indifferent or strictly self-regarding responses?

28. In fact, *Einfühlung* in its earliest usage referred to motor mimicry (Eisenberg and Strayer, *Empathy and Its Development*, 317–18).

29. Eisenberg and Strayer, *Empathy and Its Development*, 322–23.

30. Eisenberg and Strayer, *Empathy and Its Development*, 136.

31. Inattention to relational needs is a significant flaw in most developmental theories, especially Freudian theories. See Vetlesen, *Perception, Empathy, and Judgment*, 252–71.

32. Eisenberg and Strayer, *Empathy and Its Development*, 138.

33. Maurice Merleau-Ponty indicates that a child initially does not distinguish between self and Other, or between introspection and perception. Experience with caregivers is not a transfer between selves, but rather a "syncretic sociability." Bodily movements and behaviors "play across" each other, and self–Other distinctions emerge out of this nexus, which continues to operate in mature experience as well. See his "The Child's Relations with Others," in *The Primacy of Perception and Other Essays*, ed. James E. Edie (Evanston, Ill.: Northwestern University Press, 1964), 119, 133–35, 154–55.

34. Eisenberg and Strayer, *Empathy and Its Development*, ch. 7; Davis, *Empathy*, ch. 4.

35. A number of factors seem to enhance the development of empathic concern: a secure, nurturing, affectionate environment (which diminishes excessive self-concern);

modeling and identification; inductive socialization (e.g., the golden rule); and opportunities for helping behaviors and their reinforcement (Eisenberg and Strayer, *Empathy and Its Development*, 150–57).

36. In this vein we can understand the value of what has been called "service learning" in some school curricula. Here students are required to engage in actual social work in the community and to reflect on their experiences. Some might call this an unwarranted imposition of values or a circumvention of free choice in ethical matters. But we assign all sorts of activities and practices that we think are important for students' development and that we suspect they might not discover apart from schooling. In the light of our analysis, service learning is an appropriate and efficacious educational concept: It gives students avenues to ethical work that they might not recognize on their own; it exposes them to situations that might prompt empathic concern; it fosters practical and social capacities that otherwise might not emerge; and it prepares ethical habits that might be continued throughout life. On many levels, service learning is consistent with the Aristotelian idea of becoming good by doing and not simply by knowing. See Timothy K. Stanton, Dwight E. Giles Jr., and Nadinne I. Cruz, *Service-Learning: A Movement's Pioneers Reflect on Its Origins, Practice, and Future* (San Francisco: Jossey-Bass, 1999).

37. For another angle on the naturalness of empathy, see the discussions of the evolutionary advantages of empathy in Eisenberg and Strayer, *Empathy and Its Development*, ch. 3, and Davis, *Empathy*, ch. 2. For an overview of the research and issues pertaining to the adaptive character of altruism, see Neven Sesardic, "Recent Work on Human Altruism and Evolution," *Ethics* 106 (October 1995): 128–57.

38. Davis, *Empathy*, ch. 7. See also C. Daniel Bateson, "Experimental Tests for the Existence of Altruism," *Proceedings of the Biennial Meetings of the Philosophy of Science Association* 2 (1993): 69–80.

39. Because Kant would take something like mineness as saturated with self-regard, he claims that I should seek the happiness of others because a maxim excluding such efforts cannot be universalized, and not because such efforts were a concern of mine. See Kant, *Foundations of the Metaphysics of Morals*, trans. Lewis White Beck (New York: Bobbs-Merrill, 1959), 60.

40. Eisenberg and Strayer, *Empathy and Its Development*, 54. The rest of the points in this paragraph are drawn from pages 54–73.

41. For a discussion of the role of emotion in moral judgment and moral life, especially in contrast to Kantian and Habermasian postconventional systems that stress cognitive validity, see Vetlesen, *Perception, Empathy, and Judgment*, ch. 6. Mention should be made of the work of Lawrence Kohlberg. See especially his *Essays on Moral Development* (New York: Harper and Row, 1981). In effect, Kohlberg provides an empirical rather than a transcendental account of a Kantian approach to ethics, by suggesting that children pass through progressive stages of moral development, from a preconventional to a conventional and finally a postconventional level, the last being the truly moral level of comprehensive, Other-regarding thinking based in universal principles of right and contractual relations. Carol Gilligan has challenged this model as gender-biased, overly cognitive, and suppressive of a care ethic. For a detailed critique of Kohlberg, see Richard A. Schweder, Manamohan Mahapatra, and Joan G. Miller, "Culture and Moral Development," in *The Emergence of Morality in Young Children*, Jerome Kagan and Sharon Lamb, eds. (Chicago: University of Chicago Press, 1987), ch. 1.

42. Among the most significant examples are behaviors in the Nazi regime. See Vetlesen's discussion in *Perception, Empathy, and Judgment*, chs. 2, 4, 5. A key question for impartial moral theories is: What is the difference between impartiality and indifference? One presumable difference is that impartiality does not lack feelings but simply brackets them in moral considerations. But would not indifference be the preferable state measured by the aims of impartiality? Cannot an indifferent person be fully rational, even *more* rational than a person wrestling with feelings? In certain situations, the cultivation of emotional indifference might be safer, more efficient, even psychologically attractive. If we might balk at such a prospect, especially given some heinous consequences of emotional indifference, we notice the difficulties in divorcing affect from ethics. For a discussion of how a Kantian sense of duty can be implicated in immorality, see Oakley, *Morality and the Emotions*, ch. 3.

43. For a beautiful and forceful meditation on obligation as a thrown, finite call that exceeds the logistics of moral theory, see John D. Caputo, *Against Ethics* (Bloomington: Indiana University Press, 1993).

44. Heidegger, *Vom Wesen des Grundes* (Frankfurt am Main: Vittorio Klosterman, 1955).

45. The dynamic of being-toward-death opening up authentic care can also address the phenomenon of ethical transformation, or a "change of heart" issuing from dramatic occurrences or circumstances, which is difficult to explain or even deal with in most moral theories grounded in rational reflection. See Philip Blosser, *Scheler's Critique of Kant's Ethics* (Athens: Ohio University Press, 1995), 162.

46. This touches on the profound level of Nietzsche's critique of moral sentiment. An intrinsic tension in ethics is that the more we care about people, the more we want to protect them from suffering and alleviate it; yet the finitude of meaning implies that suffering can be educative and productive. Compassion should involve the phronetic balance between responding *to* suffering and learning *from* suffering. On this point, see Charles E. Scott, *The* Question *of Ethics: Nietzsche, Foucault, Heidegger* (Bloomington: Indiana University Press, 1990), 111–20.

47. See Werner Marx, *Towards a Phenomenological Ethics: Ethics and the Life-World*, trans. Stefaan Heyvaert (Albany: SUNY Press, 1992), 56–67.

48. Eisenberg and Strayer, *Empathy and Its Development*, 73. Is it possible that objections to the role of affect in ethics stem not simply from a concern about the harmful effects of the passions and threats to the stability of moral regulations, but also from an anxious resistance to the "throw" of ecstatic empathy that is perceived as a loss of control or threat to the preserves of a disengaged self? Such would be a decidedly unethical element in the modern celebration of "autonomy."

49. Marx, in *Towards a Phenomenological Ethics*, suggests an ethical basis in compassion born out of mortality, which certainly accords with my analysis. However, I do not see why indifference should be called our everyday attunement (39), or why mortality is the only basis for engendering compassion. Everyday experience can involve compassionate concern, and many things can stimulate such concern without having to encounter death. Moreover, Marx talks about a person developing a compassion for all humanity, an "all-pervading force that is alive in his overall relation to world, fellow-man, and community" (140). This is way overblown, I think, and it needs to be subjected to a Nietzschean suspicion.

50. Vetlesen makes the important point that much of indifference is traceable not to the human psyche but to modern bureaucratic institutions that neutralize or dilute concrete

responsiveness because of their abstract ordering techniques and controls (*Perception, Empathy, and Judgment*, 108).

51. One reason why indifference can be converted is that in many cases it is not a bare absence of empathic concern. It can be a reactive shadow of an ethical apprehension. Speaking for myself, if I ignore or turn away from a homeless person on the street, this response is not truly indifferent or detached, but rather a second-order response to a more original response to the ethical claim of the situation ("Here is someone in need who could be helped"). This more immediate response can be faint but nonetheless there, and it accounts for a faint sense of guilt in my second-order response.

52. And as noted in chapter 3, that there are other ways to construe rationality. In ethical conversation, "What if someone did that to you?" is an excellent dialogical question, although it might not always produce expected results (recall the power advocate willing to accept defeat). "What if everyone acted that way?" can be effective too, although the rejoinder "They won't" is not an irrational response. "If everyone acted that way, would not rational consistency collapse?" is a contrived extension of ordinary consistency into an overly abstract ordinance that cannot actually be tested. In some moral cases we can surmise unbridgeable rational differences if we consider the familiar distinction between valid and sound arguments. In the abortion debate, if killing an innocent human being is wrong, both the pro-life and pro-choice camps can supply valid arguments but disagree about a key premise involving the humanity of the fetus. Recalling Aristotle, one can certainly see an embryo as alive and potentially human, but at the same time not yet actually human. The ambiguity of not-yet-but-will-be-human allows both sides to advance valid arguments leading to opposite conclusions. How the *truth* of the embryo/human premise in each case is ascertained, is not likely amenable to a neutral measure that can adjudicate or rectify this disparity.

53. On the limits of impartiality in ethics, see Margaret Urban Walker, "Partial Consideration," *Ethics* 101 (July 1991): 758–74.

54. Richard Rorty takes moral principles not as justifications for practices but as reminders and abbreviations for a host of practices and vocabularies. See his *Contingency, Irony, and Solidarity* (Cambridge: Cambridge University Press, 1989), 59.

55. One difficulty for an ethics based in subject-centered reason is as follows. Why should the rationality of the subject be preferred over the more personal self-interests of the subject? Why should so-called rational freedom trump the more anarchic freedom of individual divergence? To simply opt for the universality of reason or presume that it must govern the self on pain of inconsistency begs the question and is not sufficient to rule out divergent subjectivity. Acting solely on one's interests need not come across as irrational. With an ekstatic, social self, on the other hand, a separable subjectivity would not stand as a baseline reference haunting all Other-regarding ethical prospects.

56. See Kant, *Critique of Practical Reason*, trans. Lewis White Beck (New York: Macmillan, 1956), ch. 1, theorems I and II.

57. See Vetlesen, *Perception, Empathy, and Judgment*, ch. 5.

58. Heidegger grants that Dasein can and should come to master its moods, but adds that this should not presume the primacy of something opposite to mood (*BT*, 175).

59. Kant would question helping someone out of sympathy rather than from duty to the moral law. See Kant, *Foundations of the Metaphysics of Morals*, 73–74, where he claims that any normal person would wish to be sympathetic, but that inclinations blocking sympathy should prompt us to transcend inclination altogether in the direction of a rational law. This contrasts with my suggestion of constructing a moral concept not by disregard-

ing affect but on the basis of *certain* affects that Kant would agree we all esteem and that seem to be in the range of our experience in some way or another.

60. I would also suggest that there is something in the ekstatic character of empathy that is implicated in the familiar sense of a moral intuition. Since authentic empathic experiences are immediate and not a matter of projection from inside the self out to the Other, such an immersion in someone's condition has a certain phenomenological self-evidence about it, in that the ethical import is directly given, as opposed to some kind of inference or surmise. Empathy as an ekstatic affect is an intuition that is not restricted to cognitive senses, and is a disclosure that is not restricted to an internal condition of the self. Accordingly, those who are comfortable talking about moral intuitions or self-evident ethical claims may be aided somewhat by the ekstatic structure of being-in-the-world. What is meant here by self-evidency, however, will not satisfy conditions of rational necessity or indubitability, but will simply indicate an immediate truth disclosed (unconcealed) to a responsive self in a particular situation. Such might be the existential background of more abstract senses of self-evidency.

61. Lawrence Blum, "Particularity and Responsiveness," in *The Emergence of Morality in Young Children*, 310–11.

62. An affect–cognition blend can also account for ways in which knowledge can affect, alter, or guide emotional states. If I am angry at an injury and then learn that it was not intentional but accidental, my anger can immediately subside. Sometimes emotions can be stilled or modified by thoughtful reflection. Sometimes emotions can be conjured up simply through rumination, memory, or imagination. All of this suggests that emotions are not entirely passive and can be considered a kind of middle voice.

63. For instance, see Peter Unger, *Living High and Letting Die: Our Illusion of Innocence* (New York: Oxford University Press, 1996).

64. Altruism is rooted in kinship ties and yet the circle can be expanded, but usually only if the circle of intimates is secure. In deteriorating circumstances the circle tends to close back. See Frans de Waal, *Good Natured: The Origins of Right and Wrong in Humans and Other Animals* (Cambridge: Cambridge University Press, 1996), 212–16. An ethics of the stranger is an urgent question, especially given the scale, mobility, and technological reach of the modern world. What do we owe the stranger? Should the stranger be taken as a potential intimate? As someone deserving our regard in any case? On this question there has arisen an interest in an ethics of generosity and gift-giving, an active response to need, and an openness to the Other, specifically the foreigner and the exile. See Alan D. Schrift, ed., *The Logic of the Gift: Toward an Ethic of Generosity* (New York: Routledge, 1997). Jacques Derrida is particularly evocative in this matter. See his *The Gift of Death*, trans. David Wells (Chicago: University of Chicago Press, 1995), and "Hospitality, Justice, and Responsibility," in *Questioning Ethics: Contemporary Debates in Philosophy*, ed. Richard Kearney and Mark Dooley (New York: Routledge, 1999), ch. 6. In the latter essay Derrida talks of an "unconditional hospitality," an unreciprocal openness to foreigners and exiles, a surrender of the mastery of one's home or nation. This is excessive, I think. It can become domination in reverse and it allows in the old perfectionist guilt over never measuring up. A phronetic balance is called for. David Wood, in the same volume (ch. 8), advises well: "Openness does not require that one leaves the door open, but that one is always willing to open the door" (117).

65. See Blum, "Particularity and Responsiveness," 330–31. As Williams suggests, reflecting on ethical life need not be identified with providing justificatory reasons or with

pondering the relations between premises and conclusions (*Ethics and the Limits of Philosophy*, 112, 154). See also Stuart Hampshire, *Morality and Conflict* (Cambridge, Mass.: Harvard University Press, 1983), 105–14.

66. Williams, *Ethics and the Limits of Philosophy*, 180.

67. Blum, "Particularity and Responsiveness," 323ff.

68. Hampshire, *Morality and Conflict*, 92ff.

69. One reason for Heidegger's reticence about ethics was his sense of tragic dwelling that he took to exceed moral categories: "The tragedies of Sophocles . . . preserve the *ēthos* in their sagas more primordially than Aristotle's lectures on 'ethics'" (*LH*, 256). Heidegger follows Nietzsche in retrieving the early Greek cultural form of tragedy to challenge the tendency in Western thought to "moralistically" pass judgment on a world of time, change, and disorder. The West has advanced different projects aiming to transcend, master, correct, or progressively rectify an enigmatic, hostile world. Heidegger diagnoses this tradition as an anxiety-driven search for refuge, a fugitive disposition in the face of finitude. Greek tragedy, on the other hand, does not exhibit such a disposition; it confronts squarely the limits of existence without hopes for any fundamental salvation, rectification, or intelligibility. Yet beyond this ontological level, tragic dramas often turn on intractable ethical conflicts, such as the conflict between kinship duties and civic duties in Sophocles' *Antigone*. See Martha Nussbaum's insightful treatment of Aeschylus and Sophocles in *The Fragility of Goodness* (Cambridge: Cambridge University Press, 1986), chs. 2–3.

Chapter Seven

Selfhood, Freedom, and Community

In this chapter I bring a Heideggerian perspective to bear on the question of self-hood, with particular attention to debates over the relation between individuality and community. My contention is that Heidegger's thought can open up fruitful negotiations between contending positions in these debates, and that his finite ontology can radicalize standard categories in such arguments and deepen the discussion of their ethical and social implications. I begin by examining the dispute between liberalism and communitarianism.

LIBERALISM AND COMMUNITARIANISM

The central issue in this debate concerns the relationship between individuality and community, between the self and the social order.[1] Liberalism is an outgrowth of the modern displacement of tradition, custom, and authority in favor of the project of critical reason. The modern self, as I have shown, is the free, rational individual, distinct from nature, inherited structures, and other selves. Human beings share a general nature of being individual subjects grounded in reflective consciousness. Each individual has a specific nature that can be discerned by rational examination and actualized through the agency of purposive, regulatory reason. In this way the liberal self is conceived as a ground prior to its ends and involvements. In the "state of nature," prior to social constraints, the individual self is essentially free. Such foundational freedom, coupled with the subject's rational capacities, underwrites the claim that human beings are *entitled* to freedom from social control and external powers. The Kantian conception of freedom, for example, is not license but the *self*-imposed moral law disclosed by the rational mind's own reflection. In this way freedom involves reason's capacity to transcend the constraints of sensuous nature and achieve self-mastery. Ethics and politics, as rational projects, can be freed from traditional constraints and elements of force in favor of deliberative discovery and construction. Human development is internally based, and so exterior forces, even when not oppressive, are inauthentic sources of the self's being.

In liberalism, the social order is construed as a "contract" between free individuals to protect their interests, a mutual recognition of individual rights guaranteed by the state, wherein each self agrees to limit its absolute freedom in order to protect the freedom of all to pursue self-development. The baseline principle in liberalism, then, is individual sovereignty, or in Lockean terms, self-ownership. The social order is a secondary sphere that is constituted to facilitate and protect the interests of individual self-formation. Such a foundational individualism underwrites the notion that social and material goods are "possessions," that we "own" rights and property, for example, which therefore are inviolable. The legitimacy of politics is then based in a rational, calculated self-interest, a mutual protection of individual possessions.[2]

Liberalism distinguishes between the right and the good, between political principles of justice grounded in individual rights and particular conceptions of the good life that can vary from individual to individual. Liberalism prefers a state that is neutral with respect to conceptions of value, thus sustaining a division between the public domain of justice and the private domain of life interests. A central feature of liberal thought is the freedom of individuals to live the life they want, so long as they do not violate the rights of others to do the same.[3] Liberalism is dedicated to the idea of respect for individual freedom and autonomy, rather than an emphasis on more communal notions of love or social bonds.

Communitarianism involves a critique of both the liberal conception of selfhood and its consequent social philosophy. Individual sovereignty and autonomy are rejected as a philosophical foundation, because no human self can actually be posited as its own ground. Each self becomes an individual in medias res, that is, not from the standpoint of detached, rational reflection or a self-asserting will, but from social, cultural, and material forces that shape the self from early on in life. The liberal notion of the free rational individual (which animates most modern moral theories) is critiqued as too thin a conception to fit many common ethical relations that are not "chosen" in a strict sense or assessed by some reasoning process (for instance, family relationships, friendships, personal loyalties, love relations). Communitarianism stresses the sociality of the self rather than the "unencumbered self" of liberal individualism.[4] Every self is situated, which is to say caught up in and formed by tradition, custom, language, family, schooling, and multiple associations. The sociality of the self is far from simply an external relation restricted to the obvious fact that humans cannot survive or develop their capacities apart from upbringing by other human beings. Communitarianism draws on a quasi-Hegelian concept of dialectical recognition, which indicates that every aspect of the self's nature is in part constituted by a confrontation with, and the recognition of, others, that we are always embedded in a transactional network of interpersonal responses, even if the response is one of rebellion.[5]

The communitarian critique of liberal social philosophy is not predicated on the sheer denial of individual freedom, but on the charge that liberalism stems from a flawed conception of the self and issues paradoxical or divisive implications when the ideal of individual autonomy is taken to reductive extremes. First of all, liberalism itself is a tradition that helps form selves, and even in its historical emergence it did not unfold out of the blue apart from prior influences in the Western tradition. Second, even a system of individual "rights" cannot be understood apart from certain "goods," or values and preferences that we are likely to hold in common. Third, liberal politics can precipitate a certain schizophrenia in citizens, who are told that some of their deepest commitments (such as religious beliefs) should be kept private, out of the public sphere of political deliberation. Finally, liberal individualism can tend toward a fragmentation or disintegration of community, especially in an inevitably competitive (capitalist) model of economic life that many have said is intrinsic to the history and perpetuation of liberal social theory.

Communitarians argue that social thought needs to stress the self's dependency on, and connections with, other selves in various associational milieus. Contrary to the liberal dissociation of politics from such milieus, communitarians call for a cultivation of "civic virtues" and a politics of the "common good." In this way, social life in the context of the state can be a vehicle for promoting and inculcating collective values.

The communitarian critique of liberal individualism is consonant in many ways with Heidegger's phenomenology of Mitsein, and so I think there is much to recommend it philosophically. Liberalism, however, could incorporate much of sociality while still affirming certain contextual strategies of individuation that can be seen as relevant to ethics and politics, and as protection against the dangers of a communal momentum that can consume or suppress individuality. Liberalism is particularly suspicious of the state—given its elements of coercion and bureaucratic forces—as the proper locus for the fostering of sociality or community. In other words, liberal politics can call itself "postsocial" rather than pre- or extrasocial.[6] Communitarians might still be suspicious of this gesture to sociality, because state-of-nature narratives (and contemporary modifications such as Rawls's original position and veil of ignorance) that have underwritten liberal theories do stipulate a nonsocial, disengaged starting point—and one can certainly question whether such provisions really can accommodate sociality in any viable way, and whether they predispose social philosophy toward certain distortions or omissions.

Liberals can still counter that it is not at all clear how community defines human existence. We inhabit many communities and group associations, along the lines of family, nation, religion, race, ethnicity, gender, language, occupation, and so on. Which of these communities best defines us? A "human community" seems too broad, and focusing on more specific communities shows that often our lives are marked by a *conflict* between some of our associations (for example, between work and family), rendering communitarian notions of collectivity and cohesion suspect. In addition, communitarianism often comes across as nos-

talgia for a lost sense of harmony that has been ruined in modern times by a grow-
ing conflict of competing factions. This historical picture, however, is illusory.
The supposed condition of harmony in the past was due more to the exclusion and
suppression of certain groups, or to the mutual seclusion of different cultural
groups within their own enclaves. With modern developments of inclusiveness,
mobility, and social interpenetration, a certain conflicted complexity would seem
to be inevitable. Genuine inclusion of all voices is likely to produce ineradicable
tensions. Global harmony is more likely the silhouette of silence or suppression.

HEIDEGGER ON SELFHOOD AND SOCIALITY

What appears evident from the above analysis is that the debate between liberalism
and communitarianism should not be seen as a forced choice between community
and individuality, or between social harmony and conflict, but rather as an indication of the complex intersection of various social forces and dynamics that cannot
be grounded in *any* locus, whether in the community or individual or identity or difference. What is needed is a philosophical analysis that incorporates both sociality
and individual divergence, and that provides a fundamental openness that subverts
stable groundings in social theory. Such an analysis can be found in Heidegger.

Here I focus more attention on Mitsein and authenticity. Some readings have
taken Dasein's authenticity to be either an asocial, heroic individualism or a con-
sumptive communalism. The former is flatly false, as I have shown, while the latter is doubtful, though conceivable, especially given Heidegger's own political
history. I want to argue that authenticity can be read as neither reductively individual nor reductively communal, but as the kind of complex, intersectional
openness that can negotiate between liberalism and communitarianism.[7]

I have established that Dasein, as being-in-the-world, is not a separate or isolated self apart from the environing-world or other Daseins. Dasein's being is the
meaning or mattering of world involvement. With the notion of "mineness,"
Heidegger offers a clear sense of individuation, not in the manner of an isolated
subject, but simply the existential meaningfulness of Dasein's endeavors. With
Mitsein, Dasein's sociality is a core phenomenon. We do not have to argue for a
social dimension to challenge individualistic models of the self, because Dasein
from early on in life is ekstatically *with* others *in* the world. Relations with others are not simply external or second-order phenomena. Individual selves co-
constitute each other and dwell in/there/with each other in various ways.[8]

We have also considered how Heidegger's conception of authenticity is radically different from traditional models of selfhood, and how inauthenticity is not
some deficient existence that should be given up.

> [T]he inauthenticity of Dasein does not signify any "less" being or any "lower"
> degree of being. Rather it is the case that even in its fullest concretion Dasein can be
> characterized by inauthenticity—when busy, when excited, when interested, when
> ready for enjoyment. (*BT,* 68).[9]

Inauthenticity is simply a concealment of Dasein's radical finitude by way of a fallen immersion in beings and a confinement to the common social patterns of *das Man*. Authenticity involves Dasein being called by and to its radical finitude. Dasein's authentic "self" is the baseline negativity of being-toward-death, and the unpositable temporal thrownness from birth, into the world, toward death. For Heidegger, "Dasein never comes back behind its thrownness" (*BT*, 330). Self-hood, then, is neither a substance nor a subject, neither an enduring essence nor a radically responsible, self-grounding agency. The negativity of authenticity, however, allows for the openness of freedom and the possibility of disrupting established patterns of life, so that an individual self might discover paths that are more appropriate to its particularity. Dasein's selfhood is better rendered as an engaged openness, rather than as a detachable subject or a fixed entity.

I have shown that authenticity consists of a double movement that opens up disclosure by way of a negative experience, or a dynamic of disorientation and reorientation. The abyssal nature of Dasein's being-toward-death generates the "throw" that opens up a world of meaning. Rather than taking things for granted or remaining absorbed in their presence, Dasein comes to see things *as* finite, which sharpens and deepens Dasein's care for things. Out of being-toward-death, Dasein as care "exists finitely" (*BT*, 378). Dasein's finitude allows for authentic individuation because the disruption of death breaks the spell of *das Man* and opens up possibilities of an individual Dasein's own particular modes of care. Individuation is another mode of "becoming finite" (*FCM*, 6), of living one way rather than another way, a distinctive way rather than a common way. In sum, it can be said that Dasein's engaged openness is shaped by the dynamic of being-toward-death and its role in authentic disclosure: The climactic finale of death serves as a flashpoint that (1) illuminates the *engagement* (the correlation of care and finitude) and (2) prompts the *openness* (world conditions now seen *as* possibilities rather than fixed actualities).

I have also suggested that *das Man* should be construed as modes of socialization and enculturation, and that authenticity is better rendered as the tension between individuation and socialization, rather than as a break with the social world on behalf of some radically unique existence.

Authentic being-one's-self does not rest upon an exceptional condition of the subject, a condition that has been detached from *das Man;* it is rather an existentiell modification of *das Man*—of *das Man* as an essential existentiale. (*BT*, 168).[10]

Authenticity is not even a departure from the "fallen" character of everyday life and its various concerns, but rather an altered bearing toward quotidian endeavors.

[A]uthentic existence is not something which floats above falling everydayness; existentially, it is only a modified way of coming to grips with that everydayness. (*BT*, 224).

In fact, everydayness and authenticity may be "structurally indistinguishable" (*BT*, 70).

There are telling ambiguities in *Being and Time* that are preferable to clearer delineations of individuality and sociality, which tend to distort the complex intersections of social life. The structure of Dasein suggests both an individual and a communal sense (*BT,* 434–39). And authenticity is described as at once a movement in terms of, for, and yet against Dasein's heritage (*BT,* 435). We can recognize this ambiguity and tension in social history. For example, great moral innovators such as Socrates, Jesus, Mahatma Gandhi, and Martin Luther King Jr. have claimed strong allegiances to tradition while at the same time challenging established practices and beliefs. The engaged openness suggested by Heidegger's notions of interpretation and historical repetition speaks to such cases. Moreover, the ambiguous, reciprocal structure of engaged openness indicates that socialization and individuation represent a bipolar tension; and as such, individuation can never be a sheer departure from the social, and the social can never be immunized from disruptions and differentiations.[11]

Authentic individuation, then, is a *modification* of how the world and being-with-others are disclosed, rather than the discovery of some "new content" (*BT,* 344). I suggest that such individuation involves the fourfold possibility of (1) *owning*, (2) *unmasking*, (3) *innovating*, and (4) *interrogating* one's cultural inheritance to varying degrees. (1) One can freely appropriate as one's "own" (*eigen*) a tradition that has been handed down, but no longer simply as handed down (*BT,* 435). For instance, one can affirm the importance of certain moral obligations, but now because their relevance and value have been registered through experience and examination, rather than simply presumed or taken on authority. (2) One can unmask the concealments, disguises, superficialities, and illusions that block a deeper understanding of cultural forces and origins (*BT,* 167, 443). For instance, the notion of freedom can show its complex ambiguities and its frequent guises on behalf of privilege, irresponsibility, or domination. (3) One can discover new possibilities that are normally impeded by the inauthentic immersion in the actual and the commonplace (*BT,* 239). (4) One can challenge the normalizing tendency to suppress "new inquiry" and "disputation" (*BT,* 213). Interrogating existing orders is intrinsic to the historical structure of being for Heidegger, but forces of social cohesion and establishment dictate that such interrogation will likely involve a certain estrangement from extant patterns.

Authenticity can be understood as a tension between received patterns and decision. And decision is a phenomenon intrinsic to the finitude of ethical dwelling. Given limit conditions and uncertainties, we must still decide how to live. Sometimes we decide to depart from an established convention, to disrupt it in our resolve.[12] Even if we have clear confidence about what is good or right, ethics in the end is action and we must decide to enact the good or right in the midst of counterpossibilities, which makes *being* ethical in the end spontaneous, without cognitive or social dictation. Dasein's ethical authenticity, then, would involve (1) the responsibility of coming to one's own decision in the midst of thrown involvements, and (2) the temporal openness of bringing to presence future possibilities in the midst of an appropriated past (repetition).

Ethical decision as an individuated, responsive moment of action can be associated with Heidegger's important concept of the *Augenblick*, the moment of Dasein's resolute taking action (*BP*, 287–89). The *Augenblick* reflects (1) the temporality of repetition, (2) the disclosive constitution of the current situation, and (3) the responsiveness to the situation's circumstances, possibilities, and contingencies. Heidegger specifically compares the *Augenblick* with Aristotle's *kairos* in the *Nicomachean Ethics* (288).[13] Accordingly, such a moment can be given an ethical sense of appropriate action that is attentive to a particular temporal circumstance. What Heidegger's account of authentic resolve adds to Aristotle is important: Aristotle simply declares that the ethical *kairos* is contingent and specific; for Heidegger, it is the *experience* of existential finitude that prompts the responsiveness to the rich specificity of the situation, which has been freed from the clutter, evasions, and generalities of inauthentic existence. Authentic ethical action charged by finitude is far from a loss of direction; it is a deliverance *from* facile abstractions and convictions *toward* the complexities of practical situations.[14]

The individuating elements of authenticity do not bring a break with the social world, because Dasein always remains situated. Even the radical individuation of being-toward-death is simply an interruption of world involvement that prepares a reorientation. Dasein's finite transcendence *is* a surpassing (*PM*, 108–9), and as such it surpasses not only beings but also *itself* understood as some discrete or self-contained entity. That is why in choosing itself authentically, Dasein chooses its being with other Daseins and other beings in the world (*MFL*, 190). Authentic individuation "does not mean clinging obstinately to one's own private wishes but being free for the factical possibilities of current existence" (*BP*, 288). Dasein's selfhood is not some kind of interior entity but rather a perpetual *thrownness* toward the world. Dasein's authentic resoluteness (*Entschlossenheit*) is connected with disclosedness (*Erschlossenheit*) and truth (*BT*, 343); resoluteness frees Dasein for its world of concerns, involvements, and social relations— by *opening up* such a world. So authentic individuation is still a mode of Mitsein; it remains a being-with-others (*BP*, 287–88) and also a concern for the authentic being *of* others (*BT*, 309).[15]

I have noted the ethical implications of authenticity, especially in its differentiation from egoism. I have also considered the relational phenomenon of *Fürsorge*, which Heidegger indicates is essential to Mitsein. I mentioned two polar modes of *Fürsorge*—standing in for people's care and releasing people to and for their own authentic care—and also mixed forms in between these two extremes. The suggestion here is that social involvement must balance between overtaking people and allowing them freedom, and we can surely see most of social life as negotiated blends in between sheer freedom and sheer control. Think of the blending of guidance, restriction, and release in relationships between parents and children, teachers and students, experts and novices, professionals and clients. Think also of the wide range of helping endeavors in times of need.

For Heidegger, *Fürsorge* is clearly implicated in authenticity. Authentic Dasein is "thrust" into *"fürsorgende Mitsein"* with others (*BT*, 344). Authenticity makes possible a "letting be" of others for their ownmost potentiality (*BT*, 344). Accordingly, authentic *Fürsorge* is a "co-disclosing" that *liberates* (*BT*, 344). It lets other Daseins be themselves, freed from everyday common assumptions and distortions.[16]

In sum, we can see in Heidegger a complex intersection of social life and individuation, connection and divergence, restriction and liberation—all incorporated within an ontological openness that (1) discloses the world's meaning, (2) essentially situates the self in the world, and (3) exhibits the world's finitude. Now I summarize how this Heideggerian configuration helps negotiate between, and improves upon, the positions of liberalism and communitarianism.

LIBERALISM AND COMMUNITARIANISM REVISITED

The strength of communitarianism is the recognition of sociality, tradition, and the larger environment of the self. The strength of liberalism is the affirmation of individuation that protects the self from being consumed by community and tradition, and that provides an interstitial supplement in the face of the inevitable variety and conflicts of community affiliations. The liberal–communitarian debate should be read not as a call for a disjunctive choice but as an argument over the *extent* of individual freedom and communal bonds in social life.[17] The thought of Heidegger provides some depth to this discussion on many levels.

From an ontological standpoint, both liberalism and communitarianism are not penetrating enough regarding the process of world disclosure (the former based in the rational individual's perceptions and cognitive faculties, the latter in social constructs that mold and guide the self). In particular, Heidegger's thinking allows an articulation of the original emergence of the ethical sphere. The very possibility of ethics, in terms of the *difference* between an ought and actuality, is made possible by Dasein's transcendence, which is not confined to extant conditions and thus is open to the possibility of altered modes of living.

Regarding the specific philosophical disputes between liberalism and communitarianism, Heidegger's sense of the radical finitude of being—world disclosure issuing from the negativity of ungrounded Dasein—provides an ontological openness that can critique proposed groundings in either the individual or the community, or even in some kind of neat synthesis or organization of individuality and community.[18] An ungrounded *ontological* openness that is simply thrust into the world's differentiated conditions implies an *ontical* complexity and ambiguity, a dynamic intersection of individuation and sociality, innovation and tradition, that cannot be brought to rest in any standpoint. Although social life is contextually and episodically orderable as a phronetic balancing of different forces, it can never be such without remainder, and so from a global standpoint it is unstable. Various social theories disclose important elements of ethical and political life (individuality, group identity, freedom, responsibility, autonomy, authority, duties, consequences, fairness, excellence, the secular, the sacred, innovation, tradition) but err in seeking a foundation in some of these elements or in some kind of systematic organization.

Heidegger can assist communitarianism with his configuration of being-in-the-world. Given the ekstatic structure of Dasein, where the self *is* situated in world involvement, we do not need to justify the social order and certain constraints on individual freedom. Facticity, thrownness, and situatedness show that Dasein cannot be conceived as separate from, or prior to, its circumstances and the larger economy of the social world. Constraints, then, are *given*, and Dasein must find its way *within* them. Furthermore, communitarianism's objections to the liberal notion of the rational self as prior to its ends are given support by Heidegger's fundamentally temporal and historical conception of being. Dasein is essentially a potentiality, a futurial being-toward in the midst of its past, which renders suspect the liberal dependence on "universal reason" detached from particular aims, legacies, and endowments.

At the same time, Heidegger can speak to the limits of sociality and therefore assist liberalism in its warnings against communal consumption of the individual.[19] The finite negativity of the self and authenticity are important elements that can counterbalance social cohesion and the connectedness of empathic regard, forces of convergence that can turn an interest in interpersonal relations into an intrusive trespass or the benevolent tyranny of undue paternalism. Evasive absences or idiosyncrasies in the Other should not prompt a mandate to evoke presence or convert to sameness.

Regarding Dasein's sociality, Mitsein is a formal structure that is not committed to any specific form of community, and so it can accommodate a variegated, conflicted set of communal associations. With authenticity built into the structure of Dasein, individuated divergence is also essential to the social environment. Such structural inclusion shows that disruption and sociality can be correlated; in other words, the "social" need not be identified with something like harmony or homogeneity, since conflict is no less a social relation.[20] One problem for communitarianism is a certain paradox regarding innovation and tradition. A given tradition that presumably molds and guides the self can be seen, from a genealogical perspective, to have originated in a creative divergence on the part of an individual who resisted and challenged prevailing social and intellectual conventions. Such a paradox can be resolved by a structural inclusion of authenticity that stipulates continuing disruption of convention and established patterns.

On another level, the human self should not be conceived as some "alienated" being that must be restored or transformed into some whole or completed condition—a theme that has taken many forms in the Western tradition. For Heidegger, part of the self's being is an anxious alienation that discloses meaning. So projects that advance a restoration of the self's "true being" as a merger that will render it whole, restored, or unified—be it in terms of God, nature, reason, spirit, instinct, community, labor, and so on—in fact fantasize a prospect that will abnegate the conditions of meaningfulness by undermining its tensional dynamics of disclosure.

FREEDOM AND RESPECT

With Heidegger's thought one can articulate a complex modification of the idea of freedom. Heideggerian freedom is an ontological openness that is not confined to a Kantian freedom construed as a rational transcendence of empirical nature. Ontological freedom is a disclosive letting-be that makes possible any and all orientations in the world (*ET*, 124ff), and as such it is prior to something like a will or self-causation (*PM*, 126–27; see also *GA* 31). The openness of Dasein is also different from an "existentialist" freedom, a sheer negativity apart from physical nature, social situations, roles, and traditions; rather, Dasein is an openness *within* such conditions, which therefore allows *both* coherence *and* variance. In this way, freedom can be affirmed, not as an absolute ground or condition within the self, but as something situated and contextual, calling for specific analyses regarding what kind of movement is at issue, in relation to what kind of constraint, and for what purpose. There are different kinds of freedom (economic, political, personal, artistic), with respect to different kinds of agents and roles (adults, children, workers, students, leaders, innovators), in relation to different kinds of constraint (physical nature, material need, social coercion, conformity), and all of these factors vary and fluctuate between and within circumstances and agents. A phenomenology of such situational balancing acts need not be founded in some kind of primal freedom of the self. Accordingly, we should not begin with a concept of freedom *from* constraints, but rather freedom *within* the various milieus that help shape the self.[21]

As long as we keep sociality in view, we can also think of freedom in relation to the liberal notion of respect, but an existential respect stemming from an ontological openness, rather than a Kantian respect that can be problematical owing to its grounding in modernist reason. Existential respect can reflect the postmodern affirmation of difference and otherness, which can accommodate a wider range of references than the liberal emphasis on the rational individual (a range that can include creative eccentricities and various group identities having to do with race, gender, religion, and so forth). A Heideggerian *Seinlassen*, or letting-be, can operate here to balance sociality with modes of release and noninterference that can protect against domination, control, and presumptive fixtures of human nature, which can be said to violate the ontological openness at the heart of Dasein and being itself. Since Dasein's "self" is ultimately ungrounded and ungroundable, never a full presence (even to itself), human beings should see themselves and others as free *from* baseline reductions and free *for* their possibilities.[22]

Existential respect can be taken as a radical expansion of the Kantian notion of respect. Kantian respect for persons refers to them as agents governed by the rational moral law, and not as concrete, factical persons in all their complexity and particularity.[23] Liberal social theory in one way or another has sustained a Kantian heritage. Although liberalism has certainly affirmed individual differences and can trump forces of consumption that might be implicit in communitarianism, it is not clear how much difference can really be accommodated by the liberal attachment to rationality as the origin of, and justification for, individual freedom; people's religious commitments, for example, have tended to be problematical in the wake of liberalism's secular leanings.[24] Herein lies the communitarian counter that social life is not always driven by individual interests and rational methods championed in the modern period. The self has many facets and modes of comportment that should not be distilled into a narrow set of faculties. And this is where feminist objections to liberalism achieve their force, in that the experience of women is not fully captured by, and may even be concealed in, models of individual self-assertion and rational self-direction.[25]

THE OBLIGATORY OPENNESS OF THE SELF

Heidegger's thought is a challenge to traditional essentialist assumptions about human nature that have played a crucial role in moral philosophy. Yet do we not need to posit or discover some kind of universal human nature to shape the idea of a common good that can overcome the divisive strife that has plagued human life? Is not the denial of a metaphysics of humanity a significant threat to ethics? These are important questions confronting postmodern thought, but my conviction has been that a nonessentialist account of human existence can effectively speak to these concerns in ethics.

As I have indicated, Dasein's radical finitude is disclosed as a transcendence, as being held out into the Nothing. The whole of Dasein is not a definable essence but an abyss that exceeds ontical conditions of beings. But the abyssal dimension of Dasein does not prompt a philosophy of "nothingness," which would be "the enemy of all culture" (*FCM*, 299). Dasein's transcendence is what makes possible wonder, questioning, and disclosure (as un-concealment). Transcendence also makes possible the disclosure of the ought as distinct from extant conditions. Finally, transcendence opens up the kind of freedom implicated in ethical decisions. Radical finitude is radical openness, the antithesis of deterministic closure.[26]

Beyond such metaethical matters, Dasein's abyssal transcendence provides a nonessentialist version of personhood that can, I think, be brought to bear against a number of ethically problematical beliefs and practices.[27] Many human abuses can be traced to reductionistic schemes of human nature, where the self is grounded in some positive property or condition, whether it is individual, group, or universal reductions (for example, egoism, ethnocentric tribalism, or Enlightenment universalism). The trouble starts when an Other is encountered (when an egoist encounters another ego, when a tribalist encounters another tribe, or when a universalist encounters difference or resistance to the presumed paradigm of "human nature").

In this regard, Dasein's transcendence provides an interesting prospect of harmonizing the "is" and the "ought" along Heideggerian lines. Since the being of the self is a kind of negativity implicated with absence, we are *wrong* when we try to reduce people to fixed or closed essences without remainder or otherness. In other words, such closure violates aletheic signs of truth. To see the human person in nonessentialist terms is to refuse all reductions, to weigh potentiality more than actuality, concealment more than full disclosure, process more than finished states, uniqueness more than universality. What humans ultimately have in common, then, is the negativity of finitude, the fact that we do *not* ultimately have a definable "essence." And this negativity can help disrupt various definitional references with which we frequently promote ourselves and demote others. Since human persons cannot finally be fixed by positive attribution, then all the abstract categories of race, gender, role, ethnicity, class, and the like that fuel so much trouble in human affairs can be intercepted by a negative correction. Such categories do have a use, but not as substantive reductions.[28]

It is important to note that designations of race, gender, sexuality, ethnicity, and a host of practical and associational settings (occupation, family, language, religion, politics, and so on) are ineradicable elements of human "identity," construed as the narrational disclosure of "who we are." Such elements cannot be bracketed in favor of some abstract conception of individuality or universal humanity grounded in a metaphysical essence or a reason-based transcendence of particularity. In the terms of my analysis, the self is both ontologically ungrounded and ontically complex in being a finite, dynamic confluence of different perspectives, each of which is constituted in part by a contrast and tension with other perspectives. Part of any identity, then, is difference. The problem is not individuation, group associations, or other settings, but rather the reductive grounding of "human nature" in any definite condition, whether it be universal, social, or individual. When "identity" is construed as some kind of self-sameness, it cannot accommodate difference, that which is other than identity. The human person should not be reduced to *any* category, even to "difference." What is needed is a sense of personhood as a dynamic, engaged openness, which is neither suppressive of differences on behalf of cohesion nor limited to differences on behalf of individuality or diversity.[29]

The human person, then, is a complicated interplay and tension between individuation, socialization, identity, and difference, a complex that is not reducible to any discrete or stable reference without remainder. The ambiguity in all this shows that personhood is at bottom a mystery that exceeds presumed definitions or descriptions—or put another way, the human person is a singularity. Singularity is something we are more likely to accept in ourselves from a first-person standpoint, indicated in our common resistance to other people's presumed grasp of who we are or what we are about; but it is something we should grant to others too. Singularity names the excess and remainder at the edges of all unstable signifiers; in other words, it names each person's own unique, irreducible, elusive existence in the midst of finite being-in-the-world, which cannot be exhausted by any positive reference. Indeed we are well aware of the singularity of others in intimate relationships. The familiarity of personal acquaintance is far from simply an accumulation of facts and descriptions that renders a person "known." It is more the case that our initial understanding of people involves more general notions or categories (gender, ethnicity, occupation, and so forth) that gradually become complicated and destabilized by the intricacies of personal lives. More often, truly "knowing" people is recognizing how their singular being exceeds conceptual structures and simple narratives. Singularity can be cashed out in ethics as a warning against fixed beliefs that are implicated in hatred, discrimination, exploitation, and abuse.[30]

Although the negativity of radical finitude can be unsettling, we should not forget the ways in which more positive ascriptions have been implicated in injustice. The rational universalism championed by the Enlightenment has had mixed results. The promotion of the free rational individual surely has had an emancipatory effect, yet scientific reason has also generated disciplinary regimes, normalization techniques, and bureaucratic controls that have tended to overwhelm individuality and heterogeneity. Moreover, the Enlightenment promotion of universal humanity was in some ways a ruse, since it was a *concealed* Eurocentrism that cashed out in practice as colonialistic paternalism and cultural genocide. What is thought to be universal or impartial can mask entrenched or unexamined biases and exclusions. Affirming differences, however, is not without its own reductionistic dangers. Tribalistic reductions to cultural differences can prompt indifference toward, or dehumanization of, other cultural groups, which can spawn the worst kind of factional strife. Undercutting these and other reductive ascriptions can have an important application in ethics gathered around a Heideggerian *Seinlassen*: In letting-be there resonate tones of openness, noninterference, recognition, respect, and release.[31]

In this context it is interesting to note an early remark of Heidegger's about death as presenting a kind of equality, in that being-toward-death and the "how" of temporality dissolves all "whats," all differences and exceptional conditions (*CT*, 21). In fact, there is also a reference to the formalism of Kant's ethics as pertaining to this temporal dynamic (*CT*, 13). Such remarks suggest ethical possibilities that can bridge human differences, but without a reduction to sameness. The negativity of death can prompt a common understanding and human concern. Our interests may differ widely, but we all share the significance of *losing* our interests. A mortal equality would not pertain to every ethical consideration but it could help shape some basic ethical bearings. The advantage of a mortal equality is that its negativity sustains an openness that need not be traced to typical egalitarian stipulations of some common form, condition, or attribute (creaturehood, rationality, identity, worth). What can draw humans together (death) does not reduce to, and can exceed, proposed conditions of equality that have rendered difference problematical in the rule of sameness. Here I draw on Heidegger's peculiar definition of the "same," which is not the identical or the common, but the "belonging together of that which differs" (*PLT*, 218). Heideggerian phenomenology is always protective of difference—without, however, dispersing into a fragmented separatism.[32]

In *Being and Time*, Heidegger clearly connects authenticity with an affirmation of difference. Heidegger follows Kierkegaard in pursuing a radically different sense of individuality compared with the traditional sense, which saw individuals as simply instances of a repeatable type or kind (this chair, this cat, this human being). For Kierkegaard and Heidegger, individuality is a radical singularity that exceeds "kinds" and that is best expressed in personal terms.[33] The "dictatorship" of inauthentic *das Man* is not only indicated in the absorption of one's own self in an indiscriminate, common mass. Others too, in *their* difference (*Unterschiedlichkeit*) and expressiveness (*Ausdrücklichkeit*), are covered up and suppressed as well (*BT*, 164). The selfhood of others cannot be understood or disclosed as simply an extension or analogue of one's own self. As Heidegger says, the selfhood of the Other is not an "alter-ego," it is an Other as *itself* (*MFL*, 188). Authenticity, then, requires letting others *be* in their distinctiveness.[34]

NEGATIVE AND POSITIVE FREEDOM

If we recall the notion of *Fürsorge*, we should not interpret letting-be as a passive, indifferent bystanding. *Letting*-be has social implications in that we often have to participate in, and actively foster, the development of difference.[35] *Fürsorge*, as authentic care, *helps* others become free for their care (*BT*, 159). There is an analogy here with the ontological function of letting-be in Heidegger's reflections on truth. Dasein's freedom as letting-be is neither a passive disengagement nor an assertive construction of the subject, but an ambiguous middle voice that participates in the unfolding of being (*ET*, 124–28). Letting-be is thus different from a pallid indifference (*Gleichgültigkeit*), which simply leaves things as they are, and which in fact is a mode of fallen everydayness, an *abandoning* oneself to one's thrownness (*BT*, 396). Indifference is distinguished from an authentic equanimity or composure (*Gleichmut*) that stems from a resolute attentiveness to one's situation and its claims in the light of being-toward-death (*BT*, 396). For Heidegger, Dasein's freedom is its capacity-to-be, which includes its capacity to be with others (*MFL*, 214).

We can notice here how Heideggerian phenomenology—with its ambiguous blending of individuality and sociality, selfhood and otherness, involvement and release—can be applied to the familiar distinction between negative and positive freedom, between freedom-from constraint and freedom-for pursuing an interest, and the recognition that honoring the former can still restrict the latter. People can be left alone and still lack the resources or opportunity to meet their needs or fulfill their potential (such is the trenchant complaint about a capitalist economy).[36] With Heidegger, one can argue that both senses of freedom are important and that neither one is primary. Negative freedom can be associated with letting-*be*, with releasing persons for their being, as opposed to domination and willful constraint. Positive freedom can be associated with *letting*-be, with attention to Dasein's potentialities and capacities for living well that can be blocked. Disclosure of both senses of freedom can be seen as an irreducible confluence that cannot be divided or ordered in a formulaic manner, because stressing either one can conceal the importance of the other. In addition, neither sense of freedom is grounded in determinate conditions of the individual self or the needs of others, groundings that would make them seem incompatible or difficult to bridge. Ontological letting-be, or Dasein's disclosive openness to being that is not subject-based, is relevant to an ontical sense of ethical regard: of both releasing the Other and caring for and about the Other. Such regard is grounded neither in the self nor in the Other; rather, it stems from Dasein's own disclosive openness *to* the Other's situation, and from Dasein's being claimed in some way by this disclosure. Being ethical is being claimed by an *interest* in both release and an involvement that releases. In social life, we cannot help but be caught up in both conditions in various ways.

DIALOGICAL SELFHOOD

The critique of individualism is more than simply a turn toward a generalized sociality. Social life and practice have a primal dialogical, conversational, transactional character that is evident beginning in childhood. As we have said, Heidegger did little to explore an interpersonal dynamic, but it is surely implied in his concept of Mitsein. There are some instances where he suggests a dialogical structure of selfhood: Authentic Mitsein is associated with a "hearing" and a "listening to each other" (*BT*, 206). He also mentions a preference for the richness and multidimensionality of direct conversations, as opposed to the relative fixity of written texts (*LH*, 219). Recall also the notion of authentic *Fürsorge* as a co-disclosure (*BT*, 344), which speaks to the reciprocity of interpersonal engagement that was exemplified in empathic relations. In general terms, communication is a speaking with one another, which is more than simply an exchange between interior selves; it is a being-with-one-another that amounts to a sharing of disclosure, a co-uncovering and co-understanding

(*HCT*, 263; *BT*, 205). Contrary to a monological self that simply ventures out, fully formed, to confront other selves, a dialogical self is formed *through* correlative engagements with others.

Much of ethical life involves mutual interrogation and exploration of social possibilities in various settings of conversation and interaction. We recognize genuinely productive outcomes in such settings that generate elucidations, new vistas, and self-alterations that would not occur apart from the dynamic of dialogue. The tensional element in authenticity can also show how ethical dialogue is often contestual; and yet, as Hegel and Nietzsche have shown, such tensions between different interests produce innovations and discoveries in the participants that would otherwise lay concealed. So even tensional strife is productive of one's being. In a developmental sense, then, ethical dialogue—as an interrogation of and with others—is an openness to otherness that is at the same time an openness to possibilities in oneself. In this respect, sociality is far from simply a collective phenomenon. One's own ethical bearings take shape in dialogical transactions.

Ethical dialogue is a transactional practice embedded in different contexts and operating by way of multiple modes of address. Ethical engagement is much more than a matter of "argumentation" from premises to conclusions and a critique of each step from the standpoint of disengaged reflection (this is more the province of *academic* practice). Ethical address must consider who is speaking, to whom, when, on what occasion, in response to what problem; also at issue are different rhetorical modes that can advance or affect a conversation. Accordingly, dialogue is a complex process that eludes clear grasp and control, and thus that cannot be understood from the standpoint of "agency." In fact, ethical dialogue is a process of mutual bestowal, and so it overrides an insistence on one's own agency.[37]

SELFHOOD AND MORAL RESPONSIBILITY

I have noted the various dimensions of the modern conception of autonomy and freedom, and how the modern self was implicated in scientific, political, economic, and technological revolutions that displaced ancient orders and orientations.[38] The philosophical problem at hand concerns metaphysical conceptions of subjectivity that buttressed historical assertions of freedom, rationality, and individuality with the figure of the autonomous subject as the measure of human nature. The historical struggle against vested and entrenched regimes benefited from the sharp counterimage of freedom at the heart of modern selfhood. Since the philosophical ground rules at the time were measured by foundationalist guarantees, it may be that given the force of ancient metaphysical warrants standing in the way of modern developments, only the counterwarrant of metaphysical freedom would be able to register any effect.

Even granting this historical and dialectical function, a Heideggerian critique of modern subjectivity targets the mythology of foundationalist freedom, which can be called a secularized, rationalized, individualized remnant of a long-standing flight from finitude and encumbrance that was born in Greek and medieval ideals of divine self-sufficiency. Modernity gathers in the free, rational, individual subject the fantasy of self-mastery and sovereignty. Self-mastery not only runs afoul of finite being-in-the-world, it also has spawned various social fragmentations and disintegrations on behalf of acute individualism, which in return has generated countermovements of rationalized or socialized controls.

Because of the foundational myth of the free self, modern ethical and political theory has always been vexed by the problem of justifying social institutions, measured against the sovereignty of the subject. Heideggerian phenomenology can bypass this problem of legitimacy by recognizing a primal situatedness in human existence. It is important to reiterate that finitude for Heidegger does not suggest some arbitrary construction or unhinged loss of bearings. Contrary to the disengaged modern subject that aims for autonomy and mastery, finitude indicates that human existence is a thrown engagement, a primal appropriation and belonging to the world. This is precisely what allows a Heideggerian orientation to circumvent the modern problematic of legitimacy in everything from epistemology to ethics. Only the starting point of a disengaged self can prompt the question concerning whether or not ethical norms are simply constructions of the human subject. In this regard we should note an important passage (*LH*, 262) where Heidegger connects *ēthos*-as-dwelling with the directives of rule and law (*nomos*). The primal belonging of being-in-the-world is what allows ethical directives to be a kind of "dispatching" that is "capable of supporting and obligating," as opposed to being "merely something fabricated by human reason." In this way, dwelling in the truth of being "offers a hold for all conduct."[39]

The finitude of ethics can speak to the limits of moral agency and to distortions in the modern ideal of autonomy.[40] We can then acknowledge the ambiguity of ethical praise, blame, and responsibility, especially in terms of the role of luck and fortune in ethical life.[41] As has been shown in different ways in this investigation, ethical practices should be understood in terms of being-in-the-world, which is constituted by thrownness, openness, sociality, and individuation—all together indicating an ambiguous blend of situatedness and development, encumbrance and release, constraint and choice, happenstance and design.

A finite sense of selfhood can address standard questions of moral responsibility without a strict sense of autonomy as the discrete origin of ethical action.[42] I would like to suggest a kind of responsibility that can be characterized as "answerability" (cf. the German *verantwortlich*), rather than what I would call moralistic "accountability." With these formulations I mean to distinguish responsibility from autonomous agency and a related sense of accountability that spawns overly acute estimations of moral praise and blame, shown in a valorization of rectitude and a demonization of transgression. A metaphysical commit-

ment to autonomous agency and freedom as the exclusive source of ethical performance distorts the complex environment of human action and permits the sim-
plistic and sometimes heinous construction of retributory targets. The ontological
openness and situated finitude advanced in this study can support ethical answerability and yet subvert moralistic locations of strict origins.

Responsibility as ethical answerability can be associated with a Heideggerian
sense of finite authenticity, especially in terms of individuated resolve as opposed
to thoughtless compliance or disjointed happenstance. In this regard, existential
phenomenology can speak to the traditional assumption that moral responsibility
requires some kind of constancy across time in order to connect an agent with
past deeds. With Heidegger we can give self-constancy an existential interpretation, as opposed to substantive accounts that are counterposed to time and
change. For Heidegger, the "unity" of the self can be indicated in the primor-
diality of mineness animating action, without having to conjure up some time-
surpassing substance. In fact, temporality itself has an existential continuity in the
sense of the "stretching" character of the lived experience of past, present, and
future (*BT*, 443). Only when time is construed as a succession of now-points does
there arise the problem of unity, because of the "breaks" between the points of
time. With Heidegger, the "negativity" of time is experienced as an existential
whole: The self *is* a stretching between past and future. Consequently, being
answerable for actions in time is built into temporality as such.[43]

There is another way to understand the relation between finite openness and
responsibility. The very notion of ethical "decisions" as existentially answerable
can be understood as intrinsically related to the "undecidability" of the ethical
sphere as distinct from causal forces, compulsions, uncontestable facts, or strict
demonstrations. We have noted the finite openness that marks ethical life: potentiality, temporality, *phronēsis*, the counterfactual ought, and the cut of either/or
facing every choice. Insisting on existential decision as the last word in such an
ungroundable sphere is one way of understanding ethical responsibility. The
problem with many traditional moral theories is that they aim to "definitize"
ethics by grounding the good or the right in some fixed scheme; and they bypass
the abyssal element of existential decision by modeling ethical thinking along the
lines of demonstrative and calculative techniques that in a way are meant to
decide things *for* us. I do not "decide," for example, that 2 + 2 = 4, or that
"Socrates is mortal" in the classic syllogism. Demonstrative "decidability" in
ethics would seem to erase or diminish the sense of "responsibility for choices"
that has long been considered an essential part of ethical life.[44] Theoretical conceptions of responsibility have tended to focus exclusively on rationality, and so
have missed or avoided the ungroundable, spontaneous dimension in decision as
an existential phenomenon. As Heidegger puts it, a decision is always correlated
with "something unmastered, hidden, confusing; otherwise it would never be a
decision" (*PLT*, 55). Ironically, then, it is the openness of ethical decisions that
makes them existentially answerable, as opposed to being fixed outcomes, pro-

grammatic functions, necessary inferences, or productions of impersonal forces (be they physical, historical, or cultural) that dictate the self's actions.

Ethical answerability undermines the tendency (gaining currency) to explain or excuse certain behaviors as the consequence of addictions, syndromes, genetic codings, or environmental scripts. At the same time, the situated, thrown finitude of being-in-the-world helps undermine a sense of responsibility taken to the unwarranted extreme of moralistic accountability based in a fictional autonomy. Such hyperbolic responsibility is indicated when we presume to assign clear and decisive blame for misdeeds to discrete agents without remainder, without any sense of ambiguity, contingency, or regret. Some human actions are clearly not "decisions" and so are not considered ethically answerable (for example, certain compulsions, afflictions, or forms of madness). Some supposedly ethical decisions are more tragic than answerable, as in cases of choosing between mutually exclusive obligations. And some ethical decisions are more clearly answerable. To illustrate these three spheres, think of the differences between killing stemming from a psychotic seizure, killing in warfare, and killing for hire.

Human action can be understood as a spectrum of answerable and nonanswerable performances, with a great portion of gray area and complex combinations, given the multiple factors in human behavior that are not within the strict control of the self (biological drives, genetic endowments, social conditioning, luck, happenstance, ignorance, fallibility, and uncertainties intrinsic to the temporal and situational contingencies of decision making). Much of this complexity is more amenable to a tragic sense of life than to moralistic accountability. Nietzsche is known for diagnosing such accountability and its presumption of autonomy as grounded in resentment over the injuries of life.[45] Autonomy permits the clear assignment of blame and punishment to a discrete site of origin, which then can alleviate anxiety and frustration in the face of a finite, tragic existence. In this way certain everyday, common attitudes toward offenses can match metaphysical conceptions of autonomous agency. Both outlooks, however, in their strictest sense can be seen as a form of transference meant to resolve existential anxiety. When bad things happen, the belief in unambiguous origins in sovereign selves permits ameliorating rituals of expiation. A tragic sense of life, however, forces an accommodation with negative conditions that cannot be fully mastered, eliminated, or adjudicated without remainder.[46]

NOTES

1. A helpful study is Stephen Mulhall and Adam Swift, *Liberals and Communitarians* (Malden, Mass.: Blackwell, 1992).
2. See C. B. Macpherson, *The Political Theory of Possessive Individualism* (London: Oxford University Press, 1962).

3. Such freedom is most clearly articulated and defended in John Stuart Mill's *On Liberty*. See his *Three Essays* (Oxford: Oxford University Press, 1975).

4. See Michael Sandel, *Liberalism and the Limits of Justice* (Cambridge: Cambridge University Press, 1982).

5. See Frederick A. Olafson's treatment of recognition in *Heidegger and the Ground of Ethics: A Study of* Mitsein (Cambridge: Cambridge University Press, 1998), 87–91.

6. Richard E. Flathman, "It All Depends on How One Understands Liberalism," *Political Theory* 26 (February 1998): 83. Rawls in his later work tries to sidestep metaphysical questions of selfhood by construing his analysis as *political* liberalism. See his *Political Liberalism* (New York: Columbia University Press, 1993). There Rawls shifts from an earlier dependence on general moral and anthropological conceptions of rational selfhood as the ground of a liberal order toward the articulation of what is constitutive for citizens in a liberal society. In some respects this shift can resonate with a Heideggerian hermeneutics and thrownness, in that it thinks *from* liberal predilections rather than *toward* them.

7. Lawrence Vogel offers a helpful discussion of this matter in *The Fragile "We": Ethical Implications of Heidegger's* Being and Time (Evanston, Ill.: Northwestern University Press, 1994), ch. 5.

8. Olafson, in *Heidegger and the Ground of Ethics,* gives a very effective analysis of Mitsein as a basis for ethics, and it improves upon Heidegger by articulating what authentic Mitsein could be like. Olafson focuses too much on communality and harmony, however, missing some of the tensional elements I am trying to consider.

9. It is important to add that authenticity is not equivalent to the genuine, and so inauthenticity is not something spurious: "On the contrary, this everyday having of self within our factical, existent, passionate merging with things can surely be genuine, whereas all extravagant grubbing about in one's soul can be in the highest degree counterfeit or even pathologically eccentric" (*BP*, 160).

10. The passive conformity of *das Man* is more the problem than the force of common social patterns; indeed, even the meaning of such patterns can become distorted by a passive conformism. On this point, see Olafson, *Heidegger and the Ground of Ethics*, 38–39.

11. For this reason, we need not accept Habermas's postconventional assumption that only "universal reason" detachable from tradition provides the possibility of cultural "critique." Habermas maintains that only the measure of idealized speech conditions can prevent discourse from being blocked by conservatism and co-opted by existing power structures. A hermeneutic openness to tradition can close off the emancipatory effect and critical capacity of modern reason to contest forces of domination. Yet, as Nietzsche has shown, critique is a complex phenomenon that is not exclusively rational. Moreover, the "bar of reason" has itself taken on features of a vested tradition. Heidegger's strong emphasis on questioning allows for new possibilities and responses to shortcomings in the tradition—but always complicit with tradition and thus different from the wholesale questioning exhibited in modernist critique and skepticism.

12. Heidegger quotes, with apparent favor, Count Yorck's promotion of individual conscience over public conscience, and of the political mission to cultivate individual perspectives in education (*BT*, 454–55).

13. For an important study that focuses on the *Augenblick* and Heidegger's relation to Aristotle, see William McNeill, *The Glance of the Eye: Heidegger, Aristotle, and the Ends of Theory* (Albany: SUNY Press, 1999).

14. Regarding situations that can either promote or limit someone's freedom, consider two basic approaches. (1) One can charge in with clean, customary definitions of freedom and constraint (where each term excludes the other), or with secure directives such as "Follow reason" or "Maximize well-being" or "Create your own values." (2) One can understand that ethical action is not clean and secure, because it involves the circulation of multiple values and guidelines tempered by the exigencies of the situation and its particular parties. Such difficulty might be an anxiety-producing loss of bearings for the first approach, yet in the second approach it is an anxiety-prompted deliverance from the fantasized comfort of clear guidance to the reality of responsive openness. It could even be said that inauthentic ethical comforts are constituted by a fugitive concealment of the difficulties of ethical action.

15. For an insightful discussion of Dasein's transcendence, freedom, and responsible choice, see Peg Birmingham, "Ever Respectfully Mine: Heidegger on Agency and Responsibility," in *Ethics and Danger: Essays on Heidegger and Continental Thought*, ed. Arleen Dallery and Charles E. Scott (Albany: SUNY Press, 1992), 109–23. See also her essay *"Logos* and the Place of the Other," *Research in Phenomenology* 20 (1990).

16. Hannah Arendt, *The Human Condition* (Chicago: University of Chicago Press, 1968), advances a social theory that owes much to Heidegger. She extends and explores further the phenomenon of Mitsein as social praxis, to correct for Heidegger's *alleged* individualized conception of authenticity owing to the social forces of *das Man* that conceal rather than open up the self. Despite my disagreement with this interpretation of authenticity, Arendt makes a valuable contribution in articulating praxis (as distinct from work and production) as a public space where selves open up and create their identities in speech and deed. Arendt is much better than Heidegger in seeing the democratic potential in existential phenomenology, in seeing history as more contingent, and sociality as more pluralized and open to otherness. Reiner Schürmann's *Heidegger on Being and Acting: From Principles to Anarchy*, trans. Christine Marie Gros (Bloomington: Indiana University Press, 1987), draws from Heidegger's *Gelassenheit* and attention to "temporal difference" the possibility of an "anarchic" politics freed from global or hierarchical governance, a finite, mortal politics that continually interrogates itself. One question, of course, is whether politics can be so open as to move beyond traditional conceptions of regulatory reason. For a balanced analysis of this issue, see Richard Bernstein, *The New Constellation: The Ethical–Political Horizons of Modernity/Postmodernity* (Cambridge, Mass.: MIT Press, 1992).

17. See Michael Walzer, "The Communitarian Critique of Liberalism," *Political Theory* 18 (February 1990): 6–23.

18. For a critique of recent attempts at mediation, see the review essay by Mary G. Dietz, "Merely Combatting the Phrases of This World: Recent Democratic Theory," *Political Theory* 26 (February 1998), 112–39.

19. Heidegger was critical of liberalism mostly because of its metaphysical commitments. For an analysis of this matter and of prospects for social liberalism that can stem from Heidegger's thinking, see Richard Polt, "Metaphysical Liberalism in Heidegger's *Beiträge zur Philosophie*," *Political Theory* 25 (October 1997): 655–79.

20. See my discussion in *A Nietzschean Defense of Democracy: An Experiment in Postmodern Politics* (Chicago: Open Court, 1995), ch. 4.

21. Leslie Paul Thiele provides a helpful distinction between freedom *in* speech and freedom *of* speech, freedom *in* action and freedom *of* action. See *Timely Meditations:*

Martin Heidegger and Postmodern Politics (Princeton, N.J.: Princeton University Press, 1995). An important article that sets out a contextual formula for freedom is G. MacCallum, "Negative and Positive Freedom," in *Liberty*, ed. D. Miller (Oxford: Oxford University Press, 1991), 100–22.

22. The Kantian notion of persons as "ends" rather than things can certainly fit a Heideggerian outlook. Yet in Heidegger, the notion of end can be broader and richer than the Kantian association with reason and autonomy. Dasein as end is more than an end "in itself"; it is a sheer being-toward and the openness of possibility. For this reason I resist Vogel's attempt (in *The Fragile "We"*) to press Heideggerian authenticity into a Kantian mold of persons as ends in themselves. Dasein construed as sheer possibility would not be amenable to the Kantian notion of an ideal sphere of moral perfection as a reference for action. See Kant, *Foundations of the Metaphysics of Morals*, trans. Lewis White Beck (New York: Bobbs-Merrill, 1959), 61, and *Critique of Practical Reason*, trans. Lewis White Beck (New York: Macmillan, 1956), 118.

23. Heidegger does not disparage Kant's concept of respect, however. See Heidegger's nuanced and supportive analysis of Kantian notions of moral personhood and respect in *BP*, section 13. There Heidegger calls Kant's account of respect "a brilliant phenomenological analysis of the phenomenon of morality" (133). Section 14, however, faults Kant for confining the ontology of the self to subjectivity. See also *BT*, 366ff, where Heidegger critiques Kant's conception of the self as being caught up in the modern framework of the subject as *res cogitans*. I suggest that there is a conceivable imperative that might be drawn from an existential version of respect: Never reduce persons to full presence without remainder or otherness. Such a formulation would be richer than a Kantian reduction to reason and could attend better to the complexity of ethical relations. Moreover, the Mitsein element in existential respect can better account for the motivation to respect others than can a subject-based ethics. For extended discussions of the prospects for ethics in light of Heidegger's response to Kant, see two works by Frank Schalow, *Imagination and Existence: Heidegger's Retrieval of the Kantian Ethic* (Lanham, Md.: University Press of America, 1986) and *The Renewal of the Heidegger–Kant Dialogue: Action, Thought, and Responsibility* (Albany: SUNY Press, 1992).

24. Religion, of course, plays an enormous role in many people's ethical lives, and elements of religious life can be defended against secularist biases in modern thought. Yet in developed societies, ethics cannot be grounded in religion. There must be a central place for moral philosophy, which can certainly make room for religion, but which must be able to address nonreligious attitudes and the wide variety of religious belief systems.

25. Feminist philosophy has experienced a division between an "equity" approach and a "difference" approach. Equity feminism argues against gender inequality and the subjugation of women by extending traditional conceptions of justice and rights to include women. Difference feminism has argued that there is something distinctive about women's moral experience (relatedness and care), which is missed or even concealed in models of justice and rights that reflect men's traditional interest in separation and individuation. Recent developments have argued for attention to both justice and care. Some representative works on these matters are Claudia Card, ed., *Feminist Ethics* (Lawrence: University Press of Kansas, 1991); Virginia Held, *Feminist Morality: Transforming Culture, Society, and Politics* (Chicago: University of Chicago Press, 1993); and Alison M. Jaggar, *Living with Contradictions: Controversies in Feminist Social Ethics* (Boulder, Colo.: Westview, 1994). Two significant works in the continental tradition are Judith Butler, *Gender*

Trouble: Feminism and the Subversion of Identity (New York: Routledge, 1990), and Seyla Benhabib, *Situating the Self: Gender, Community, and Postmodernism in Contemporary Ethics* (New York: Routledge, 1992).

26. Heideggerian phenomenology is not reducible to the kind of modernist objectivity and causal necessity that make freedom problematical from the outset, nor does it have to locate freedom in the refuge of a subject detached from empirical nature (which then makes action in the world structurally problematical). As in Aristotle, we can simply articulate a phenomenology of decision as distinct from compulsion, without having to pay homage to a foundational scheme of natural causality.

27. See my extended discussion of this matter in *A Nietzschean Defense of Democracy*, ch. 8.

28. Nazi atrocities and racist policies violated all the aletheic signs of truth sketched in chapter 2, and inhabitive signs as well (given the various wild theories about history and biology, not to mention the catastrophe unleashed upon the world).

29. Heidegger critiques both individualism and collectivism as equally grounded in a human-centered subjectivism, differing only in scale (*LH*, 244–45).

30. John D. Caputo gives suggestions for ethics in this regard in *Radical Hermeneutics* (Bloomington: Indiana University Press, 1987), chs. 9–10. Emmanuel Levinas presents a powerful account of the self as a singularity. The elusiveness of the Other is an important antidote to the rule of the same and universality in Western thought. It provides a basic starting point for ethics by stipulating an original limit on the self's freedom and power with regard to the Other. It lets the Other be heard *as* Other, rather than as a subject of explanation or assimilation into community. Yet reversing the power of self and Other in this way does not avoid difficulties haunting the original binary. Levinas seems to say that the self begins as self-asserting freedom and is then countered by the Other. My proposal of an ekstatic self would call this into question. Moreover, the face of the Other comes across as a mysterious, quasireligious, absolute force that is not exhausted by existing human faces, which I find hard to understand. And the Other places an infinite obligation on the self that can never be satisfied. This appears to me to be a kind of passive–aggressive domination in reverse.

31. Derrida addresses the ethical possibilities in letting-be in "Violence and Metaphysics: An Essay on the Thought of Emmanuel Levinas," in *Writing and Difference*, trans. Alan Bass (Chicago: University of Chicago Press, 1978). See also Charles E. Scott, *The* Question *of Ethics: Nietzsche, Foucault, Heidegger* (Bloomington: Indiana University Press, 1990), 202–10. Caputo examines justice in terms of the tension between universals and singularities in "Hyperbolic Justice: Deconstruction, Myth, and Politics," *Research in Phenomenology* 21 (1991): 3–20. See also my essay "Human Nature in a Postmodern World," *Human Studies*, vol. 17, no. 3 (1994): 363–71. Stephen K. White examines Heidegger's thought in relation to a "responsibility to otherness" in *Political Theory and Postmodernism* (Cambridge: Cambridge University Press, 1991), ch. 4.

32. In line with Heidegger's notion of an original community animated by the nearness of death, Jean-Luc Nancy meditates on the possibility of a "community of mortals" in *The Inoperative Community*, ed. Peter Connor (Minneapolis: University of Minnesota Press, 1991). There Nancy suggests the idea of an "impossible" community bounded by death, a mythical, self-limiting community that is never consummated in some kind of social whole or unity, but rather constituted by finitude. I want to add, however, that mortality is not sufficient to engender a feasible sense of community. Awareness of death can just as

easily generate fear, division, and discord (which was Thomas Hobbes's position). That is why the generation of meaning out of finitude needs articulating. The phenomena of empathy, *Fürsorge*, and letting-be analyzed in this study go a good way toward shaping a viable sense of social bearings based in finitude.

33. See Richard McDonough, "Heidegger on Authenticity, Freedom, and Individual Agency: An Aristotelian Model," *International Studies in Philosophy,* vol. 32, no. 2 (1998): 77. Heidegger, however, does not follow Kierkegaard in hypostatizing singularity at the expense of sociality. This helps make sense out of an otherwise odd-sounding claim of Heidegger's that *das Man* is a modification of authentic selfhood (*BT*, 365). For Heidegger, individuation and socialization are in perpetual confluence.

34. This is why Levinas is wrong in claiming that Heideggerian ontology repeats the rule of the same.

35. See White, *Political Theory and Postmodernism*, ch. 7. It should be noted that the German verb *lassen* has active connotations beyond a mere "allowing." It can involve having or getting something done.

36. An excellent study that explores different senses of freedom in liberalism is David Johnston, *The Idea of a Liberal Theory: A Critique and Reconstruction* (Princeton, N.J.: Princeton University Press, 1994).

37. P. Christopher Smith, *Hermeneutics and Human Finitude: Toward a Theory of Ethical Understanding* (New York: Fordham University Press, 1991), 130, 151.

38. As Charles Taylor points out, a critique of modernism should not overlook its many benefits and humane developments: the spread of knowledge; a moral imperative to reduce suffering; the emancipation of people from enslavement, domination, and authoritarian rule; and the encouragement of self-expression. See *Sources of the Self: The Making of Modern Identity* (Cambridge, Mass.: Harvard University Press, 1989), ch. 22.

39. This helps undercut worries in the face of Heidegger's notorious critique of humanism. As I have noted, for Heidegger both individualism and collectivism are based in a human-centered, self-asserting subjectivity, differing only in scale. The essence of human existence, for Heidegger, is "more" than human in this subject-centered sense, and the "more" is not some kind of addition, but being open to, and thrown from, being (*LH*, 244–45). This "more" is precisely what can sustain a primal sense of belonging to norms that is not simply a human construction.

40. See Bernard Williams's evocative study of ancient and modern conceptions of agency in *Shame and Necessity* (Berkeley: University of California Press, 1993).

41. See Bernard Williams, *Moral Luck* (Cambridge: Cambridge University Press, 1981).

42. Here I take up a sense of responsibility *for* one's actions, which is distinct from the prior discussion of responsibility *to* others. Both senses benefit from Heidegger's notion of a primal, ekstatic, thrown openness to the world. In this way the self *is* responsible from the start, and so one is freed from the modern problematic of justifying *why* the self should be obligated to others, or explaining *how* the self is responsible for its actions.

43. Mention should be made of how Heidegger's conception of open selfhood, while allowing a sense of existential continuity, also undermines a kind of rigidity that can be problematic in ethical life. Heidegger calls resoluteness a loyalty (*Treue*) to oneself, not as a constant presence but as a steadiness (*Ständigkeit*) that is open to anxiety and possibility (*BT*, 443). In other words, the self is not a fixed entity, but a continual and continuing openness that retains a kind of continuity in that sense. This helps underwrite the flexibility implicit in the engaged openness stressed in this investigation, which speaks to the

mix of responsiveness, involvement, commitment, contingency, adaptability, and experimentation that marks ethical existence. Heidegger indicates that Dasein's resoluteness is always situated rather than free-floating; yet it should avoid rigidity and be open to various possibilities that might arise in a situation, and even be free to "take back" a resolution if need be (*BT*, 355, 443).

44. Derrida develops this connection between ethical decisions and undecidability in his afterword to *Limited Inc.*, ed. Gerald Graf (Evanston, Ill.: Northwestern University Press, 1988).

45. See *Beyond Good and Evil* and *On the Genealogy of Morality*, in *Basic Writings of Nietzsche*, ed. Walter Kaufmann (New York: Random House, 1966).

46. A dose of tragic sensibility is certainly needed to help stem the tide of litigation, incrimination, and diagnostic reportage that dominates so much of the American scene. It seems that whenever bad things happen we cannot rest until someone is held liable or some explanation is found to make sense out of transgressions.

Chapter Eight

Ethical Existence and Limits

For the purpose of summation and preparation for some final reflections, I review the general features of ethical existence that I have drawn from Heideggerian phenomenology. Human beings come into the world with natural capacities for ethical development that must be nurtured in the social environment. Caregivers help shape this development in a transaction of nature and nurture informed by historical/cultural inheritances. There are better and worse ways of fostering these ethical potentialities.

The early social environment exhibits two principal goods and sources of ethical meaning: freedom and care, born in natural expressions of self-interest and empathy for others. Because these natural bearings can move in different directions and come into conflict, the tensional pluralism of ethical life is evident from early on owing to the conjunction and intersection of diverging goods. The social environment negotiates and orchestrates this tensional mix without the strict regulation of an overarching formula or scheme. Out of a tripartite self-world, with-world, and environing-world, language development allows the articulation of ethical meanings and opens up the stretches of temporality that facilitate moral instruction and permit an expansion of the original social milieu.

So from the start the human self is shaped by ethical bearings, initially in terms of enculturation, habituation, and prereflective competence. Such early shaping is not a one-sided conditioning regime, but a drawing out of capacities that is saturated with an intrinsic openness. Mature development advances ethical possibilities and can be characterized as a thrown, engaged, situated openness.

At the heart of ethical existence is the finitude of meaning. Norms involving modes of shelter and release take shape in a world of dangers, losses, pains, and constraints. Ethical bearings are concerned with existential weal and woe in social life, with caring about one's own and others' faring in a finite world. In addition, experiences of estrangement and disruption uncover and accentuate the meaning of ethical bearings, help explicate their tacit sense, and open space for interrogation.

195

Ethics is a mode of being-in-question, an interpretive interrogation in the midst of historical inheritances and temporal structures. It involves life narratives and the engagement of complex choices. It is a blend of thrown inhabitance, affect, cognition, responsiveness, and dialogical transaction, a blend that animates the questions, searchings, motivations, and decisions in ethical life.

Human existence displays an intrinsic capacity for ethical responsibility, construed as a primal, ekstatic openness-to-others-that-matters. Such responsiveness to others is the existential source of obligation, conscience, and guilt, which generate the *claim* of ethics. Such a claim cannot collapse into communalism, however, because part of responsibility is letting others be, measured by the obligatory openness and singularity of the human person.

Moral virtues unfold in a complex field of desires, and can be called an owned sense of ethical bearings. Virtue involves the capacity to live well with others, which includes an appropriation of one's own possibilities, a responsiveness to others, and courage in the face of finitude. In general terms, virtues are ways of being that function as balancing acts in the midst of tensional possibilities. Some examples of virtuous dispositions that fit the atmosphere described in this investigation can be sketched in the following forms of ethical counsel.

Be caring and responsive, rather than indifferent, but not to the extent of losing yourself in others. Be yourself, rather than a replication of social expectations, but not so far as to abandon sociality or revel in cheap eccentricity. Be respectful of others' freedom, rather than controlling or reductive, but not so far as to miss responsibilities and appropriate judgments. Be open, rather than dogmatic, but not so far as to rest in cynical skepticism or miss the call for decision and commitment. Be courageous, rather than disabled by fear of losses or pains, but not so far as to bring disintegration. Be compassionate, rather than cruel or disengaged, but not so far as to block the necessary lessons of suffering. These and other virtues are formal indications that cannot be directed by strict formulas or theoretical governance; they are enacted by a discerning performance in concrete circumstances.

Reflection, reasoning, and moral principles are not to be ruled out or superseded in ethics. Such forces can operate in conjunction with, or at the limits of, virtue and empathic concern. Moral principles, however, cannot be divorced from virtue and empathy, which are ingredient in the genesis, animation, and performance of moral principles. Impartial rationality and principles find their most appropriate setting in the political sphere. Yet both ethical and political practice exhibit intrinsic limits, contingencies, and conflicts that undermine the projects of rationalized governance (or even reflective equilibrium) envisioned by much of modern moral theory.

Consider the following elements of finitude that suggest the global instability of the social sphere: (1) differences, ambiguities, and mutual tensions in various conceptions of the good; (2) the absence of an uncontested foundation for decision making; (3) the scarcity of goods and resources, raising problems of distribution; (4) the contingency of ethical and political decisions, owing to persistent trade-offs and uncertainties about future outcomes; (5) the complexity of ethical situations that makes balancing interests hard to gauge; (6) the irregularity of particulars when it comes to decisions and judgments according to principles; (7) ongoing oscillations in the spectrum of social categories between openness and order, authority and conscience, equality and merit, inclusions and exclusions, individuality and group identities, freedom and responsibility; (8) luck, fortune, and happenstance, which cloud the assignment of responsibility and desert; (9) failure in aiming for the good, or instigating harmful effects in doing good; and (10) extreme or degraded environments that can ruin ethical bearings or their potential.

The virtue of Heidegger's notion of finite dwelling is that it forces us to give up the idea that such conditions of finitude are deficiencies. This *is* the ethical world, and the myth of pure presence must be surrendered in moral philosophy no less than in ontology. The problem with ethical beliefs that insulate the good from limit conditions is not simply a philosophical flaw. There is an irony that history has demonstrated all too often: The "purer" the concept of the good, the greater the capacity to do evil on its behalf. With a definitized ideal, the world now appears fallen and in need of reform; when elements in the world continue to resist or fall short, there arises the potential to commit terror in the name of salvation.

My analysis has stressed the nonfoundational, dialogical, performative character of ethical life, exhibited in ongoing exchanges, discoveries, negotiations, and decisions. Such practices unfold as experimental balancing acts, even when principles are in play. For many moral theorists, this profile would likely come across as a form of decisionism, in the sense of an arbitrary voluntarism, where nothing can be ruled out. This concern, however, is still informed by modernist subjectivity. In my sense, the decisional, performative element moves within a situated, socialized background, and it must be engaged, responsive, informed, and open to question. And my suggestion of inhabitive truth in ethics works against an unhinged openness. Ethical truth can be located in appropriate decisions, which do not have to mean "correct" or "justified" decisions, but something like the attentive ethical discernment of *phronēsis*, the capacity for responsive and responsible choice. As radically finite, however, ethical discernment comes with something of a tremble.

Given the practical task of having to make ethical decisions, how long would we have to wait if we would only be confident in acting when backed by an indefeasible guarantee? We surely do not presently have such backing, yet the social world has not collapsed into chaos. And what is to be said of someone who is not satisfied with an ethical bearing until and unless it is guaranteed? In Heideggerian terms, this seems like an anxiety-prompted flight from the finitude of existence, a kind of ethical cowardice. Even if we could achieve a guarantee, we might want to turn it down if Heidegger is right that meaning, even the meaning of being rational, is animated by the negativity of finite limits.

The force of finitude both generates ethical meaning and prompts the fugitive tendency to definitize ethics. My analysis opens up the possibility of a kind of humility that can be brought to bear in ethical dwelling. In social life we face the following tension: We cannot exist without ethics, without advancing certain assessments, preferences, and judgments; yet ethics must abide without decisive guarantees and modes of certainty that in most respects are simply a refuge from anxiety. In this regard we should note Heidegger's critique of "good conscience," understood as a condition of moral certainty and rectitude. Heidegger calls good conscience a "tranquilizing suppression" of the primal sense of guilt and conscience born in being-toward-death (*BT*, 338). Such a critique also can be directed at the arrogance of foundationalist moral theories that aim to secure and master the ethical environment. On a psychological level, ethical humility can work against cocksure self-righteousness and the vilification of transgressors. Both attitudes fall prey to the error of assuming full presence in human selves without remainder. One possible effect of attending to the correlation of being-toward-death, care, and ekstatic throwness is a sensitivity to the pathos of human attachments and fears that are implicated in much unethical living. We might develop more empathic understanding and then be less prone to demonize people.

Such ethical humility, however, need not recoil from making judgments. Yet judgments need not be rigid or unambiguous because they are saturated with limits, which undermine sanctimonious judgments without ambivalence or regret. Ethical humility also opens up the possibility of, and capacity for, forgiveness.[1] Such humility would be an ethical version of a Heideggerian sense of thrown openness that cannot be fully mastered or controlled, and that therefore has built into its structure an intimation of incompleteness and a warning against final stories.

Ethical humility is the antidote to both paternalism and terror. When there are clear and secured conceptions of the good and its transgression, there arise the motivation and confidence to control people for their own good, despite their resistance, a resistance that is usually attributed to a kind of false consciousness. If recalcitrance persists, there can arise the impulse to commit terror, the elimination or silencing of a demonized Other. As has been indicated, such is the vicious irony of history, that a host of cruelties, oppressions, and slaughters have been committed in the name of moral rectitude.

I want to conclude with a brief reflection on gratitude. Heidegger connects *Denken* with *Danken*, or thinking with thanking (*PM*, 231–38), and he talks about an "originary thanking" as the "echo of being's favor"(*PM*, 236). On an ontological level, this linkage reflects Heidegger's alternative to modern subjectivity's vision of sovereignty, shown in its self-grounding epistemology and its impulse toward technological mastery. Dasein's throwness indicates that humans cannot and should not aim for mastery of being.

Man is rather "thrown" from being itself into the truth of being, so that ek-sisting in this fashion he might guard the truth of being, in order that beings might appear in the light of being as the beings they are. Man does not decide whether and how beings appear, whether and how God and the gods or history and nature come forward into the clearing of being, come to presence and depart. The advent of beings lies in the destiny of being. But for man it is ever a question of finding what is fitting in his essence that corresponds to such destiny; for in accord with this destiny man as ek-sisting has to guard the truth of being. Man is the shepherd of being. It is in this direction alone that *Being and Time* is thinking when ekstatic existence is experienced as "care." (*LH*, 234)

Heidegger's emphasis on thrown finitude and the "arrival" character of temporal futurity sustains the notion that what is worthy and meaningful in life is not the product of an autonomous subject, but is in some deep sense *given*, in the sense of a gift. Such givenness prompts the receptive bearing of thankfulness in response to the favor of being. With all the supposed "losses" implied in a finite ontology, one positive consequence is an enhanced meaningfulness in the face of unmeaning, which is an alternative to nihilistic despair. And in view of the loss of "control" implied in the eclipse of the sovereign subject, the world's meaningfulness is taken in the spirit of gratitude.[2]

Heidegger's ontological conception of thanking can be associated with an ethics of gratitude. Part of finitude is that the human self is not the complete master and mover of its fate; in many ways it is beholden to circumstances beyond itself. In this way, Dasein's guilt (*Schuld*)—which Heidegger calls being the basis of a nullity, in the sense that the self is not self-grounding—can be understood as a debt, as being indebted (*schuldig*) to one's culture, history, and upbringing. In other words, one is beholden to forces and persons *other* than oneself in various ways. Accordingly, some of the presumptive obligations that were discussed earlier can be enriched and animated with a concomitant presumptive gratitude, owing to a primal sense of indebtedness for occasions of bestowal. Heidegger's ontological sense of thankfulness for being can serve as a founding disposition for ethics, a primal mood of grateful reception and openness to the world, to others, and to the fragile marvel of human possibilities.[3]

NOTES

1. Forgiveness entails not being bound by the past and one's injuries; it is an openness to the future and new possibilities. See Paul Ricoeur, "Memory and Forgetting," and John D. Caputo, "Reason, History, and a Little Madness," in *Questioning Ethics: Contemporary Debates in Philosophy*, ed. Richard Kearney and Mark Dooley (New York: Routledge, 1999), chs. 1 and 7.

2. Heidegger's image of thankfulness is certainly consonant with religious dispositions, yet it has the advantage of not having to depend on, or be associated with, particular religious views of the world.

3. Given that Heidegger's thinking calls for an openness to the world in a manner meant to counter the Western fixation on mastering nature, it will likely be a disappointment to some that I have limited my discussion of ethics to the human sphere. In particular, Hei-

degger's thought has much to offer environmental ethics. What is especially relevant is Heidegger's deep meditation on modern science and technology, on the far-reaching questions of how the world is understood and the place of human beings in the world. Environmental ethics cannot be restricted to the difficult choices and questions of priorities facing modern societies in the wake of technology and its effects on human life and the environment. Prior to problems created by technology are the more profound problems of how and why nature is conceived as merely a set of manipulable, calculable, and serviceable objects; of how and why other, more intrinsic, dimensions of the world get concealed. This is particularly significant with respect to the human treatment of animals. For an excellent study that explores various avenues of environmental philosophy partly in the spirit of Heidegger's thought, see Michael E. Zimmerman, *Contesting Earth's Future: Radical Ecology and Postmodernity* (Berkeley: University of California Press, 1994). My exclusion of environmental and ecological issues is by no means a dismissal of their importance. My preoccupation with human relations is simply a provisional exploration of basic ethical concerns that have long been the province of moral philosophy. This in no way presupposes an anthropocentric orientation. Indeed, the notion of world-disclosive, ekstatic dwelling rules out confining ethical questions to a "human" domain.

Epilogue

Heidegger and National Socialism

Could it not seem offensive to bring the thought of a confirmed Nazi to bear on the question of ethics? Since Heidegger saw his commitment to National Socialism as unfolding out of his project of thinking, are not my efforts in this book tainted by this fact? Two main questions must be addressed concerning Heidegger's politics. First, did his vision of National Socialism match the vision of Adolf Hitler's regime? Second, was his commitment to fascism a necessary consequence of his philosophy? The answer to both questions, in my opinion, is no. If I thought that fascist politics was the only possible outcome of Heidegger's thought, I could not have written this book. Even if we cannot separate Heidegger the man from Nazism, his philosophy harbors a rich wellspring of other possibilities, which I hope my text has helped to open up. Indeed, if my work is at all persuasive, I think it can be said that certain elements in Heidegger's political vision were not consistent with basic elements of his philosophy that I have tried to articulate in this investigation.

What are we to make of Heidegger's Nazism and its aftermath? I can only offer some brief reflections and cannot hope to present a comprehensive response to this difficult question.[1] One thing is clear: Heidegger's "official story," that he ceased his affiliation with the Nazi regime after a one-year period as rector of Freiburg University in 1933, and that he was a voice of moderation then and thereafter, is not true.[2] Heidegger was enthusiastic about National Socialism as the salvation of German culture, and he saw himself as a kind of philosophical *Führer* who would show the way for the political leadership.

It should not be forgotten that Germany in the 1930s was going through enormous economic and political upheaval. In a time of crisis, Heidegger's idealized vision of National Socialism can be understood as a response to four supposed threats: American materialism, Russian communism, Enlightenment universalism, and rational individualism, all posing interrelated threats to what Heidegger took to be authentic German culture and a proper engagement with being. Chief among

201

Heidegger's concerns were the following: (1) that being would be reduced to economic resources and technological controls (Americanism and communism); (2) that the social order and high culture would be ruined by consumerism and the celebration of private experience (Americanism and individualism); and (3) that a particular culture and heritage would be overcome by a rationalized, global construct (communism and universalism). It should also be noted that Heidegger did not support the Nazi regime's racialism, biologism, militarism, or supremacism.[3] And eventually he came to see German Nazism as simply another version of modern anthropocentric technocracy, and thus as having nothing to do with the "inner truth and greatness" of National Socialism as he saw it (*IM*, 199).

Yet in his early fervor for the movement, Heidegger displayed an alarming propensity for a kind of collectivism that outdid most versions of communitarianism in the degree to which it pitted a "people" against the individual. The ambiguous relationship between individuation and sociality that has been documented in this investigation became lost in Heidegger's myopic promotion of the German *Volk* in his notorious rectoral address.[4] And then this startling passage: "The individual, wherever he may stand, counts for nothing; the destiny of our people in its state counts for everything."[5] Such statements are difficult to understand because of the following anomaly: Being-in-question was an essential feature of Heidegger's ontology, and confident, secure groundings were continually subjected to criticism; how could Heidegger have been so assured and reductive in his political thinking?[6] Despite various passages in his writings that critique a crude nationalism and folkism,[7] many of his political remarks are heinous, and in my mind incoherent when measured against the atmosphere of his philosophical texts. The question, of course, is whether to attribute this to a personal idiosyncrasy or to insist on rereading and decoding the texts. It seems to me that the concept of authenticity should have interrupted the hypercollective tone of Heidegger's Germanism and his authoritarian embrace of the *Führerprinzip*.[8] It is admittedly difficult to discount the possibility that *Being and Time* was fundamentally and excessively communitarian in spirit, but I still believe that the text shows avenues that can and should undermine the kind of path Heidegger took in the 1930s.

Even though Heidegger's phenomenology stemmed from the concreteness of the lived world and took its initial bearings from everyday experience, Heidegger was given over to a lofty, dramatic, historical narrative, of the kind that has been common in the Western tradition and that is just as susceptible to distorting and surpassing the lived world as are metaphysical constructs. After *Being and Time* Heidegger began to articulate a global sense of the historicality of being, in terms of a more original experience of being in the Greek world followed by a series of concealments of this experience, especially in the modern world. The particular crisis facing German culture in the 1930s prompted Heidegger to see his times in grandiose historical terms, and to find in National Socialism the prospect of delivering German culture from modernist forces toward a more authentic experience of being.

Heidegger's rhetoric at the time reflected a highly charged narrative of primal origins, corruption, crisis, new beginnings, and salvation, which moved him to interpret the Nazi revolution in heroic, world-historical terms. This grandiose excitement in a time of crisis brought Heidegger to believe in the need for a collectivist, authoritarian political order. I think he was blind to the dangers of such a politics and to its inconsistency with crucial elements of his philosophy: especially authentic individuation, ontological openness, and thrown finitude (this last element always being counterposed to the modernist predilection for controlling the life-world). In short, National Socialism was a political project that was bound to fail the test of finitude. Heidegger made an important philosophical contribution in espousing a finite dwelling in the richness of the world, to counter modern excesses of instrumentalism, materialism, consumerism, and technological control. Yet an authoritarian social order in the service of this cause is bound to obviate the openness to negativity and limits that uncovers the richer experience of the world in the first place.

Another way to understand the shortcomings of Heidegger's political vision involves his preference for *poiēsis* over *praxis*, for creative bringing-forth over engaged social practice.[9] Like many thinkers who have called for radical cultural change, Heidegger saw the state in artistic terms, as a creative advent fashioned by heroic founders (*IM*, 152–53). Seeing the state as an "artwork" fits a sense of revolutionary politics, a fundamental recasting of the social order from the ground up. Such a political vision is much like a Platonic *poiēsis* stemming from the insight of a visionary, rather than a more Aristotelian *praxis* that works out an interactive, collaborative shaping of the social order in the midst of existing conditions.[10] For all his interest in Aristotle's ethics, Heidegger never really followed through on Aristotle's emphasis on *praxis*, and was given over instead to a kind of political Platonism.[11] For whatever reason, Heidegger did not appreciate the way in which a democratic *praxis*—understood as an ongoing, open-ended, interrogative, dialogical engagement with existing conditions—can be more appropriate to a situated finitude and less susceptible to the danger of catastrophic ruin or tyrannical control that always haunts revolutionary politics.[12]

On the matter of Heidegger and the German *Volk*, there is nothing intrinsically wrong with Folk-thinking, in the sense of affirming cultural particularity. Behind current movements of multiculturalism and identity politics lies the notion that group identifications of all sorts are part of human existence and that ethnic traditions enhance and enrich human lives. But within an embrace of particularity lies the danger of tribalism, where a myopic fixation on one's own group can obscure or cancel out the dignity and humanity of other groups. I believe that Heidegger's sincere commitment to National Socialism came from his interest in freeing a Folk for their authentic culture. But the Nazis were tribalists whose main aims were the domination and annihilation of *other* Folk. What was likely missing in Heidegger and what is especially needed today is a phronetic balance that affirms a cultural heritage as essential to one's world, but without a reductive attachment that takes one's culture as the full limit of one's world. In other words, a culture can be a finite presence that remains open to, and keeps open a space for, other cultures.

Heidegger is surely responsible for supporting a despicable political regime. Yet if we exclude the racist and supremacist elements of Nazism from Heidegger's outlook, we see something distinguishable from the monstrosity he so blindly endorsed. To put it simply, Heidegger was an antidemocratic, conservative nationalist, which was very common among German intellectuals of his era.[13] If the war and the Holocaust had not happened, what would be thought of Heidegger's politics? Most people would still be critical, but the level of intensity would be greatly diminished. But the war and the Holocaust did happen, and so Heidegger's words and deeds become retrospectively more ominous in the light of this terrible fact. Try this experiment: Take any American political speech you like, substitute German references, and see if the tone darkens ("Ask not what Germany can do for you, but what you can do for Germany"). I am not trying to sanitize Heidegger or deny that his thought was culpable and dangerous. I am only saying that the culpability and danger have been overstated.[14]

As Michel Foucault would say, all political viewpoints are dangerous. Of course, some systems are less dangerous than others, but even liberal democracies have their dangers, as Karl Marx and Friedrich Nietzsche have forcefully shown. What bothers me is not the criticism of Heidegger but the hypocrisy in some of it. Americans are rightly proud of their democratic heritage, but we are usually quiet about how our nation was founded on conquest and enslavement. Although we have owned up to the evils of slavery and its aftermath, we are almost completely silent about the fate of Native Americans, which is arguably the worst sustained story of genocide in human history. And we should not ignore how some of the assumptions in our "enlightened" tradition made such atrocities possible, or at least easier to sanitize.[15]

Many have been offended or troubled by Heidegger's postwar "silence" on the Holocaust and his failure to apologize for his involvement with National Socialism. His indirection and misdirection on these matters have been a spur for much reflection on responsibility and the role of intellectuals in public life. To me, Heidegger's postwar bearing was unnerving and strange. Surely some kind of public reckoning was called for. But by the same token, why have Marxist intellectuals not been called upon to apologize for their complicity with the evils of Stalinism? Is it that they might be permitted to say that Stalinism had nothing to do with the "inner truth and greatness" of communism?

Some have sensed an implicit contrition in the changed bearing of Heidegger's postwar thinking. He turned from an early heroic project of cultural renewal to a more meditative *Gelassenheit*, a renunciation of philosophical ventures and all modes of assertive willing toward a quasireligious atmosphere of reverence and waiting for the "sendings" of being. Accordingly, Heidegger announced the "end of philosophy" because he thought it could not extricate itself from subjectivist willing and the technological control of beings. Can one take this shift as evidence for Heidegger's sincere admission of his (and the West's) failure in perpetuating a project of willful domination that brought on catastrophe? Or is this global metanarrative of failure a form of denial, a psychological defense mechanism and refuge from the burden of owning up to his earlier commitment and responsibility? Although there is some truth in both proposals, I think there is more truth in the second. I sense in some of Heidegger's world-historical pronouncements certain psychological symptoms. Think of the incredible arrogance behind the "end of philosophy." Because *his* philosophy was caught up in catastrophe, philosophy comes to an end!

A certain diagnostics of Heidegger's postwar bearing can be important not simply because of Heidegger's own case, but also for what it can tell us about philosophy and thinking in general terms. For all Heidegger's attention to the concreteness of being and the lived world, he was still susceptible to a kind of aestheticism and Platonic essentialism, both of which sustain a disengagement from factical life that harbors philosophical and ethical dangers. In this matter it is important to remember Kierkegaard's analysis of aesthetic existence as a self-absorbed objectification of the world, detached from the burdens of concrete, ethical involvement.[16] Aesthetic existence involves more than simply sensuous enjoyment; it includes reflective apprehension of artistic beauty, and even the reflective gaze of theoretical comprehension.

Here we get some guidance in deciphering what is problematic in much of Heidegger's postwar rhetoric. John Caputo is right on target in diagnosing much of Heidegger's thought as a "phainesthetics," shown in Heidegger's long-standing fixation on the Greek sense of *phainomenon* (that which shows itself), in the atmosphere of captivation before the self-showing of being's bestowal, and in the poetic participation in advents of language.[17] Such aestheticism can also be implied in Heidegger's talk of "essences." Although Heidegger insisted that essence for him is nothing metaphysical, nevertheless *how* Heidegger spoke of essence betrayed a kind of Platonism that is no less disengaged from concrete life.

This is especially evident in one of Heidegger's rare remarks about the Holocaust, where he described modern agriculture as a motorized food industry that is "in essence" the same as the manufacturing of corpses in extermination camps (*GA* 79, 27). What Heidegger was trying to say concerned the global effects of technicity and its objectification of being, and he may have thought he was spotlighting the heinous dehumanization in the camps. But the equation is dumbfounding and shocking, if only because of the crucial difference between feeding people and killing people.[18] In another instance, Heidegger insisted that the "real plight" of dwelling is greater than the need for housing; *real* "homelessness" is human alienation from a primal dwelling with being (*PLT*, 161).

What is going on here? In one sense Heidegger could simply be extolling the importance of thoughtful reflection in focusing our thinking amidst concrete particulars, and in drawing attention to deep issues of historical and existential import at the heart of particular concerns. But the jarring juxtapositions measured by what is "essential" show something else. Why would any human being talk this way? In my opinion, Heidegger is simply another example of a long-standing philosophical disposition that is properly diagnosed as a special mode of aesthetic indulgence. Philosophical aestheticism can take many forms, and I suggest that it stems from an interest in, or need for, an experience of some deep insight, truth, image, or vision that is elevated beyond the everyday, and that brings the exaltation of having discovered something profound. Philosophical insight is not the problem, but rather a kind of monastic concentration that can prompt a philosopher to pronounce on what is "really" or "essentially" going on behind mere events in the world. What would be lost if philosophical reflection was simply taken in pragmatic terms, as an orientation for living in all its forms, nothing more and nothing less? What kind of person needs more than this? Again, I think the answer is found in variations of monasticism, in a certain comfort, satisfaction, and excitement found in turning from an active life to a contemplative life. And in the spirit of Nietzsche's critique of asceticism, we can notice in philosophical monasticism a kind of anesthetic effect. And in line with my suggestion that indifference might be a kind of cowardice in the face of human suffering, the anesthetic effect is germane to ethical considerations.

I think it is highly plausible that Heidegger's essentialism was a kind of anesthetic indifference to keep the pains of life at bay. For me what is ethically problematical here is not simply the indifference as a flight response—which is quite common in human life and likely necessary in some respects—but rather the philosophical conceit. I might turn away from a homeless person, but I could not bring myself to talk of the "more essential" homelessness behind this person's need for shelter. It is enough to own up to certain limits in my ethical capacity without the exalting and ameliorating supplement that I am making some important contribution in meditating on what is "really" going on. Such a supplement is not only complicit with indifference, it is embarrassingly self-serving. I am not trying to trash Heidegger here. He is certainly not alone in being susceptible to philosophical aestheticism. And I hope that my book has shown that Heidegger's own thought can be brought to bear against such a tendency.

Heidegger's essentialism and the mythopoetic character of his later thinking can be seen as an ironic departure from his earlier conception of philosophy as formal indication. Heidegger probably thought that his later meditations were still in keeping with the facticity of life. Indeed Heidegger's thought from beginning to end was always *about* concrete existence, but he fell prey to a typical syndrome that can afflict intellectuals and academics, wherein thought has more life than the life-world, so that *how* one thinks about the life-world can manifest its own peculiar disengagement. Heidegger's reflections on the modern world remain one of the great contributions of Western philosophy, but much of his later thought bypassed his earlier "indicative" criterion and brought out some embarrassing lapses of judgment.

There is a good deal in Heidegger's later thinking that does not suit my own philosophical tastes: epochal thinking, momentous beginnings and endings, deep diagnostics of historical crises, and a mythopoetic, almost messianic/prophetic anticipation of deliverance. Too much arcanery, histrionics, and eschatological thrills for me. If one were to strip all of this from Heidegger's thought, I believe that nothing of importance would be lost, and what would remain is his profound and productive phenomenology of finite being-in-the-world. The later essential-ism and aestheticism are in a way a consummation of Heidegger's long-standing demurral on questions of practical life, particularly in ethics. But as I hope I have shown, this tendency is due more to Heidegger's own bearing as a human being, because his thought has enormous potential for advancing practical philosophy.

NOTES

1. There are a host of important treatments of this topic, including the following: Gunther Neske and Emil Kettering, eds., *Martin Heidegger and National Socialism* (New York: Paragon House, 1990); Michael E. Zimmerman, *Heidegger's Confrontation with Modernity: Technology, Politics, Art* (Bloomington: Indiana University Press, 1990); Richard Wolin, *The Politics of Being: The Political Thought of Martin Heidegger* (New York: Columbia University Press, 1990); Richard Wolin, ed., *The Heidegger Contro-versy: A Critical Reader* (Cambridge, Mass.: MIT Press, 1991); Tom Rockmore and Joseph Margolis, eds., *The Heidegger Case: On Philosophy and Politics* (Philadelphia: Temple University Press, 1992); John D. Caputo, *Demythologizing Heidegger* (Bloomington: Indiana University Press, 1993); Hans Sluga, *Heidegger's Crisis: Philos-ophy and Politics in Nazi Germany* (Cambridge, Mass.: Harvard University Press, 1993); Fred Dallmayr, *The Other Heidegger* (Ithaca: Cornell University Press, 1993); James F. Ward, *Heidegger's Political Thinking* (Amherst: University of Massachusetts Press, 1995); Berel Lang, *Heidegger's Silence* (Ithaca: Cornell University Press, 1996); Julian Young, *Heidegger, Philosophy, Nazism* (Cambridge: Cambridge University Press, 1997); and Miguel de Beistegui, *Heidegger and the Political* (New York: Routledge, 1998).

2. See Hugo Ott, *Martin Heidegger: A Political Life*, trans. Allan Blunden (New York: Basic, 1993).

3. See Zimmerman, *Heidegger's Confrontation with Modernity*.

4. See Wolin, *The Heidegger Controversy*, 29–39.

5. Cited by Ott in "Martin Heidegger als Rektor der Universität Freiburg i.Br. 1933/34," *Zeitschrift des Breisgau-Geschichtsvereins* 103 (1984): 117.

6. Caputo points to this problem in "Spirit and Danger," in *Ethics and Danger: Essays on Heidegger and Continental Thought*, ed. Arleen Dallery and Charles E. Scott (Albany: SUNY Press, 1992), 45. See also Charles E. Scott, *The* Question *of Ethics: Nietzsche, Foucault, Heidegger* (Bloomington: Indiana University Press, 1990), ch. 5. I agree with de Beistegui that in Heidegger there was always a bit of the priest, and thus the surrender of a questioning spirit at certain levels of his thought (de Beistegui, *Heidegger and the Political*, 4).

7. See Véronique Fóti's analysis in "Aletheia and Oblivion's Field: On Heidegger's Parmenides Lectures," in *Ethics and Danger*, 71–82.

8. See Jacob Rogozinski, "Dispelling the Hero from Our Soul," *Research in Phenomenology* 21 (1991): 62–80.

9. For a discussion of the priority of *poiēsis* in a later work, see *PLT*, 213–29.

10. See Samuel IJsseling, "Heidegger and Politics," in *Ethics and Danger*, ch. 1, and de Beistegui, *Heidegger and the Political*, 160–62.

11. On this question see Hannah Arendt, *The Human Condition* (Chicago: University of Chicago Press, 1968), and Richard Bernstein, *The New Constellation: The Ethical–Political Horizons of Modernity/Postmodernity* (Cambridge, Mass.: MIT Press, 1992), ch. 4.

12. I make a similar case against Nietzsche's aristocraticism in *A Nietzschean Defense of Democracy: An Experiment in Postmodern Politics* (Chicago: Open Court, 1995). Leslie Paul Thiele presents a good case for democratic possibilities in the light of Heidegger's thought in *Timely Meditations: Martin Heidegger and Postmodern Politics* (Princeton, N.J.: Princeton University Press, 1995).

13. See Sluga, *Heidegger's Crisis*.

14. For a concise and even handed treatment of various critical perspectives and responses in the matter of Heidegger's politics, see Richard Polt, *Heidegger: An Introduction* (Ithaca: Cornell University Press, 1999), 152–64. I also recommend this work as a cogent and accessible overview of Heidegger's thought.

15. An "irrational" or "backward" people can be "freed" for their true humanity by colonial rule, or sacrificed to a "manifest destiny."

16. See Kierkegaard, *Either/Or*, vol. 1, trans. David F. Swenson and Lillian Marvin Swenson (Princeton, N.J.: Princeton University Press, 1959).

17. Caputo, *Demythologizing Heidegger*, 142ff.

18. Caputo gives a nuanced and powerful critique of Heidegger's essentialism in this context in chapter 7 of *Demythologizing Heidegger*. To conjoin extermination and agriculture as essentially the same has the effect of neutralizing and silencing the cry of the victim (143).

Bibliography

Anton, John P., and Anthony Preus, eds., *Aristotle's Ethics*. Albany: SUNY Press, 1991.

Arendt, Hannah. *The Human Condition*. Chicago: University of Chicago Press, 1968.

Aristotle. *Nicomachean Ethics*. Trans. Terence Irwin. Indianapolis: Hackett, 1985.

——. *Eudemian Ethics*. Trans. Michael Woods. Oxford: Clarendon Press, 1992.

Arnhart, Larry. *Darwinian Natural Right: The Biological Ethics of Human Nature*. Albany: SUNY Press, 1998.

Austin, J. L. *How to Do Things with Words*. Cambridge, Mass.: Harvard University Press, 1975.

Ayer, A. J. *Language, Truth, and Logic*. Mineola, New York: Dover, 1952.

Benhabib, Seyla. *Situating the Self: Gender, Community, and Postmodernism in Contemporary Ethics*. New York: Routledge, 1992.

Bernstein, Richard. *Beyond Objectivity and Relativism: Science, Hermeneutics, Praxis*. Philadelphia: University of Pennsylvania Press, 1983.

——. *The New Constellation: The Ethical–Political Horizons of Modernity/Postmodernity*. Cambridge, Mass.: MIT Press, 1992.

Bloom-Feshbach, Jonathan, and Sally Bloom-Feshbach, eds. *The Psychology of Separation and Loss*. San Francisco: Jossey-Bass, 1987.

Blosser, Philip. *Scheler's Critique of Kant's Ethics*. Athens: Ohio University Press, 1995.

Broadie, Sarah. *Ethics with Aristotle*. New York: Oxford University Press, 1991.

Bruner, Jerome. *Child's Talk*. New York: Norton, 1983.

Butler, Judith. *Gender Trouble: Feminism and the Subversion of Identity*. New York: Routledge, 1990.

Capaldi, Nicholas. *Hume's Place in Moral Philosophy*. New York: Lang, 1989.

Caputo, John D. *Radical Hermeneutics*. Bloomington: Indiana University Press, 1987.

——. *Against Ethics*. Bloomington: Indiana University Press, 1993.

——. *Demythologizing Heidegger*. Bloomington: Indiana University Press, 1993.

Card, Claudia, ed. *Feminist Ethics*. Lawrence: University Press of Kansas, 1991.

Cicchetti, D., and P. Hesse, eds. *New Directions for Child Development*. San Francisco: Jossey-Bass, 1982.

Crisp, Roger, and Michael Slote, eds. *Virtue Ethics*. Oxford: Oxford University Press, 1997.

Dallery, Arleen, and Charles E. Scott, eds. *Ethics and Danger: Essays on Heidegger and Continental Thought*. Albany: SUNY Press, 1992.

Dallmayr, Fred. *The Other Heidegger*. Ithaca, N.Y.: Cornell University Press, 1993.

Davis, Mark H. *Empathy: A Social Psychological Approach*. Boulder, Colo.: Westview, 1996.

de Beistegui, Miguel. *Heidegger and the Political*. New York: Routledge, 1998.

de Waal, Frans. *Good Natured: The Origins of Right and Wrong in Humans and Other Animals*. Cambridge: Cambridge University Press, 1996.

Derrida, Jacques. *Writing and Difference*. Trans. Alan Bass. Chicago: University of Chicago Press, 1978.

——. *Limited Inc*. Ed. Gerald Graf. Evanston, Ill.: Northwestern University Press, 1988.

——. *The Gift of Death*. Trans. David Wells. Chicago: University of Chicago Press, 1995.

Descartes, René. *Discourse on Method*. Part VI of *The Philosophical Works of Descartes*, vol. I. Trans. Elizabeth S. Haldane and G. R. T. Ross. Cambridge: Cambridge University Press, 1969.

Descola, Phillippe, and Gísli Pálsson, eds. *Nature and Society: Anthropological Perspectives*. New York: Routledge, 1996.

Dewey, John. *Human Nature and Conduct*. Vol. 14 of *John Dewey: The Middle Works, 1899–1924*. Ed. Jo Ann Boydston. Carbondale: Southern Illinois University Press, 1988.

Dreyfus, Hubert L. *Being-in-the-World: A Commentary on Heidegger's* Being and Time. Cambridge, Mass.: The MIT Press, 1991.

Eisenberg, Nancy, and Janet Strayer, eds. *Empathy and Its Development*. Cambridge: Cambridge University Press, 1987.

Gadamer, Hans-Georg. *Truth and Method*. Trans. G. Barden and J. Cumming. New York: Seabury Press, 1975.

——. *Philosophical Hermeneutics*. Trans. David E. Linge. Berkeley: University of California Press, 1976.

——. *The Idea of the Good in Platonic–Aristotelian Philosophy*. Trans. P. Christopher Smith. New Haven, Conn.: Yale University Press, 1986.

Gilligan, Carol. *In a Different Voice: Psychological Theory and Women's Development*. Cambridge, Mass.: Harvard University Press, 1982.

Guthrie, W. K. C. *A History of Greek Philosophy*. vol. I. Cambridge: Cambridge University Press, 1962.

Habermas, Jürgen. *The Theory of Communicative Action*. Two volumes. Trans. Thomas McCarthy. Cambridge, Mass.: MIT Press, 1984, 1987.

——. *Moral Consciousness and Communicative Action*. Trans. Christian Lenhardt and Shierry Weber Nicholson. Cambridge, Mass.: MIT Press, 1990.

——. *Justification and Application: Remarks on Discourse Ethics*. Trans. Ciaran Cronin. Cambridge, Mass.: MIT Press, 1993.

Hampshire, Stuart. *Morality and Conflict*. Cambridge, Mass.: Harvard University Press, 1983.

Hatab, Lawrence. *Myth and Philosophy: A Contest of Truths*. Chicago: Open Court, 1990.

——. *A Nietzschean Defense of Democracy: An Experiment in Postmodern Politics*. Chicago: Open Court, 1995.

Held, Virginia. *Feminist Morality: Transforming Culture, Society, and Politics*. Chicago: University of Chicago Press, 1993.

Hickman, Larry, ed. *Reading Dewey: Interpretations for a Postmodern Generation*. Bloomington: Indiana University Press, 1998.

Hodge, Joanna. *Heidegger and Ethics*. New York: Routledge, 1995.

Holland, Nancy J. *The Madwoman's Reason: The Concept of the Appropriate in Ethical Thought*. University Park: Pennsylvania State University Press, 1998.

Hume, David. *A Treatise on Human Nature*. Oxford: Clarendon Press, 1978.

Hursthouse, Rosilind, Gavin Lawrence, and Warren Quinn, eds. *Virtues and Reasons: Philippa Foot and Moral Theory*. Oxford: Clarendon Press, 1995.

Jaggar, Alison M. *Living with Contradictions: Controversies in Feminist Social Ethics*. Boulder, Colo.: Westview, 1994.

Johnston, David. *The Idea of a Liberal Theory: A Critique and Reconstruction*. Princeton, N.J.: Princeton University Press, 1994.

Joós, Ernest. *Dialogue with Heidegger on Values: Ethics for Times of Crisis*. New York: Lang, 1991.

Kagan, Jerome, and Sharon Lamb, eds. *The Emergence of Morality in Young Children*. Chicago: University of Chicago Press, 1987.

Kant, Immanuel. *Critique of Practical Reason*. Trans. Lewis White Beck. New York: Macmillan, 1956.

——. *Foundations of the Metaphysics of Morals*. Trans. Lewis White Beck. New York: Bobbs-Merrill, 1959.

——. *The Doctrine of Virtue*. Trans. Mary J. Gregor. Philadelphia: University of Pennsylvania Press, 1964.

——. *Kant's Political Writings*. Ed. Hans Reise. Cambridge: Cambridge University Press, 1970.

Kearney, Richard, and Mark Dooley, eds. *Questioning Ethics: Contemporary Debates in Philosophy*. New York: Routledge, 1999.

Kierkegaard, Søren. *Either/Or*, vol. 1. Trans. David F. Swenson and Lillian Marvin Swenson. Princeton, N.J.: Princeton University Press, 1959.

Kisiel, Theodore. *The Genesis of Heidegger's* Being and Time. Berkeley: University of California Press, 1993.

Kisiel, Theodore, and John van Buren, eds. *Reading Heidegger from the Start: Essays in His Earliest Thought*. Albany: SUNY Press, 1994.

Kockelmans, Joseph. *On the Truth of Being*. Bloomington: Indiana University Press, 1984.

Kögler, Hans Herbert, and Karsten R. Stueber, eds. *Empathy and Agency: The Problem of Understanding in the Human Sciences*. Boulder, Colo.: Westview, 2000.

Kohlberg, Lawrence. *Essays on Moral Development*. New York: Harper and Row, 1981.

Lang, Berel. *Heidegger's Silence*. Ithaca, N.Y.: Cornell University Press, 1996.

Levin, David M. *The Body's Recollection of Being*. London: Routledge & Kegan Paul, 1985.

——. *The Opening of Vision*. New York: Routledge, 1988.

——. *The Listening Self*. New York: Routledge, 1989.

Levinas, Emmanuel. *Totality and Infinity*. Trans. Alphonso Lingis. Pittsburgh: Duquesne University Press, 1969.

——. *Otherwise than Being or Beyond Essence*. Trans. Alphonso Lingis. The Hague: Martinus Nijhoff, 1981.

MacIntyre, Alasdair. *After Virtue*. South Bend, Ind.: University of Notre Dame Press, 1981.

Mackie, John L. *Ethics: Inventing Right and Wrong*. New York: Penguin, 1977.

Macpherson, C. B. *The Political Theory of Possessive Individualism*. London: Oxford University Press, 1962.

Marx, Werner. *Is There a Measure on Earth? Foundations for a Nonmetaphysical Ethics*. Trans. Thomas J. Nenon and Reginald Lilly. Chicago: University of Chicago Press, 1987.

———. *Towards a Phenomenological Ethics: Ethics and the Life-World*. Trans. Stefaan Heyvaert. Albany: SUNY Press, 1992.

McDowell, John. *Mind and World*. Cambridge, Mass.: Harvard University Press, 1994.

McNeill, William. *The Glance of the Eye: Heidegger, Aristotle, and the Ends of Theory*. Albany: SUNY Press, 1999.

Merleau-Ponty, Maurice. *The Phenomenology of Perception*. Trans. Colin Smith. London: Routledge & Kegan Paul, 1962.

———. *The Primacy of Perception and Other Essays*. Ed. James E. Edie. Evanston, Ill.: Northwestern University Press, 1964.

Mill, John Stuart. *On Liberty*. In *Three Essays*. Oxford: Oxford University Press, 1975.

Miller, David. *Liberty,* Oxford Readings in Politics and Government. Oxford: Oxford University Press, 1991.

Mulhall, Stephen, and Adam Swift. *Liberals and Communitarians*. Malden, Mass.: Blackwell, 1992.

Murdoch, Iris. *The Sovereignty of Good*. New York: Schocken, 1970.

Nancy, Jean-Luc. *The Inoperative Community*. Ed. Peter Connor. Minneapolis: University of Minnesota Press, 1991.

Nenon, Thomas, and Lester Embree, eds. *Issues in Husserl's* Ideas II. Boston: Kluwer Academic, 1996.

Neske, Gunther, and Emil Kettering, eds. *Martin Heidegger and National Socialism*. New York: Paragon House, 1990.

Noddings, Nel. *Caring: A Feminine Approach to Ethics and Education*. Berkeley: University of California Press, 1984.

Nietzsche, Friedrich. *Basic Writings of Nietzsche*. Ed. Walter Kaufmann. New York: Random House, 1966.

Nussbaum, Martha. *The Fragility of Goodness*. Cambridge: Cambridge University Press, 1986.

———. *Love's Knowledge: Essays in Philosophy and Literature*. Oxford: Oxford University Press, 1990.

Oakley, Justin. *Morality and the Emotions*. New York: Routledge, 1992.

Olafson, Frederick A. *Heidegger and the Ground of Ethics: A Study of* Mitsein. Cambridge: Cambridge University Press, 1998.

Ott, Hugo. *Martin Heidegger: A Political Life*. Trans. Allan Blunden. New York: Basic, 1993.

Polt, Richard. *Heidegger: An Introduction*. Ithaca, N.Y.: Cornell University Press, 1999.

Raffoul, François. *Heidegger and the Subject*. Trans. David Pettigrew and Gregory Recco. Atlantic Highlands, N.J.: Humanities, 1998.

Rasmussen, David. *Universalism vs. Communitarianism*. Cambridge, Mass.: MIT Press, 1990.

Rawls, John. *A Theory of Justice*. Cambridge, Mass.: Harvard University Press, 1971.

———. *Political Liberalism*. New York: Columbia University Press, 1993.

Reiner, Hans. *Duty and Inclination*. Trans. Mark Santos. The Hague: Martinus Nijhoff, 1983.

Ricoeur, Paul. *Hermeneutics and the Human Sciences: Essays on Action, Language, and Interpretation*. Trans. John B. Thompson. Cambridge: Cambridge University Press, 1981.

——. *Oneself as Another*. Trans. Kathleen Blamey. Chicago: University of Chicago Press, 1992.

Rockmore, Tom, and Joseph Margolis, eds. *The Heidegger Case: On Philosophy and Politics*. Philadelphia: Temple University Press, 1992.

Rorty, Amélie Oksenberg, ed. *Essays on Aristotle's Ethics*. Berkeley: University of California Press, 1980.

Rorty, Richard. *Contingency, Irony, and Solidarity*. Cambridge: Cambridge University Press, 1989.

Ross, W. D. *The Right and the Good*. Oxford: Oxford University Press, 1930.

Sandel, Michael. *Liberalism and the Limits of Justice*. Cambridge: Cambridge University Press, 1982.

Schalow, Frank. *Imagination and Existence: Heidegger's Retrieval of the Kantian Ethic*. Lanham, Md.: University Press of America, 1986.

——. *The Renewal of the Heidegger–Kant Dialogue: Action, Thought, and Responsibility*. Albany: SUNY Press, 1992.

Scheler, Max. *Formalism in Ethics and Non-Formal Ethics of Values*. Trans. Manfred S. Frings and Roger L. Funk. Evanston, Ill.: Northwestern University Press, 1973.

Schneewind, J. P. *The Invention of Autonomy: A History of Modern Moral Philosophy*. Cambridge: Cambridge University Press, 1998.

Schrag, Calvin O. *The Resources of Rationality: A Response to the Postmodern Challenge*. Bloomington: Indiana University Press, 1992.

——. *The Self after Postmodernity*. New Haven, Conn.: Yale University Press, 1997.

Schrift, Alan D., ed. *The Logic of the Gift: Toward an Ethic of Generosity*. New York: Routledge, 1997.

Schürmann, Reiner. *Heidegger on Being and Acting: From Principles to Anarchy*. Trans. Christine Marie Gros. Bloomington: Indiana University Press, 1987.

Scott, Charles E. *The* Question *of Ethics: Nietzsche, Foucault, Heidegger*. Bloomington: Indiana University Press, 1990.

Sherman, Nancy. *The Fabric of Character*. Oxford: Clarendon Press, 1989.

——. *Making a Necessity of Virtue: Aristotle and Kant on Virtue*. Cambridge: Cambridge University Press, 1997.

Sherman, Nancy, ed. *Aristotle's Ethics: Critical Essays*. Lanham, Md.: Rowman & Littlefield, 1999.

Sluga, Hans. *Heidegger's Crisis: Philosophy and Politics in Nazi Germany*. Cambridge, Mass.: Harvard University Press, 1993.

Smith, Barbara Herrnstein. *Belief and Resistance: Dynamics of Contemporary Intellectual Controversy*. Cambridge, Mass.: Harvard University Press, 1997.

Smith, Nicholas H. *Strong Hermeneutics: Contingency and Moral Identity*. New York: Routledge, 1997.

Smith, P. Christopher. *Hermeneutics and Human Finitude: Toward a Theory of Ethical Understanding*. New York: Fordham University Press, 1991.

Sokolowski, Robert. *Moral Action: A Phenomenological Study*. Bloomington: Indiana University Press, 1985.

Stanton, Timothy K., Dwight E. Giles Jr., and Nadinne I. Cruz. *Service-Learning: A Movement's Pioneers Reflect on Its Origins, Practice, and Future*. San Francisco: Jossey-Bass, 1999.

Stein, Edith. *Zum Problem der Einfühlung*. Halle, Ger.: Buchdruckerei des Waisenhauses, 1917.

Stocker, Michael. *Valuing Emotions*. Cambridge: Cambridge University Press, 1996.

Taylor, Charles. *Sources of the Self: The Making of Modern Identity*. Cambridge, Mass.: Harvard University Press, 1989.

Thiele, Leslie Paul. *Timely Meditations: Martin Heidegger and Postmodern Politics*. Princeton, N.J.: Princeton University Press, 1995.

Unger, Peter. *Living High and Letting Die: Our Illusion of Innocence*. New York: Oxford University Press, 1996.

Vetlesen, Arne J. *Perception, Empathy, and Judgment: An Inquiry into the Preconditions of Moral Performance*. University Park: Pennsylvania State University Press, 1994.

Vogel, Lawrence. *The Fragile "We": Ethical Implications of Heidegger's* Being and Time. Evanston, Ill.: Northwestern University Press, 1994.

Ward, James F. *Heidegger's Political Thinking*. Amherst: University of Massachusetts Press, 1995.

White, Stephen K. *Political Theory and Postmodernism*. Cambridge: Cambridge University Press, 1991.

Wiggins, David. *Needs, Values, Truth*. 3rd edition. Oxford: Oxford University Press, 1998.

Williams, Bernard. *Moral Luck*. Cambridge: Cambridge University Press, 1981.

——. *Ethics and the Limits of Philosophy*. Cambridge, Mass.: Harvard University Press, 1985.

——. *Shame and Necessity*. Berkeley: University of California Press, 1993.

Wolin, Richard. *The Politics of Being: The Political Thought of Martin Heidegger*. New York: Columbia University Press, 1990.

Wolin, Richard, ed. *The Heidegger Controversy: A Critical Reader*. Cambridge, Mass.: MIT Press, 1991.

Young, Julian. *Heidegger, Philosophy, Nazism*. Cambridge: Cambridge University Press, 1997.

Zimmerman, Michael E. *Heidegger's Confrontation with Modernity: Technology, Politics, Art*. Bloomington: Indiana University Press, 1990.

——. *Contesting Earth's Future: Radical Ecology and Postmodernity*. Berkeley: University of California Press, 1994.

Index

215

being-in-question, 11, 14, 28–29; in ethics, 59–60, 87–88
being-in-the-world, 2–3, 11, 16ff; as an ethical environment, 63–66, 185
being-toward-death, 25–26, 120, 150–51, 173
benevolence, 117, 128, 131
Benhabib, Seyla, 191n25
Benso, Silvia, 98n64
Bentham, Jeremy, 52
Bernasconi, Robert, 113n13
Bernstein, Richard, 49n13, 189n16, 208n11
Birmingham, Peg, 189n15
Blosser, Philip, 98n61, 165n45
Blum, Lawrence, 167n61 and 65, 168n67
Bok, Sisela, 96n42
Broadie, Sarah, 114n15
Brogan, Walter, 113n1
Bruner, Jerome, 48n1
Butler, Judith, 190–91n25

Capaldi, Nicholas, 95n36
Caputo, John D., 165n43, 191n30–31, 199n1, 205, 207n1 and 6, 208n17 and 18
care, 16, 17, 24–25, 31, 77, 126–28, 155ff
care ethics, 77
causality, 23, 191n26
certainty, moral, 197–98
character education, 133n2
child development, 66–71, 112, 126, 134n16, 163,33; and empathy, 145ff, 149; and language, 34, 69–70
child rearing, 14; and ethics, 66–71
childhood, 66; Heidegger on, 67
children, 83–84
Chismar, Douglas, 162n11
circumspection (*Umsicht*), 17–18
collectivism, 202, 203
commitment, 46, 48, 50, 150
communism, 201–2, 204
communitarianism, 77, 170–72, 176–78, 179
community, 151, 171, 191n32
compassion, 140–41, 151–52, 165n46 and 49. *See also* empathy

conscience, 79–83, 96n52, 97n53, 150, 188n12; Heidegger's conception of, 25, 79–80, 96n49 and 51
consciousness, 20–21, 138
consequentialism, 52–53, 117, 135n23. *See also* utilitarianism
conservatism, 88
contingency (in ethics), 131
contract, 170
courage, 119, 120, 128–30; and anxiety, 129; and compassion, 151–52; as negative capability, 129
cowardice, 129–30
creativity, 110, 123–24, 177; and normalcy, 123–24, 134n9
curiosity, 135n19

Dahlstrom, Daniel O., 31n5
Dallmayr, Fred, 207n1
das Man, 25, 26–27, 32n14, 78, 123, 133n6, 173, 182, 188n10, 192n33
Dasein, 11, 21; and transcendence, 25, 179–80
Davis, Mark H., 162n4, 7, and 12, 164n38
death, 181–82, 191n32
de Beistegui, Miguel, 207n1 and 6
decision, 48, 60, 86, 174–75, 186–87
deontology, 53, 62, 117
Derrida, Jacques, 167n64, 191n31, 193n44
Descartes, René, 2, 9–10
desire, 85–86, 114n16, 124–28; authentic, 126–28
destruction of tradition, 15
de Waal, Frans, 167n64
Dewey, John, 133n3
dialogue (dialogic), 60, 183–84
Dickens, Charles, 95n39
Dietz, Mary G., 189n18
difference, 154, 180, 182
Dilthey, Wilhelm, 162n15
disinterest, 149–50
Dreyfus, Hubert L., 32n13, 94n23
dwelling, 3, 16, 20–21, 31, 90, 119, 134n10, 148, 185, 205

education, 133n2, 164n36
egoism, 52, 61, 81, 117, 151, 180

160–61, 166n52; existential rationality,
92n10; instrumental, 10; modern, 9–10,
55, 92n10, 158; monological, 20
reciprocity, 140, 156, 157, 183–84
recognition, 170
Reiner, Hans, 98n65
relativism, 49–50n14
religion, 179, 190n24, 199n2
repetition (*Wiederholung*), 28–29, 88
resoluteness, 175
respect, 170, 178–79, 190n23
responsibility, 82–85, 150, 184–87; as
answerability, 185ff; and
undecidability, 186–87
Ricoeur, Paul, 49n7, 96n51, 199n1
right-good distinction, 53, 56, 170, 171
Rogozinski, Jacob, 208n8
Rorty, Richard, 95n39, 166n54
Ross, W. D., 93n16
Rouse, Joseph, 49n13
Rousseau, Jean-Jacques, 137, 140

Sandel, Michael, 188n4
Sartre, Jean-Paul, 11
Schalow, Frank, 96n47, 190n23
Scheler, Max, 98n61
Schneewind, J. P., 91n1
Schopenhauer, Arthur, 137, 140, 153
Schrag, Calvin O., 92n10, 136n24
Schürmann, Reiner, 6n1, 189n16
science, 47, 49n10 and 13; and
disenchantment, 10; and ethics, 75–76;
and existential meaning, 22–23;
modern, 9–10
Scott, Charles E., 6n1, 98n63, 165n46,
191n31, 207n6
selfhood: and continuity, 186; dialogical,
183–84; and finitude, 173ff; in
Heidegger, 172–76; and inwardness,
93–94n19; modern, 149, 169, 184–85;
and openess, 153–54, 172ff, 176–78,
180ff, 192n43; situated, 169–70, 177;
ungrounded, 25–26, 178–79, 180ff
self-interest, 128, 152
self-sufficiency, 185
self-world, 17, 63

separation anxiety, 67–68, 126
service learning, 164n36
Sherman, Nancy, 95n40, 135n23
skepticism, 52
Sluga, Hans, 207n1, 208n13
Smith, Barbara Herrnstein, 50n14
Smith, Nicholas H., 96n41
Smith, P. Christopher, 114n23, 192n37
sociality, 20–21, 44, 64, 132, 150ff,
163n33, 170ff, 177; and selfhood,
172ff, 176–78
socialization, 26–27, 68; and
individuation, 27, 69–71, 78–79, 173ff
Socrates, 59, 117, 174
Sokolowski, Robert, 98n65
state, the, 171
state of nature, 169, 171
Stein, Edith, 162n15
Stocker, Michael, 162n3
strangers, 160, 167n64
subject-object binary, 2, 9–10, 16, 18, 19,
37, 51–52, 63, 72, 81, 89
subjectivism, 42, 47–48, 72, 81
subjectivity, 22, 29–30, 51, 81, 89–91,
127, 166n55, 184–85, 198–99
suffering, 153, 160–61, 165n46
Swift, Adam, 187n1
sympathy, 163n17, 166n59

Taylor, Charles, 31n2–3, 79, 91–92n5,
94n19, 96n45, 98n60, 192n38
technology, 10, 30, 32n18, 200n3
temporality, 15, 27–29, 186; and ethics,
74, 85–86
terror, 198
Thiele, Leslie Paul, 189n21, 208n12
thrownness (*Geworfenheit*), 22, 25, 72,
83–84, 150, 156, 165n48, 173, 198
torture, 158–59
tradition, 27, 54, 57, 88, 174, 177;
deconstructing moral tradition, 60–62
tragic, the, 108, 161, 168n69, 187
tribalism, 180, 181, 203
trust, 84
truth, 36–48; as correspondence, 36–38; in
ethics, 47–48, 61, 63, 64, 74–77, 84,

About the Author

Lawrence J. Hatab is a professor in the Philosophy Department at Old Dominion University, where he has been teaching since 1976. He is the author of *Nietzsche and Eternal Recurrence: The Redemption of Time and Becoming* (University Press of America), *Myth and Philosophy: A Contest of Truths* (Open Court), and *A Nietzschean Defense of Democracy: An Experiment in Postmodern Politics* (Open Court). He has also published more than twenty articles, mostly on Nietzsche and Heidegger. He is a recovering academic and hopes to be jargon-free someday.